Accounting and Finance Policies and Procedures

Update Service

BECOME A SUBSCRIBER!
Did you purchase this product from a bookstore?

If you did, it's important for you to become a subscriber. John Wiley & Sons, Inc. may publish, on a periodic basis, supplements and new editions to reflect the latest changes in the subject matter that you **need to know** in order to stay competitive in this ever-changing industry. By contacting the Wiley office nearest you, you'll receive any current update at no additional charge. In addition, you'll receive future updates and revised or related volumes on a 30-day examination review.

If you purchased this product directly from John Wiley & Sons, Inc., we have already recorded your subscription for this update service.

To become a subscriber, please call **1-877-762-2974** or send your name, company name (if applicable), address, and the title of the product to:

mailing address: **Supplement Department**
John Wiley & Sons, Inc.
One Wiley Drive
Somerset, NJ 08875

e-mail: **subscriber@wiley.com**
fax: **1-732-302-2300**
online: **www.wiley.com**

For customers outside the United States, please contact the Wiley office nearest you:

Professional & Reference Division
John Wiley & Sons Canada, Ltd.
22 Worcester Road
Etobicoke, Ontario M9W 1L1
CANADA
Phone: 416-236-4433
Phone: 1-800-567-4797
Fax: 416-236-4447
Email: canada@wiley.com

John Wiley & Sons, Ltd.
The Atrium
Southern Gate, Chichester
West Sussex PO 19 8SQ
ENGLAND
Phone: 44-1243-779777
Fax: 44-1243-775878
Email: customer@wiley.co.uk

John Wiley & Sons Australia, Ltd.
33 Park Road
P.O. Box 1226
Milton, Queensland 4064
AUSTRALIA
Phone: 61-7-3859-9755
Fax: 61-7-3859-9715
Email: brisbane@johnwiley.com.au

John Wiley & Sons (Asia) Pte., Ltd.
2 Clementi Loop #02-01
SINGAPORE 129809
Phone: 65-64632400
Fax: 65-64634604/5/6
Customer Service: 65-64604280
Email: enquiry@wiley.com.sg

Accounting and Finance Policies and Procedures

Rose Hightower

WILEY

John Wiley & Sons, Inc.

Copyright © 2008 by John Wiley & Sons, Inc. All rights reserved.
Published by John Wiley & Sons, Inc., Hoboken, New Jersey.
Published simultaneously in Canada.

For general information on our other products and services, or technical support, please contact our Customer Care Department within the United States at 800-762-2974, outside the United States at 317-572-3993 or fax 317-572-4002.

Wiley also publishes its books in a variety of electronic formats. Some content that appears in print may not be available in electronic books.

For more information about Wiley products, visit our Web site at http://www.wiley.com.

Library of Congress Cataloging-in-Publication Data:

Hightower, Rose.
    Accounting and finance policies and procedures / Rose Hightower.
        p.   cm.
    Includes index.
    ISBN 978-0-470-25962-7 (paper/website)
        1. Corporations—Accounting.   2. Accounting—Standards—Forms.   3. Accounting—Handbooks, manuals, etc.—
Authorship.   I. Title.
    HF5686.C7H53   2008
    657—dc22

Printed in the United States of America

10 9 8 7 6 5 4 3 2 1

About the Author

Rose Hightower

Rose is an energetic proactive program manager with extensive Fortune 500 experience in identifying and resolving challenges in accounting and finance, process management, and organizational development. Her career reflects results-oriented leadership with strong, creative problem-solving and analytical skills. Rose uses over 30 years of business experience working with small and corporate clients to improve their efforts and direction in leadership development.

Rose is the executive owner of IDÆAL Consulting Solutions International, LLP. IDÆAL is an acronym for Instruction, Design, Evaluation, Assessment for Leadership. The name symbolizes a business that pays attention to the end-to-end process. With experienced consultants, the business model is to serve clients through structured project engagements, leaving clients with the tools and skills necessary to continue.

After 20+ years at IBM, in 1998 Rose began her consulting business with associates who specialized in specific business processes. Many of the engagements involved (re)designing of specific accounting and finance processes. Medium- and large-sized companies realized improvements and value to the bottom line.

IDÆAL's philosophy is to manage an engagement as a project and to transfer skill leaving a program, which continues its contribution to the client. As part of the project management process, documentation is critical. Researching best practices and customizing it to meet specific client situations, IDÆAL created a library of documentation, which became the basis for sound policies and procedures.

Clients who wanted to establish or improve their documentation began asking for generic policies and procedures. They wanted to use the sample documentation as a base to develop, compare or revise their current documentation. Generally, "for-profit" companies do not publish their policy and procedure manuals. The IDÆAL library of documents and the result of many successful Program implementations served as the input for this Manual. This Manual is the first step in adopting an end-to-end documentation program.

You may contact the author by visiting www.idealpolicy.com.

About the Web Site

As a purchaser of this manual, *Accounting and Finance Policies and Procedures,* you have access to the supporting web site: www.wiley.com/go/hightower

The web site contains everything within the book. This download is an accumulation of Microsoft Word, Excel, and PowerPoint documents.

The password to enter this site is: policies

Contents

How to Use this Manual

This manual is structured as the final product. By using the downloads from the URL, everything including this preface should be adapted to fit into your Company's culture and environment. The Manual includes a Preface, Introduction, Program policies and procedures and Policy and Procedure content.

- The Preface should be structured as a note from the Chief Executive Officer or Chief Financial Officer to set the "tone from the top", identifying the importance of having this manual and program. The objective of the Preface is to establish that this manual is "not just another initiative or project" and once complete, all employees, especially Accounting and Finance employees, are expected to comply.

  o At this point, you may want to consider the organization which will oversee the Company's policy and procedure program. Will it be one person to serve as Program Manager and individuals who serve as functional liaisons when they are needed? Will it be a department to assess, manage and monitor various stages and aspects of the program? Will there be a Policy and Procedure oversight committee who has leadership and ownership responsibility for all documents issued? Each of these alternatives comes with a cost and their own benefits.

  o The Senior Executive sponsor (the one signing the Preface page) shall mandate the policy and procedure program and authorize the Program Manager to execute the mandate.

  o In accordance with Records and Information Management policies and procedures, documents within the Policy and Procurement Manual must be retained in accordance with the Records and Information Management policy and procedure. Since the documents are encouraged to be widely circulated internally, each document must be classified as "Internal Use Only".

- The Introduction establishes and launches the manual and should identify the:

  o Manual's framework and organization. Consider your organizational and functional structure when assessing various organization methods. As part of the introduction, consider including or referencing the organization chart and how policy and procedure ownership is determined.

    Policy and procedure manuals are generally organized based on the functional distribution of labor; for example: Sales, Marketing, Communication, Research and Development, Manufacturing and Distribution, Human Resources, Legal, and Accounting and Finance. Since all of the company's transactional activity has an impact on Accounting and Finance, this section must be made available to the entire company with the accounting and finance procedures cross referenced within the other functional policy and procedure manuals.

- o Scope of what you would like to see covered within this manual. It is at this point, you will need to know if you want a linked and aligned hierarchy with Policy, Procedure, Work Instruction, Forms and Other documents.

  If you are just beginning this process the best place to start is to begin where you are. If there is no formal documentation, my advice is to start with the basics and expand. Go to your annual report and list those items within the Management Discussion and Analysis (MD&A) where it states that you have a policy, such as Revenue, and make sure you have those on the list. Look to the P&L and B/S for those accounts where there are large balances and consider documenting those transaction those balances get there. This approach is indicative of a top-down approach.

  If you are starting with decentralized processes and haphazard, inconsistent and perhaps incomplete processes, don't worry; this is typical of most companies. Identify, list or gather all the documents which you can readily locate.

  As the program is implemented, documents can be added as they become known. You know your business best, so go to the major functional areas and ask them for the instructions they use to complete work, orientation packages they use to train new employees and the results from recent process audits.

  If you have inherited a huge volume of documentation, it must be reviewed and sorted based on its functional use, ownership and aging of the documents. Using the 80/20 rule, about 80% of the volume will probably be out of date and out of compliance with today's business procedures. In order to develop the project plan, begin with a vision of the end result. What type of manual do you want to have and what is the tentative list of topics to begin with? Update or withdraw the legacy procedures, once the new framework has been put into place.

- o Policy and procedure numbering system and how it was determined. If you plan on having a living manual, then consider developing "smart numbering" to allow for growth.

- Documents must have a reference number, so they may be easily sorted within the Policy and Procedure database. Following are two examples for numbering:

  - o Documents identified by functional organization, such as Sales referenced as SA, Research and Development as RD, Human Resources as HR and Accounting and Finance as AF. An additional scheme may be required to further organize or define policies and procedures within a functional organization. For example, AF and then AP for Accounts Payable and a number to indicate the specific procedure.

  - o Documents identified in sequential order as to when they are issued. Although this approach is valid when documents are hosted on an internal website and where other sorting and search options are available.

- o When considering how sophisticated you need to get with smart numbering, you need to gain consensus as to the volume of documents and the scope of what is to be covered, how it will be accessed and who will use it.
  - o Table of Contents. As a living Table of Contents, this document should be easy to update and maintain and list all of the relevant documents that each employee needs.
  - o Getting Started presentation. You need a presentation which describes the overall initiative and the benefits of participating in the project. The presentation communicates the project rollout to other executive sponsors, document owners and as awareness for individual departments.

- Program Policies and Procedures. It may seem strange, but you will need a "Policy and Procedure" to establish the Policy and Procedure Program. These documents establish the mandate that this is a Company initiative and is owned by all employees.

The Program Policies and Procedures include documentation to cover the following:

- Create, Revise, Issue Policies and Procedures and a recommended template.

- Request to Deviate from Issued Policies and Procedures. This policy and procedure grants permission to users for temporary or permanent deviations. Using this discipline allows:

  a. Executives and senior managers to know about and measure constraints in different areas of the business
  b. Internal controls to be added, which may be required to monitor or mitigate any risks the deviation may cause and assists with internal control testing and/or internal audits
  c. The program manager to measure compliance with issued policies.

- Rescind issued policies and procedures. To complete the audit trail for formal documents, having a review and approval for those documents which can and should be rescinded in important.

- Policy and Procedure content including those policies and procedures the company have approved for issuance.

This manual provides sample documents which could be personalized and customized to meet your company's needs. Using the URL, download the book and customize it. Replace my company's IDÆAL, LLP's (used at the beginning of each document) name with your Company's name. Follow the document layout and adjust the scope and process flow using your Company's language and procedure.

Everything contained within the book is contained within the URL download. The URL contains a complete manual. To download the product, follow the download instructions.

This download is an accumulation of Microsoft Word, Excel and Powerpoint documents named and numbered in accordance with the Table of Contents. The downloadable files are distributed on an "as is" basis without warranties of any kind.

Preface

To: Company Controller or Document Program Manager:

This manual provides you with sample documents which must be personalized and customized to meet your company's needs. Using the download from the URL . . . replace my company's IDÆAL, LLP's (used at the beginning of each document) name with your Company's name. Follow the document layout and adjust the scope and process flow using your Company's language and procedure.

These documents should be used as a starting point for constructing or documenting your Company's policies and procedures.

Welcome to an exciting process. As you work through the process, the outcomes will present you with insights and opportunities about your Company that you may not be currently aware. Use this manual as a starting point to assess the maturity of the accounting and finance processes. As you address each of the processes, if the documentation process comes "easy" (i.e., is currently available, is followed by most if not all of your Company's subsidiaries and locations; is measured and used as a basis for continuous process improvement) then the process is mature and there will be no surprises.

Documentation is the backbone of the company, which indicates that the company is run "with purpose" and "not by accident". The quality and strength of the documentation is an indicator of the quality and strength of the Company.

Congratulations on taking this step and acquiring this valuable resource. The Post Script (PS) gives you some helpful background information about getting started. Enjoy the journey.

Rose Hightower
April 2008

Before Getting Started

Before getting started, a word about policy, process and procedure, program and the level of detail you would like to see.

Policy statements and Procedural instructions must be aligned: A policy is a statement identifying the authoritative direction and control; it is a business rule that must be followed throughout the Company. A procedure is a set of instructions, listing the steps, which need to be performed, to execute the authoritative direction and control specified in the policy statement. The procedure is what is tested for compliance with Sarbanes-Oxley act (SOX) and Internal Audit purposes. If the procedure is in compliance, the policy is deemed to be followed. Therefore, the procedure should link back to your company's internal control testing and internal audit programs.

Following is more on policy statements, procedures and work instructions.

- Policy statements may describe the business "concepts", "principles", and must be worded as a directive, providing authority, direction and control for a specific area of the business. Think of Policy statements as "thou shall" statements which must be followed in order for the company to be managed "with purpose."

- Process describes the procedures which connect operational or transactional functions together such as:

  o Sales leads to sales quotes to sales order processes include such procedures related to sales gathering leads with the aid of marketing and working the sales process until the customer is presented with a quote and closing the deal to with a sales order

  o Sales order to fulfilling the product or service delivery to customer acceptance to issuing an invoice to collecting on that invoice with the cash process and includes the procedures related to the Company receiving and assessing sales orders through the contracting phases, through the delivery phases, through the invoicing phase, through to collections and cash

  o Procuring raw materials, inventory, equipment, goods and/or services, through the procurement request, authorization, issuing the purchase order to receiving and accepting the goods and/or services to receiving the vendor's invoice and reconciling and paying the invoice processes which includes procedures related to assessing company purchasing/asset acquisition needs through approval, procurement, delivery, asset control, accounts payable and cash disbursement

  o Raw materials to finished goods processes which includes procedures related to receipting raw material inventory and materials management through the production/operational cycles until there are finished goods and final inventory available for sale. This process includes inventory movement, physical counts, costing methodologies, and reserves for obsolete, excess and scrap.

- o Human Resource recruitment to post employment processes which includes procedures dealing with Human Resources and includes recruitment, hiring, training, performance management, termination and post employment
- o Managing business information processes include procedures related to master data design, data collection, data storage, data access and distribution. Converting data to information for accounting and finance is reflected in recording transactions, producing in process and end of cycle reports for analysis, reconciliation, and effective and timely decision making.

- Procedures are subsets of processes; however, depending on how processes are defined, procedures may be the process itself. For example, on one hand, Accounts Receivable is a process including such sub-processes or procedures as Credit Administration, Collection and Cash Applications. On the other hand, Accounts Receivable is a procedure of the sales order to cash receipts process. Because one is a subset of the other and can be further subdivided, you may see the words "process" and "procedure" used interchangeably.

- Work instructions are procedure details and often are at a level where employees are directed where and when to "click" or where and when to locate certain information.

A program includes all of the above and generally has a specific scope; such as Inventory Management program defined as converting raw materials into finished goods, the Physical Inventory count program defined as identifying inventory and conducting physical counts and valuation. Whereas a process is the continuous loop of the cycle, a program is defined as one pass-through of the process or a process event.

I suggest establishing consensus as to the level of detail you would like to see in the procedures and be consistent.

Another decision you will have to make either for each document individually or for all, is whether the policies and procedures need to relate to specific:

- countries, regions or geographies or to all, i.e., globally

- business units as defined by products and services the company provides or to all Company legal entities

- functional business areas within Accounting and Finance such as Treasury, Tax, Corporate, Accounting and Finance administration

Addressing this topic early, assists with the determination of how you would like to organize the documents within a Table of Contents.

Before we establish the Program, we need to further define where and how the Program fits into the Company's governance, risk and compliance strategy and the audience the documents will serve.

Policies and procedures are considered a governance tool for a Company to establish direction, provide control and communicate those parameters to its employees. A component of risk is the measurement or degree of control expressed within the Company's documentation and the resulting implementation of that direction. A Company's capacity and tolerance of risk may be defined within its policies and procedures, however it is measured through a variety of tools including Sarbanes-Oxley testing. Compliance is a measure of adherence to and the accuracy of implementation that a given policy or procedure defines. Generally in today's environment, compliance is the domain of internal audit, while Sarbanes-Oxley testing and risk falls within the Internal Controls function. Therefore, policies and procedures are a starting point for a governance, risk and compliance program.

A word about ISO9000 documentation: the documentation, although similar to policies and procedures, is not the same. ISO requires more work instruction and desk type documentation. That is documentation which is very specific to the task at hand. For the Accounting and Finance Policy and Procedure Program, we are looking for a broader perspective and the highest common process denominator used by the business.

A word about where the documents will reside: There are many competitive off-the-shelf software applications which will help to organize your Accounting and Finance policies and procedures. Following is some food for thought when comparing software products and their features or when designing an in-house application:

- Hierarchy of documents and the ability to link one document with another

- Adding Company specific messages to the application so that employees may be informed as to the items which are new or have changed

- Change access rights to the application must be by authorized personnel only

- View access rights to the documentation must be available to all employees, however if there is a feature which allows for certain documents to be viewed by a specific group or individually identified employees, that may be beneficial for some company formats. Example, your company may not want all employees to know about the Executive Travel Reimbursement.

- Aging reports for documents in draft or in circulation, i.e., those documents not yet approved for issuance

- Aging reports to identify how long a document has been issued without being updated or revalidated for accuracy and completeness

- Customizable "workflow" or authorization workflow so that documents may be forwarded to specific subject matter experts or process owners for review and approval

- Document version control during the review and approval process in order to keep track of who provided which input

- You should compare costs to ensure that there are enough licenses so that an appropriate number of users whether specifically named or concurrent may access the database at the same time

- You should compare costs and accessibility benefits between Web based vs. server based applications

- You should consider if an on-site system administrator or application training be required

Getting Started with the Program

First define the Program, it is recommended that at a minimum, the Program should have elements to address the

- Program's Mandate as defined by the Principles, Charter, Vision, Mission, Goals,

- A Plan to execute on delivering the content and managing the Program, which requires following a work plan and keeping to the time schedule and measuring progress, and

- Delivering a product that is consistent in format, quality and is relevant and useful to its audience

A Program Charter documents the goals and objectives of the program and <u>authorizes</u> the Program Manager to implement and execute the Program.

When putting together your Program Charter, it is wise to consider the principles which serve as the underlying foundation and framework. Principles could be based on standards, rules and/or behaviors.

- Standards-based principles refer to the terms and conditions such as accepting documentation as long as there is an identified process owner, cross functional collaboration, review and approval.

- Rules-based principles include matching documentation with the citations which govern specific activities such as: complying with and referencing FAS 151 for inventory

- Behavior-based principles direct employee behavior such as a procedure which requires employees to identify that the goods and/or services have been received prior to Accounts Payable, processing the payment to the third party vendor.

Consider how a policy and procedure about verifying the physical inventory count would differ depending on the type of principles adopted.

- Standards-based: might indicate that 1/3 of the inventory must be counted each quarter with high-valued inventory counted twice during a fiscal year.

- Rules-based: might emphasize the valuation, classification of the inventory as well as when it must be written down or written off.

- Behavior-based: might emphasize the roles and responsibilities of each person who comes in contact with the inventory and materials management.

While a good policy and procedure would contain references to all of the principles, the documentation format and content would vary depending on the audience. Before the content is scoped out, thinking about the audience and planning for the way the information will be presented is an important step. This is not just a stylistic option, but rather an extension of "tone from the top" communication.

As with any new program or to revitalize and/or redirect an existing Program, consider establishing a Vision, Mission and Goals. Aligning the vision, mission and goals means to ensure that there is a direct cause and effect of one item leading to another. For additional information reference the chapter on the Program's Mandate.

For example: In order to support a Company's vision of *"To be the Company's central source and resource for issuing Accounting and Finance Policies and Procedures"* create a visual counterpoint such as: "Imagine a company where any employee could locate the policy, procedure and related forms and instructions, ensure they are following the rules and/or enter a question or request to deviate from those rules"

Following this Vision, an aligned Mission statement might be: *"To establish and maintain an Accounting and Finance Policy and Procedure Program"* by performing activities *"to Consolidate existing documentation under one repository (database)".* Notice that there is a direct cause and effect from the statement of being, i.e., Vision to the action i.e., Mission. Establish as many action statements as you need to support achieving the Vision.

An obvious goal would be to ensure that *"Policies and Procedures will not reside anywhere else, i.e., a metric of 0 unofficial repositories".* For each mission or action objective, there should be a corresponding goal; all the time, ensuring that as the goal is achieved, it is a measure of the action, i.e., Mission and Goals contributes toward achieving the Vision.

If everything is truly aligned, then the benefit statements will link to the external rules and regulations and produce good governance. It is not an accident that the program benefits are linked to comply with Governance statements.

As example: *Standardize policies and procedures* in order to:

- *Improve the effectiveness and efficiency in processing accounting transactions*

- *Guide the interpretation and analysis for improved financial reporting*

- Comply with external reporting requirements from external auditors, Securities and Exchange Commission and Financial Accounting Standards

Other operational benefits will improve bottom-line profitability and will include:

- Considering cross-functional operational needs when managing transactional flow and decision making

- Using a common language or at least understanding the differences in language use with an ability to reconcile the differences

- Closing the loop on operational process handoffs and reducing the risk of control deficiencies

The policy statement is often the most difficult aspect to determine. I find that unless the policy is driving the process, it is better to begin with the process flow, representing the current state and back into the policy statement(s) i.e., look for guiding principles or business rules which are embedded within the procedure.

When developing a policy and procedure document, having a flowchart of the process or a process description is a good place to start.

The process flow may be different from the information flow or the workflow. Unless it is a mature process which has been proven and where little or no continuous improvement (effectiveness or efficiency actions) is required, I suggest beginning with the process. A process is a **definable, repeatable, predictable, measurable** set of activities or tasks that produce or navigate the work. A process view that includes:

- A plan i.e., performing the tasks with purpose, not by accident

- Execution or implementing the tasks and choosing checkpoints where decisions are required

- Analysis where data becomes information and information becomes courses of action

A process description begins with the input requirement triggers. Ask yourself what criteria or situation prompts the beginning of this process. Spend some time with the triggers and situations which begin the process. **Ensure there is a direct cause and effect on the process.**

In developing process descriptions, you don't have to get too detailed. I try to define processes using a few pages and no more than a dozen steps. Each step may be further defined as a sub process, procedure or work instruction. **You have to work to keep it simple.** This approach focuses your thoughts on the cause and effect of each step and assists with keeping the procedure succinct.

If you are using flowcharts keep the process flowcharts simple and easy to read. Simple process flowcharts are defined as the highest common denominator which links processes across all of the Company's subsidiaries and departments. Simple process flowcharts include only a few design elements.

- Square boxes represent process areas; since this box structure represents work, define square boxes using verbs

- Diamond shape boxes represent decision junctions; word this box in the form of a close-ended question and remember to address yes and no decision outcomes

- Database icons to represent stored information to highlight information access and flow

Once you are happy with the process flow, step back and take a look. "**What do you want to tell your employees about the process?**" should be the basis for the policy statement.

Another hint – each handoff (i.e., movement from one box to another) is an opportunity for an internal control or process measurement point.

Use this opportunity to review the process and search for areas which may streamline the process (i.e., cut out steps), add control-steps (i.e., link with your Sarbanes-Oxley initiatives) and/or better define roles and responsibilities.

PROJECT PLAN FOR THE PROGRAM

As with any good project planning approach the following steps should be taken. The presentation attached to this manual gives examples of the various tools which should be customized and adapted to your specific organizational needs.

Following are some helpful hints for creating a successful project. The presentation material which follows expands on a few of these hints. This manual is not designed to elaborate on or provide a project management course.

There should be a project sponsor, in this case, we are looking for an executive sponsor such as the Chief Executive Officer (CEO) or Chief Financial Officer (CFO) to serve as advocate. A good Program Manager will often have the necessary Project Management skills and may serve as Project Manager for this project. Project Team members often include the CFO's direct reports.

Before the project can be scoped out, it is important to assess the current environment and establish the scope not only for the project but for the program. In order to adequately address the scope, the audience or recipients of the Accounting and Finance Policies and Procedures as well as the beneficiaries of the program must be identified.

It is important to identify the deliverables for the project as well as the program. For example, the project deliverables would be to have a defined Accounting and Finance Policy and Procedure Program established and implemented. The product deliverable for the Program would be to produce individual Accounting and Finance policies and procedures.

Once the current and future states have been identified in enough detail to produce a list of actionable activities, a work breakdown schedule may be developed with the actions assigned to those who have the skills and authority to execute them.

A process flow of how the Program will be executed should be prepared and serves as both a communication and implementation tool.

For those named to participate within the Accounting and Finance Policy and Procedure Program, consideration and delivery of the education and skills required to successfully perform their roles and responsibilities must be arranged.

Progress must be monitored and communicated to the team members and executive sponsors.

The content of what the program will include must be determined, so that at the end of the project, the program begins.

For additional program information or support, contact me as the Policyguru@ optonline.net or via http://www.idealpolicy.com.

Developing the Table of Contents

One of the last steps before you can get started is to determine the list of documents or table of contents which will make up the universe of Accounting and Finance Policies and Procedures.

The Table of Contents can be developed from the following types of techniques:

- Brainstorm key or important topics

- Examine the Chart of Accounts

- Annual report and other outward facing communication – see your external website for "policy" statements

- FASB pronouncements

Accounting policies and procedures follow US Generally Accepted Accounting Principles (GAAP) and include the ones which are identified within your annual report and other outward facing documentation. Finance policies and procedures document the way internal transactional processing, analysis and decision-making is conducted within your Company. Together Accounting and Finance policies and procedures define the Company's culture and environment not only recognizing the "tone from the top" but more importantly, how that "tone" translates to executing work.

Then of course there are non-Accounting and Finance policies and procedures critical to the Accounting and Finance processes these include and are not limited to: Insider Trading, Post-Employment Benefits, Procurement, Records and Information Management, Travel, Entertainment and Expense. These documents may not be "owned" by Accounting and Finance functions, however, they are very important to Accounting and Finance personnel because these affect the methodology and controls on how Accounting and Finance employees execute their roles.

Once a preliminary list for the table of content topics is determined, classify, group and prioritize the topics to be issued, revised or rescinded. Assign each document an owner and schedule the work.

The Program Manager should monitor this list and report on its progress to the executive sponsor. Because this is a dynamic process, expect the topics on the list to change. Responding to this change is part of the Program Manager's skill.

HIERARCHY OF DOCUMENTS

The hierarchy of documents links policies to procedures to work instructions. One could link the hierarchy of documents to an organization chart identifying process owners and cross-functional teams which participate in the design, execution, approval, monitoring and reporting of the Company's core processes. A smart policy and procedure program includes organizing the documentation into a "smart" hierarchy such as account classification, business unit or geography responsibility.

Following are a few examples of "smart" hierarchies.

ACC	Refers to Accounting policies and procedures organized by and using the same numbering convention as the Chart of Accounts.
1xx	Refers to Asset accounts as identified in the Chart of Accounts
101	Cash related documents
101.1	Cash and Banking policy and procedure
101.2	Investing excess Cash and Marketable Securities
141	Fixed Assets, Long Lived Assets, Property, Plant and Equipment
141.1	Acquiring Fixed Assets
141.6	Disposing of Fixed Assets

FIN	Refers to Finance policies and procedures organized by the type of policy and procedure with some documents identified as more important than others. So as not to confuse this numbering with the one above, the numbering may be shown as: FIN101.
1xx	Delegation of Authority
101.1	Delegation of Authority for purchasing goods and/or services from third party vendors
101.2	Delegation of Authority for acquiring goods and/or services used as part of Cost of Sales
101.3	Delegation of Authority for acquiring or disposing of fixed assets
241.1	Account Analysis and Reconciliation
421.1	Financial Planning and Analysis
421.2	Financial Planning and Analysis – guidance
421.3	Financial Planning and Analysis – key indicators
421.6	Financial Planning and Analysis – forecasting

ACF	Refers to Accounting and Finance policies and procedures organized by functional area. This approach works well where the functions have clearly defined roles and responsibilities and the documentation is intended to support that specific functional area only.
Axx	Introduction and overview of the Program policies and procedures
Bxx	Accounting related policies and procedures listed in alphabetical order, sequentially numbered based on when they were issued, organized by functional area
	Policies and procedures listed in Alphabetical order
BA01	Accounts Payable
BA02	Accounts Payable
	Policies and procedures listed in sequential order based on when they were issued
B01	Financial Code of Ethical Conduct
B02	Account Reconciliation
	Policies and procedures organized by functional area
BAxxx	Corporate with policies and procedures requiring global adminstration
BBxxx	General Accounting
BCxxx	Treasury
BDxxx	Tax

ACF	Refers to Accounting policies and procedures organized by Geography. This organization lends itself to a decentralized organization where each region has different procedures probably based on different systems and reporting needs. A variation of this approach could be adopted for a conglomerate which has independent business units.
1xx	Global policies and procedures
101	Business Combinations and Consolidations
101.1	Accounting for Mergers and Acquisitions
2xx	North America policies and procedures
3xx	Europe, Middle East and Africa policies and procedures
4xx	Latin America
5xx	Asia and the Pacific region

It takes time and forethought to determine the type of numbering scheme that is suitable for your company. It requires that there is a long term plan as to how the Program will be organized and run. To select a documentation hierarchy methodology which is right for your Company, you have to know who you are and what you want from the Program.

Select a documentation hierarchy which is right for your Company. In order to figure out what is right for your company, begin with an evaluation of "who you are". A "Who you are" analysis typically considers:

- How is the company organized and who retains ownership; for example, business units, geography, functional processes

- How is process ownership defined; for example, along organizational lines of command, at the desk level

- What drives your Company, in other words when making decisions who or what is the primary consideration; Customers, Product lines, Competition, Shareholders, Employees

- How does work get done; for example, through project management on an event by event basis, process management using a continuous loop of activities

Answering these questions and aligning the responses ensures the document management Program will have the appropriate content, business unit representation in the review and approval process, and document classification.

Self Assessment

A strong documentation program including the company's policies and procedures indicates that the company is run "with purpose" and "not by accident". The quality and strength of the documentation is an indicator of the Company's health and fitness.

Documentation is not only a "nice to have" but it is a "need to have". It is not about the quantity but rather the quality of documented processes which are required. Regulations require that the transaction as well as the documentation be:

(a) accurate; that is, say what you do, do what you say and prove it

(b) complete; that is, involving interaction across functions to link the end to end process

(c) valid; that is, contain controls to ensure that the data and information is error free

(d) authorized; that is, reviewed and approved by executive sponsors

(e) obeyed; that is, tested and audited with differences considered as weaknesses requiring remediation

Ask the process owners, representatives from the Internal Control and Internal Audit to participate and "grade" the "health" of the documentation program. In addition, ask them for a few comments as to what works well, what needs improvement, what would they like to see? The Program Manager uses this as input to produce a Program plan.

In order to measure the "health" of your company's program, following is a scorecard. The scorecard graduates from ad hoc, that is with little or no documentation through to a systematic and integrated approach toward achieving Best in Class status.

- An ad hoc approach occurs when . . . Documentation is provided when needed as a reactive response when deficiencies are uncovered from the testing or audit process

- Awareness is achieved when . . . Documentation is managed in functional silos and generally encompasses a bottom-up, "say what you do" approach. Don't be surprised if your company ranks here. This is where most companies operate.

- Deployment is considered to have occurred when . . . A systematic approach is applied to the basic processes as defined by external requirements such as the Securities and Exchange Commission (SEC), Sarbanes-Oxley, and includes some cross functional participation and some executive sponsorship. The documentation process still comes at the end and is reactive. A subject matter expert is assigned the task of documentation manager.

- An integrated stage is where most companies chose to operate and this is achieved when . . . An effective systematic approach defined by the Company's key processes which includes cross functional review and approval. The company's business has been "mapped" into key processes with each process having an executive sponsor and owner. A Policy and Procedure Program Manager is a valued resource who identifies opportunities, leads individual projects and coordinates the Program.

- The Best in Class and fully embedded program occurs when an effective systematic approach, fully responsive to its multiple requirements integrates instruction, design and development, evaluation and assessment, and leadership into managing the Accounting and Finance Policy and Procedure program.

Stage	Description
Ad hoc 0–20%	A **reactive response** to deficiencies uncovered from internal control testing or auditing
Awareness 21–40%	Documents **managed in functional silos** ex. Accounts Payable (AP) policies for AP employees
Deployed 41–60%	**An approach is applied** to meet the basic requirements as defined by external requirements
Integrated 61–80%	A **systematic approach** where the Company's key processes are mapped and documented using **cross functional participation**
Embedded 81–100%	An effective systematic approach, **fully responsive** to the Program's multiple requirements

A healthy policy and procedure program means that there is ongoing vigilance and research comparing your company's individual policies and procedures to: what is going on inside the company, i.e., measure internal compliance and to the regulations and best practices used by other companies within your industry, i.e., monitor external regulations and competitive comparisons. Note that not only will adherence to the document's content be measured, but the documentation program itself must also be evaluated for internal compliance and compared to external best Program practices.

The scale moves from ad hoc to a disciplined approach, from a scope of some to all and with deployment being measured as reactive to embedded. Bottom line, the Program requires all the phases of Program Management and all the skills of a good Program and Project Manager.

PROGRAM

	Policy and Procedures	
Procedure No. A01	Section: Introduction	Page 1 of 6
	Program Mandate	
Department Ownership	Issue/Effective Date:	Replaces previously issued

Prepared by: Date	Approved by: Date	Authorized by: Date

Governance

According to the International Federation of Accountants (IFAC) Governance refers to a set of responsibilities and practices exercised by management with the goal of providing strategic direction and tactical guidance to ensure that company goals and objectives are achieved, risks are identified and managed appropriately, and resources assigned responsibly.

The Company has defined three levels of governance:

- For Market Stability and to protect investors, external — or big G—Governance originates from laws and regulatory organizations such as the SEC, Financial Accounting Standards Board (FASB) Public Company Accounting Oversight Board (PCAOB).

- Corporate—or little g—Governance is defined and initiated from the Executive Team and the Board of Directors and exercised by Internal Control over Financial Reporting (ICOFR).

- Internal or Business Governance is marked by the integration of little g governance into the internal practices and processes required to get the work done.

At all three levels of governance, governance is about providing authoritative direction and control for leadership, integrity and accountability. The Accounting and Finance Policy and Procedure Program is about satisfying little g governance at the Corporate and internal practice and process level.

Critical to communicating and implementing governance, documentation is the <u>foundation</u> which defines the purpose, scope, and content for the policies and procedures to be implemented.

- Using a top-down approach, documentation communicates and provides the principles, rules and behaviors of the greater employee population. Documentation is used to communicate and <u>provide authority to employees to act</u> within defined parameters.

- Using a bottom-up approach, documentation informs management of the steps required to process transactions, and with review and analysis, these steps indicate where and when processes need to be revisited or transformed.

At this point it is useful to differential between the Program and the product of the Program's efforts, the Accounting and Finance Policy and Procedure documents. Project Management is concerned with a defined deliverable that has a beginning and an end. The Program follows a process to ensure the consistent execution of each of the projects. The Program is made up of projects to document specific processes. However, the Program itself is a process and must be documented. The rest of this chapter concerns itself with the Program's processes and documentation.

The Program secures its mandate from the Program's Charter, Vision, Mission and Goals.

	Policy and Procedures	
Procedure No. A01	Section: Introduction	Page 2 of 6
	Program Mandate	
Department Ownership	Issue/Effective Date:	Replaces previously issued

Program's Charter

Policies and procedures are a function of corporate governance and, as such, must be sponsored and approved by executive leadership, implemented at the business area level with responsibility and accountability for compliance held at every level.

Corporate policies are established to provide a high-level overall plan defining general goals and acceptable procedures. Corporate procedures define a particular way of accomplishing a task and include authority levels, controls, and areas of responsibility.

Business area or functional policies must be aligned and support corporate policies while applying local laws and regulations. Business area or functional procedures document the implementation of corporate procedures.

IDÆAL, LLP's policies and procedures are prepared and coordinated by the Corporate Policy and Procedure department with support and counsel of the policy and process owner and related stakeholders. Only policies and procedures issued or delegated by this organization with proper approval can be considered a company policy and as such is expected to be followed by all employees.

Selected business area representatives are invited to participate as part of the Policy and Procedure Review Committee (Committee), in the preparation, review, and approval of policies and procedures. These individuals must be appointed by the executive leadership team.

The Committee assists the Policy and Procedure department in overseeing the integrity of the Company's Policy and Procedure Program as well as the Company's outward facing statements which may be considered company policies and procedures.

Committee Membership and Representation

The Committee will be composed of at least five members representing the executive leadership. Members of the Committee must represent Legal, Finance, International, and the business areas. The chairperson of the Committee is generally the Policy and Procedure Program Manager. Committee members shall be appointed, for a period of at least one year. It is the responsibility of the chairperson of the Committee to schedule meetings and provide the Committee with a written agenda for all meetings. Decisions will be based on group discussion and consensus.

Meetings and Other Actions

The Committee shall meet at least quarterly and as often as it determines appropriate to carry out its obligations under this Charter. The Committee shall periodically report on its activities to the executive leadership and make such recommendations and findings as it deems appropriate.

Policy and Procedures		
Procedure No. A01	Section: Introduction	Page 3 of 6
	Program Mandate	
Department Ownership	Issue/Effective Date:	Replaces previously issued

Meetings of the Committee may be held in person or by teleconference. Action may also be taken by the Committee without a meeting if all members consent by electronic transmission with the minutes of the proceedings of the Committee. The Committee shall document and monitor their proceedings and actions.

The Committee shall meet periodically in executive sessions with management, including the Chief Financial Officer and General Counsel, internal auditors, and others the Committee deems appropriate to discuss the general framework, strategy, and direction for policy and procedure documentation.

Goals, Responsibilities, and Authority

The Committee shall have the authority, to the extent it deems necessary or appropriate, to secure the participation of subject matter experts and advisors.

The Corporation shall provide appropriate funding and resources to the Policy and Procedure department as well as to the Committee in order to execute its responsibilities.

The Committee shall review and reassess the adequacy of this charter at least annually and recommend any proposed changes to executive leadership for approval. The Committee shall review its own performance at least annually.

Scope and Objective

The Policy and Procedure Program may encompass any Company activity and is responsible for the following activities:

* Review and appraise the soundness, adequacy, and application of Company and business area policies and procedures.

* Review and test the process scope and compliance with statutory, regulatory, and internal policy requirements.

* Prepare and coordinate approval and implementation for policies and procedures.

Program's Vision

A vision is a forward-looking statement which when properly constructed provides direction and inspiration for the Program. For this Program, our vision is to be the Company's central source and resource for issuing Accounting and Finance Policies and Procedures.

Policy and Procedures		
Procedure No. A01	Section: Introduction	Page 4 of 6
	Program Mandate	
Department Ownership	Issue/Effective Date:	Replaces previously issued

Imagine a company where any employee could:

- locate the policy, procedure and related forms and instructions

- ensure they are following the rules and/or enter a question or request to deviate from the rules

Imagine a company where there is a management resource center and a program to ensure Policies and Procedures are:

- approved by a cross functional team

- aligned with external reporting certifications, internal controls, audits and process management

Program's Mission

The mission statement provides direction and action as to how the vision statement will be achieved. Each of the higher-level actions must be de-constructed to lower level action items which will ensure a successful implementation.

The Program's mission is to establish and maintain an Accounting and Finance Policy and Procedure Program in order to:

A. Consolidate existing documentation under one repository (database)

B. Review the existing documentation for relevancy, timeliness, accuracy, consistency

C. Align with Company goals and performance objectives

D. Include rollout Communication, Education and Training

E. Be led by a qualified Program Manager

A. Consolidate existing documentation under one repository (database) has the following individual actions:

- Eliminate redundant and "unofficial" sites (including emails, Websites and binders) where policies and procedures are retained

- Create/acquire a Web-based application with search capabilities available to all employees–anytime, anywhere

- Flexible enough to support: documentation hierarchy, workflow authorization, instruction, question and answer

Policy and Procedures		
Procedure No. A01	Section: Introduction	Page 5 of 6
	Program Mandate	
Department Ownership	Issue/Effective Date:	Replaces previously issued

B. Review the existing documentation to address:

- Relevancy – Is the Company still in that line of business? Does the process exist the same way today?

- Timeliness – Is the documentation current?

- Accuracy – Does the documentation reflect current rules, regulations and Company direction?

- Consistency – Do all related processes and business areas follow the same process?

C. Align with Company goals and performance objectives by considering the following criteria:

- Reflect and comply with laws and regulations

- Reflect the Company's culture, philosophy and ethics

- Measured and tested for compliance

- Certified by the process owners and business areas

- Used to promote process effectiveness and efficiency through continuous improvement

D. Include rollout Communication, Education and Training where and as appropriate:

- Communicate as the documents are issued, revised or rescinded

- Provide instruction, education and training to support the policy and procedure concepts and implementation

- Provide a feedback mechanism to ensure employees have a way to provide comments, ask questions and locate support

E. Led by a qualified Program Manager who has:

- Qualified with Accounting and Finance technical knowledge

- Demonstrated experience within various aspects of the business and industry

- Demonstrated proficiency in process and project management

- Demonstrated proficiency in communication and relationship management skills

Program Goals

In order for goals to be effective, they must be specific and measurable. Deciding what to measure takes careful consideration and definition. The objective is to choose a few goals which are directly related to the vision and mission.

Policy and Procedures		
Procedure No. A01	Section: Introduction	Page 6 of 6
	Program Mandate	
Department Ownership	Issue/Effective Date:	Replaces previously issued

The goal of the Program is to implement a program that is considered "Best Practice" within our Company and across the industry externally benchmarked.

In our company, Internally, "Best Practice" considers the following criteria and has corresponding measures:

- Policies and Procedures not residing anywhere else (i.e., a metric = 0 unofficial repositories)

- Program Manager has service level agreements with each process owner and business area. Process owners and business areas are defined in accordance with the Company's organization charts and may contain measures such as 40 process owners and 6 business areas and May include non-Accounting and Finance process owners

  - The program manager's goals might include being responsive to internal customer needs with measured Customer Satisfaction levels such as achieving a 100% Customer Satisfaction as per a survey

  - Maintain log and resolve all unsatisfactory issues with the documentation within a defined time period, such as 30 days

  - Practicing continuous process improvement by establishing process metrics for the Program itself and to collect data and trends for

    - Efficiency i.e., cycle time to respond to inquiries, to issue documents

    - Effectiveness i.e., process-oriented defects counted as revisions within a six-month period

As agreed in the mandate, Externally, "Best Practice" means:

- Benchmark the process and approach with external companies of like size and industry

- Target two benchmark activities per year. This might include corresponding with other companies or conducting on-site exchange visits.

- Use the information collected during these exchanges for process improvements to the Program itself

- Promote our best internal practices externally via:

  - Published articles e.g., target twice (2) per year

  - Speaking / presentation engagements e.g., target three times (3) per year

In order to keep track of the Program's progress, the Program Manager must collect data and report on the program's goals and status of achieving the mission. The Program Manager forwards this report to the executive sponsor and other interested parties who have ownership in achieving the Program's success and benefits.

	Policy and Procedures	
Procedure No. A02	**Overview—Getting Started:** **Presentation**	Page 1 of 12

Note to Readers: The PowerPoint presentation may be found as a download from the URL www .wiley.com/go/hightower with comments for the presenter and the content of the slides presented here. Customize the presentation to address your company's operational environment.

This presentation includes the basics and tools used in project and program management. The presentation should be used as a basis for planning the Program and its related communication. This presentation includes sections that address the:

A. Vision, Mission, and Goals of the Policy and Procedure Program

B. Environment

C. Project Plan

D. First Steps

A. Vision, Mission, and Goals of the Policy and Procedure Program

A program's Vision, Mission, and Goals should be aligned; that is, when one area shows success, others areas also prosper. The Vision describes a state of "being" and should be worded as a desired end point. Often described within the vision is an ultimate benefit the Company wishes to receive from the program. Mission describes a state of "doing"; by contrast, these are action statements at the highest levels. Often, these statements mimic the process flows with inputs, process, and outputs. In order for alignment to occur, what is being directed as "action" (i.e., Mission) should be a direct link to achieving the future state of "being" (i.e., Vision). As with any journey, Goals or mileposts are required to monitor direction and measure progress. The Goal should be established with the purpose of demonstrating that the vision has been achieved. True alignment is indicated by having all efforts be considered a "value add" to the Mission, Goal, and, ultimately, the Vision.

Vision

- To be the Company's central source and resource for issuing Accounting and Finance Policies and Procedures
  a. Imagine a company where any employee could:
    - Locate the policy, procedure, and related forms and instructions
    - Ensure they are following the rules and/or enter a question or request to deviate from the rules
  b. Imagine a company where there is a management resource center and a program to ensure that policies and procedures are:
    - Approved by a cross-functional team
    - Aligned with external reporting certifications, internal controls, audits, and process management

Mission

- To establish and maintain an Accounting and Finance Policy and Procedure Program to:

  a. Consolidate existing documentation under one repository (database)

  b. Review the existing documentation for relevancy, timeliness, accuracy, and consistency

  c. Align with Company goals and performance objectives

  d. Include rollout communication, education, and training

  e. Be led by a qualified program manager

Note to Reader: Each step of the mission is expanded to provide additional detail. This additional detail is used to assist with the project/program plan and may be further defined in the work breakdown schedule (or list of tasks).

- To establish and maintain an Accounting and Finance Policy and Procedure Program:

  a. Consolidate existing documentation under one repository (database)

    - Eliminate redundant and "unofficial" sites (including e-mail, folder, web, and binder) where policies and procedures are retained.

    - Create/acquire a web-based application with search capabilities available to all employees—anytime, anywhere.

    - Flexible enough to support: documentation hierarchy, workflow authorization, instruction, question and answer.

- To establish and maintain an Accounting and Finance Policy and Procedure Program:

  b. Review the existing documentation for:

    - Relevancy: Is the Company still in that line of business? Does the process exist the same way today?

    - Timeliness: Is the documentation current?

    - Accuracy: Does the documentation reflect current rules, regulations, and Company direction?

    - Consistency: Do all related processes and business areas follow the same process?

- To establish and maintain an Accounting and Finance Policy and Procedure Program:

  c. Align with Company goals and performance objectives

    - Reflect laws and regulations

    - Reflect the Company's culture, philosophy, and ethics

Procedure No. A02	**Policy and Procedures** **Overview—Getting Started:** **Presentation**	Page 3 of 12

- Measured and tested for compliance
- Certified by the process owners and business areas
- Used to promote process effectiveness and efficiency through continuous improvement

- To establish and maintain an Accounting and Finance Policy and Procedure Program:
  - d. Include rollout communication, education, and training
    - Communicate as issued, revised, or rescinded
    - Provide instruction, education, and training to support the policy and procedure concepts and implementation
    - Provide a feedback mechanism to ensure employees have a way to provide comments, ask questions, and locate support

- To establish and maintain an Accounting and Finance Policy and Procedure Program the Program must be:
  - e. Led by a qualified program manager who:
    - Is qualified with Accounting and Finance technical knowledge.
    - Has demonstrated experience within various aspects of the business and industry.
    - Has demonstrated proficiency in process and project management.
    - Has demonstrated proficiency in communication and relationship skills.

Goals

- To build and align the goals, have the Vision and Mission handy.
  - Vision: To be the Company's central source for issuing Accounting and Finance Policies and Procedures
  - Mission: To establish and maintain an Accounting and Finance Policy and Procedure Program
  - Goals: To achieve a program that is considered "Best Practice" within our Company and across the industry (externally benchmarked)
    - Internally, "Best Practice" means:
      - Policies and procedures not residing anywhere else [metric = 0 unofficial repositories]
      - Program manager has service-level agreements with each process owner and business area [with an estimated 40 process owners and 6 business areas]
        - May include non–Accounting and Finance process owners

<table>
<tr><td rowspan="2">Procedure No. A02</td><td>**Policy and Procedures**</td><td rowspan="2">Page 4 of 12</td></tr>
<tr><td>**Overview—Getting Started:**
Presentation</td></tr>
</table>

- Responsive to internal customer needs with measured customer satisfaction levels [100% customer satisfaction as per a survey]

  - Log and resolve all unsatisfactory issues.

  - Practice continuous process improvement by establishing process metrics.

    - Efficiency/Cycle time to respond to inquiries, to issue documents

    - Effectiveness/Defects counted as revisions within a six-month period

- Externally, "Best Practice" means:

  - Benchmark the process and approach with external companies of like size and industry:

    - Target two benchmark activities per year

    - Use benchmark information for process improvement

  - Promoting our best internal practice externally via:

    - Published articles—target two per year

    - Speaking/presentation engagements—target three per year

B. Environment

Note to Reader: The Environment section of the presentation identifies "Who you are" as a company, as a project, as a program. This section aids in defining the scope or definition of the work to be performed. It may seem redundant to have a "Who you are" section within a presentation to your peers and management; yet the number one reason why projects/programs fail is that the scope of work is not clearly defined. Take a hard look at the starting point and understand what the key issues are that could be stopping the company from having a successful implementation of this project.

Describe the company's current environment:

- #___ of business areas

- #___ Identified processes and process owners

- #___ Accounting and Finance professionals who rely on policies and procedures

- #___ Estimated number of policies

- #___ Estimated number of procedures

- #___ Estimated number of work instructions

- # ___ Audits and internal control findings that identify the lack of policy and procedures

Policy and Procedures		
Procedure No. A02	**Overview—Getting Started:** **Presentation**	Page 5 of 12

Issues

- Inconsistent definition and classification of policies, procedures, and work instructions

- Processes without process ownership

- Some documentation not updated for several years

- Subsidiaries and acquisitions may or may not have a policy and procedure manual or local documentation

- Chief Financial Officer, Corporate Controller, and Chief Accounting Officer rely on the integrity of the Accounting and Finance Policy and Procedure Program

Strengths, Weaknesses, Opportunities, Threats (SWOT)

Strengths

- No significant audit findings

- Executive and senior management understand the need and are willing to assign resources and review and approve all policies

- Accounting and Finance Policy and Procedure Program manager named

Weaknesses

- Limited financial audit presences

- Accounting and Financial policies are merged within other documentation.

- Company culture is only at the awareness stage for the benefits of continuous process improvement.

Opportunities

- Documentation generally exists on intranet web sites.

- Some business units have local manuals and resources available for use.

- Link and align Accounting and Finance policy and procedure objectives (Mission) with Company objectives.

Threats

- Executive and senior management attention and interest may stray due to other business concerns.

- Resources (central repository and process ownership assignment) may be delayed or go unfulfilled.

- Timing and scope of external reporting requirements

	Policy and Procedures	
Procedure No. A02	Overview—Getting Started: Presentation	Page 6 of 12

Note to Reader: After the SWOT analysis, be sure to gain commitment that the project and program as you have conceived it are worthwhile. Identify the program benefits, and be sure these can be achieved (i.e., aligned) by implementing the Mission, measured by the Goals, and will be a tangible expression of the Vision.

Program Benefits

- Standardize policies and procedures to:

  - Improve the effectiveness and efficiency in processing accounting transactions.

  - Guide the interpretation and analysis for improved financial reporting.

  - Improve the information available (timeliness and consistency) when making decisions.

  - Comply with external reporting requirements from external auditors, Securities and Exchange Commission, and Financial Accounting Standards.

C. Project/Program Plan

Note to Reader: Following is an introduction to project management and includes some of the techniques and details that a program manager would provide to the project manager. A project has start and end dates and begins with the current state and ends with when the design and development of the program is established and ready for full deployment. However, the program, like a process, goes on in a cyclical manner, ever improving its scope and output to meet changing Company needs. Once the program is established, there should be steps to allow for its continued enhancement. The following addresses a basic plan required to establish both the project and program.

Program Benefits

- Project: Establish an Accounting and Finance Policy and Procedure Program.
- Program: Establish an ongoing process for the project.
  - a. Deliverables
  - b. Work breakdown schedule
  - c. Timeline
  - d. Flowchart
  - e. Roles and responsibilities
- **a.** Project/Program Deliverables
  - Project and program time, budget, resources
  - Central repository
  - Content and database

	Policy and Procedures
Procedure No. A02	**Overview—Getting Started:** Page 7 of 12
	Presentation

- Define and gain agreement on the program and the process
- Prepare and gain approval to issue the documentation
- Issue and communicate
- Educate and train
- Measure and report

b. Work Breakdown Schedule

- Project and program time, budget, resources
  - Determine and gain approval for project start/end date and key dates for major milestones
  - Assess required resources including alternative scenarios
  - Determine and gain approval for project budget
- Central repository
  - Make or buy decision
  - Develop and install
  - Assign a system administrator
  - Train users
- Content and database
  - Define scope and document hierarchy
  - Define current and proposed table of contents
  - Assess and evaluate documents
  - Prioritize documents for validation/updating and migration to content database
- Define and gain agreement for program
  - Roles and responsibilities
  - Central review committee
  - Types of documents within the scope
  - Document format
- Define and gain agreement on the process
  - Source of documents
  - Preparation and approval procedures
  - Assessment and evaluation criteria and process

	Policy and Procedures	
Procedure No. A02	**Overview—Getting Started:** **Presentation**	Page 8 of 12

- Assign responsibility for developing new documents
- Approval reviews and sign-offs
- Document retention
- Prepare and gain approval to issue the documentation
  - Initiator and process owner to discuss
  - Circulate the preliminary draft document among the initiator, process owner, and document contact
  - Circulate the draft document to a cross-functional list of stakeholders
  - Circulate the final draft to senior management for approval and issuance
  - Prepare the final draft for issuance
  - Measure time from initiate to issue
  - Measure the number of revisions within six months
- Issue and communicate
  - Determine the types of communication that are required/wanted
  - Release the final document to the central repository
  - Send out broadcast e-mail to all who have a need to know
  - Send out follow-up e-mail or arrange to meet with those who are directly affected
  - Measure effectiveness of communication
- Education and training
  - Determine when/if education and training is required
  - Determine make/buy the material (including job aids if required)
  - Develop/acquire the material
  - Test the material
  - Roll out the education and training
  - Measure education and training coverage
  - Measure education and training effectiveness
- Measure and report
  - Project measurements
    - Work in progress and percent of completion measures

<table>
<tr><td>Procedure No. A02</td><td>**Policy and Procedures**
Overview—Getting Started:
Presentation</td><td>Page 9 of 12</td></tr>
</table>

- Timeline
- Budget and resource use
- Program measurements for continuous improvement
  - # trends__ identified processes and process owners
  - # trends__ Accounting and Finance professionals who rely on policies and procedures
  - # trends__ estimated number of policies
  - # trends__ estimated number of procedures
  - # trends__ estimated number of work instructions
  - # trends__ audits and internal control findings that identify the lack of policies and procedures

c. Timeline
  - Project timeline
    - Start date: Now
    - End date: Target 6 months
  - Program timeline
    - Begins when the project is complete

Note to Reader: Following is an example of a Gantt chart, typically used with project management to visualize the tasks and timeline as to when these tasks are due to be completed. The column on the left lists the main tasks, and the numbered row across the top is a unit of time measurement (could be days, hours, or months).

	1	2	3	4	5	6	7	8	9
Develop Project Plan	▓								
Secure Budget and Resources		x							
Develop/Acquire Central Repository		▓							
Define Content Format and Scope		▓							
Define Program and Process		▓							
Assess Current Documentation			▓	▓					
Migrate Available Documentation to Repository				x					
Prioritize Workload to Revise/Issue Documents			▓	▓	▓	▓	▓	▓	
Measure and Report to Management			▓			▓			▓

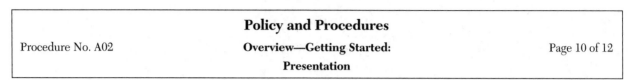

Policy and Procedures

Procedure No. A02   **Overview—Getting Started:**   Page 10 of 12
                                     Presentation

d. *Note to Reader:* Following is a process flowchart of the Policy and Procedure Program with the roles and responsibilities of the various participants listed below the flowchart.

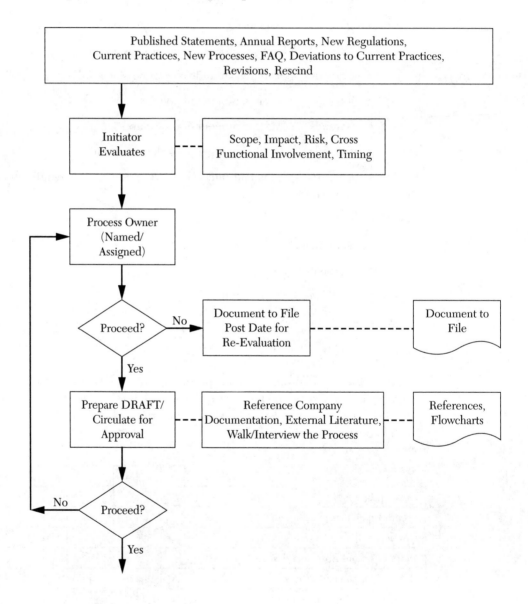

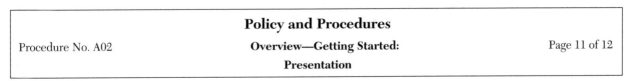

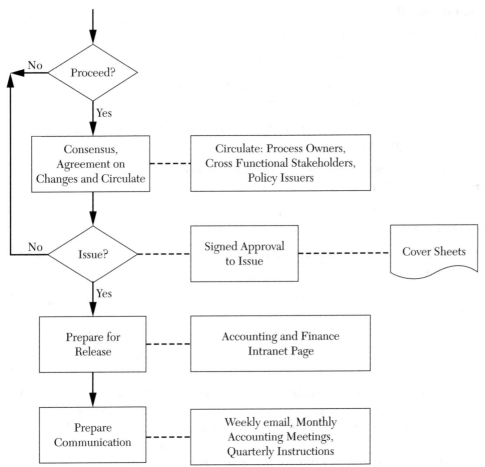

e. *Roles and Responsibilities*

- Project manager—to employ project management techniques in managing a successful project

- Systems administrator—oversees the management of the document repository

- Program manager—to employ program management techniques in managing a successful program; oversees the management of the repository's content

- Document initiator—conducts preliminary investigation as to the scope of the proposed document and gains process ownership approval to proceed

- Process owner—is responsible for the worldwide end-to-end process, including documentation, and serves as the Policy and Procedure sponsor

- Document contact—is a Policy and Procedure person who is responsible for monitoring the document through the draft, approval, and issuance process

- Cross-functional review—those subject matter experts who are or will be affected by the policy and/or procedure

- Senior manager—serves as the executive sponsor for the document and approves all documents issued by his/her process owners

D. First Steps

Note to Reader: Make sure that the last slides are action oriented, with immediate steps to be taken by the participants in the room. After you have inspired and motivated your audience, make sure they know where and how to begin. Don't lose the momentum.

- Ensure that there is an executive sponsor for the project and ongoing program.

- Develop and gain approval for the project plan, identifying scope, time, budget, and resources.

- Work the project and program plan.

Thank you

For additional information on project or program planning, contact

IDŒAL via http://www.idealpolicy.com

	Policy and Procedures	
Procedure No. A03a	Section: Introduction	Page 1 of 5
	Create, Revise, Issue Policies and Procedures	
Department Ownership	Issue/Effective Date:	Replaces previously issued

Prepared by: Approved by: Authorized by:
Date   Date   Date

Scope

The Accounting and Finance Policy and Procedure manual is prepared and maintained to reflect the Company's accepted practices and norms as well as regulatory requirements that must be integrated within Company processes.

The Accounting and Finance Policy and Procedure manual is prepared and maintained to comply with U.S. Generally Accepted Accounting Principles (U.S. GAAP) and related Federal, State and local non-US government requirements, rules or laws.

The manual applies to all IDÆAL LLP's legal entities, subsidiaries and business units.

Policy

It is IDÆAL's (Company) policy that accounting and finance employees (full or part time), understand and comply with the policies and procedures. Employees shall ensure that third party service providers, temporary help, contractors and suppliers are required to understand and comply with the policies and procedures appropriate to their responsibility and interaction.

Issued policies must be approved by cross-functional reviews that include relevant stakeholders (such as Sales, Marketing, Operations, Legal, Human Resources, Information Technology).

The Program shall be designed to:

1) Serve as the primary resource for official Company policies, procedures and technically specific instruction.

2) Standardize the method of preparation, review, issuance, revision, maintenance and audit of all official Company Policies and Procedures.

3) Ensure that existing documentation is accurate by having the process owner validate an issued document at least every two years.

The Documentation shall be designed to:

4) Evaluate and issue documentation which shall be designed to provide authoritative direction and control, safeguard the assets of the company and assign accountability.

5) Incorporate rules and regulations from governing authorities such as:

   a) Securities and Exchange Commission (SEC) rules and regulations including SEC staff accounting bulletins (SAB's) and the provisions of the Sarbanes-Oxley Act

b) The standards set forth under U.S. Generally Accepted Accounting Principles (GAAP)

c) The Foreign Corrupt Practices Act (FCPA) of 1977 and its amendments

d) The Internal Revenue Service (IRS) and other tax regulatory agencies both foreign and domestic

e) Other non U.S. and US Federal, State and local government requirements, rules or laws

6) Facilitate the issuance of financial statements and other outward facing Company pronouncements

Procedure

The following procedure identifies the:

A) Format to be used when preparing policies and procedures (PnP)

B) Preparation and Review process

A) *Format*

The person responsible for preparing the PnP should be the process owner or subject matter expert. Following the chain of command, the Chief Financial Officer's direct report responsible for the process must approve the PnP. The Chief Financial Officer is responsible for all Accounting and Finance PnP authorizes the document for issuance. The names, titles and dates of these preparers and reviewers are included as the first part of each document.

Each policy and procedure should be written with the following general headings and descriptions.

- *Scope* (optional) – Policies should be global or worldwide in scope unless otherwise stated. Special instructions or guidance may be applicable for individual countries vs. U.S. Domestic operations. Acceptable exceptions should be prefaced with a statement such as "subject to local laws and regulations" or other reason as to why there are / may be differences.

- *Policy* – The policy statement should reflect the Company's principle, plan or course of action. Background information is optional if it helps the reader understand the Company's goal in issuing the policy. The policy statement should begin with "It is Company policy that . . ." Additional information should be included to clarify or explain the policy statement. If this is significant, it may be prefaced with a subtitle of Policy Guidelines.

- *Procedure* – The procedure refers to the method in which the policy is implemented. List the key steps (generally between four and eight) required for the policy to be carried out. Consider using tables or a matrix to convey complex information or a flowchart for complex procedures.

- *Controls/Areas of Responsibility* – This section identifies specific actions or areas in charge of ultimate compliance with the procedure. Controls should be Sarbanes-Oxley compliant

Policy and Procedures		
Procedure No. A03a	Section: Introduction	Page 3 of 5
	Create, Revise, Issue Policies and Procedures	
Department Ownership	Issue/Effective Date:	Replaces previously issued

and may refer to specific checkpoints that ensure operational effectiveness, efficiency, specific measures or key process indicators. Controls generally address such areas as: validation of and access to the information, authorization levels, and separation of duties.

- *References* (optional) – References related to the policy may be included as cross references to other internally related policies and procedures and/or external sources citations.

- *Contacts* – Contacts refers to a functional area(s) with subject or process matter expertise and generally refer to the process owner.

- *Revision History* (optional) – This section applies to those PnP that have been revised. The section identifies the date and brief description of the revision. Revalidation of the policy is required at least every two years.

- *Exhibits* (optional) should be included when they are referenced within the text and add value to the understanding of complex policies and/or procedures or when standardized forms are required to support the procedure.

Each policy and procedure should follow the guidelines as described in the Exhibit. PnP should be labeled and treated as "Internal Use Only".

Unless otherwise approved, the font style (e.g., Arial), size (e.g., 11), line spacing (e.g., single space), indentation and use and style of bullets must be consistent for all documents.

B) *Preparation and Review*

Any employee or department may recommend a policy or procedure. PnP may be initiated as a result of new procedures, additions, changes or clarifications to operational processes, the Financial Accounting Standards Board, Worldwide Chart of Accounts (or summary trial balance equivalent), audit findings, frequently asked questions, the review schedule or for other reasons.

Requesting a new PnP – The originator of a procedure should prepare a draft outline and submit it to the Chief Accounting Officer (CAO) or a designate. The originator should provide basic information as to why the policy is requested and in outline form complete the template.

Revising an issued PnP – The process owner may initiate revision or the Program Manager may ask the process owner to validate a document for revision. Revised documentation shall follow the same review and approval process as defined for issuing a new PnP.

Review process – As part of the procedure to Create, Revise and Issue a Policy and Procedure an assessment should be conducted to determine if any (directly or indirectly related) existing policies require updating or withdrawal.

Policy and Procedures		
Procedure No. A03a	Section: Introduction	Page 4 of 5
Create, Revise, Issue Policies and Procedures		
Department Ownership	Issue/Effective Date:	Replaces previously issued

The review process includes the following steps:

1) Iterative reviews between the CAO and the process owner until agreement is reached on the content.

2) Cross functional peer reviews that include other departments within accounting and finance as well as other departmental stakeholders such as Legal, Internal Controls, sales and Information Systems until consensus is reached

3) Senior Management review and authorization. All policies must be approved by the CFO. Procedures must be reviewed by the Executive and/or Sr. Manager of the business area. For audit and authorization purposes, this review includes receipt of a signed document.

Revisions are updated with minor changes to an issued PnP - If an existing policy is to be revised, the revised area should be marked (e.g., in the margin or using the highlight and track changes tool within MSWord) and forward to the CAO or designate for evaluation and approval. Minor revisions may occur at any time and unless the content has changed, additional reviews and approvals are not required.

Maintenance and Validation of issued PnP - At least every two years, all issued PnP should be reviewed for completeness, accuracy, relevancy and the document shall be re-issued.

Issue PnP – Once approved, Accounting and Finance policies must be issued and posted on the Company's document repository for all official documents.

Communication – Once issued, policies should be communicated to the Accounting and Finance population as well as those who have a need to know. Documentation should be accessible to all employees. Additional communication includes and is not limited to:

- Weekly, monthly and/or quarterly announcements identifying newly issued, updated and with-drawn documents

- Business unit announcements through regularly scheduled staff meetings and business unit intranet sites

- Special/occasional broadcast emails announcing significant changes to the policy and procedure

- Accounting and Finance Policy and Procedure intranet site

Rescind issued policies - When an existing PnP is to be withdrawn, it must be documented and formally communicated. The CAO and the business areas should agree that the PnP should be withdrawn. To withdraw a policy or procedure, refer to the procedure for rescinding a policy.

Policy and Procedures		
Procedure No. A03a	Section: Introduction	Page 5 of 5
	Create, Revise, Issue Policies and Procedures	
Department Ownership	Issue/Effective Date:	Replaces previously issued

Internal Controls/Internal Audit - Internal Controls/Internal Auditing are responsible for the periodic audits of the Company's policies and procedures. Internal Controls/Internal Audit shall use the Accounting and Finance PnP as a basis for conducting testing and evaluating risk. Compliance with all policies and procedures is expected.

Control/Areas of Responsibility

The originator is responsible for providing the basic information and sponsoring the PnP through the issuing process.

Document reviewers should be chosen as subject matter experts, accounting or finance representatives or other related interested parties/stakeholders responsible to comment on the accuracy, necessity and scope of the proposed policy and procedure. They are responsible for providing a comprehensive review and authorization to issue in a timely manner.

The Chief Financial Officer (CFO) is the sponsor for all Accounting and Finance PnP; while procedures and other documents must be sponsored by the global process owner designated by the CFO. The Chief Financial Officer (or a designate) shall assign an Accounting and Finance Program Manager to oversee the execution of the Program and assign appropriate resources.

The Chief Accounting Officer (CAO) ensures PnP comply with U.S. GAAP with PnP program responsibilities reporting directly to the CAO.

A comprehensive list of current and proposed PnP should be maintained by the PnP program manager.

If a business unit or functional business area cannot comply with an issued PnP, a request for deviation must be submitted to the Chief Accounting Officer for review and approval.

Contact

Chief Financial Officer
Policy and Procedure Program Manager

Policy and Procedures		
Procedure No. A03b	Section: Introduction	Page 1 of 2
	\<Template — Name of Document\>	
Department Ownership	Issue/Effective Date:	Replaces previously issued

Prepared by:	Approved by:	Authorized by:
Date	Date	Date

Header Input:

- Procedure number: Should follow the reference or numbering scheme of the program.

- Section: Identifies how the manual is organized into segments.

- Document title:

- Document ownership: Identifies the functional organization or department which has responsibility for process ownership.

- Issue/effective Date: Generally is the same date; however, the effective date may differ and should be identified. When the effective date is different than the issue date, the procedure may have to address a transition plan.

Footer Input:

- Document classification (e.g., Internal Use Only) may vary depending on your Company's information handling guidance.

- Additional contact information generally identifies the program manager.

Scope

The scope identifies the intended audience and the range of content that is included or excluded from the discussion and/or which business areas or activities are included or excluded.

Policy

Write the policy statement as appropriate for the intended audience. This should be written in terms of business rules that mandate or constrain actions and should avoid procedural details.

Policies refer to a methodology used to guide present and future business management decisions. The policy serves as a guide to decision making, mandate or constrain actions, under a given set of circumstances. Policies are the belief and ethical framework used to implement Company objectives and reach Company goals.

The following optional segments may be included as appropriate to the policy section:

- Objectives should be used, especially if the policy statement is written as a company "intention" rather than a "direction."

- Background/guidance may be used to reference the accounting or technical literature that supports the policy statement.

- Guiding principles may be used when the policy statement is broad and requires clarification.

Procedure

Procedures refer to a specific way to implement the policy.

Procedures may represent a series of steps that, when followed, ensure a consistent approach for action and are used to produce a desired result or outcome. A documented procedure defines a series of interrelated steps that address "who, what, when, where, and how" an outcome is achieved.

Procedures may be classified into process steps such as initiation, budget, analysis, transaction entries, reconciliation, documentation, and reporting; in other words, plan, do, check and act.

Include definitions to key or unique terms as appropriate.

Control/Areas of Responsibility

Controls identify the management controls used to monitor compliance.

Areas of Responsibility identify those critical ownership areas where responsibility needs to be highlighted. Do not duplicate responsibility descriptions or references made within the body of the document.

Contact

Identify by title the person **or** department responsible for overseeing this document. You may want to include an executive sponsor and an operational contact.

Exhibit

This section is optional and may include lists, references, forms, or other information which enhances understanding or otherwise assists with implementation of the procedure.

Policy and Procedures		
Procedure No. A04	Section: Introduction	Page 1 of 4
Request to Deviate from Policies and Procedures		
Department Ownership	Issue/Effective Date:	Replaces previously issued

Prepared by: Approved by: Authorized by:
Date   Date   Date

Scope

This policy requests permission to deviate from Company-approved policies and procedures. Under no circumstances will this application extend to violating the law.

Policy

The Company recognizes that due to the changing nature of business activities, computerized systems, and accounting and finance regulations, immediate compliance with policies and procedures may not be possible. It is IDEAL LLP's (Company) policy to document and assess deviations from the approved and issued policies and procedures.

An approved deviation exempts the subsidiary or functional business area for audit noncompliance; however, it remains the subsidiary's or functional business area's responsibility to mitigate risks that may impact the control environment. Deviations must be renewed and approved annually.

Procedure

The subsidiary or functional business area requesting the deviation should determine the nature, extent, and risk of noncompliance.

- The nature relates to whether the deviation is temporary or permanent. Temporary deviations generally result from timing delays in implementing certain aspects of the policy or procedure. Permanent deviations generally result when there is no anticipated approach or date for operational compliance.

- The extent relates to scope of the deviation. Occasionally, there may be aspects of an announced policy and procedure that require additions or changes to resources and/or systems. A deviation may be requested for this transition period. Permanent deviations may exist when the policy and procedure does not correspond to local external regulatory requirements that limit or prohibit implementation.

- The risk relates to sizing the impact of noncompliance and includes both quantitative as well as qualitative aspects.

<table>
<tr><td colspan="3" align="center">**Policy and Procedures**</td></tr>
<tr><td>Procedure No. A04</td><td align="center">Section: Introduction</td><td align="right">Page 2 of 4</td></tr>
<tr><td colspan="3" align="center">**Request to Deviate from Policies and Procedures**</td></tr>
<tr><td>Department Ownership</td><td align="center">Issue/Effective Date:</td><td align="right">Replaces previously issued</td></tr>
</table>

The subsidiary or functional business area should research, review, and analyze alternative approaches and the associated costs and resources required to comply with the policy and procedure. Cost vs. benefit considerations may include but are not limited to:

- Outsourcing the function or procedure in question

- Acquiring or upgrading to the necessary resources (e.g., hiring and/or training for skill)

- Using work around reports to produce top-level journal entries

- Identifying the penalties and consequences of noncompliance

- Evaluating the impact to other subsidiaries or functional areas

The subsidiary or functional business area should complete the "Request to Deviate from Approved Policies and Procedures" form (see Exhibit). The subsidiary's or functional business area's general manager or functional head and controller or financial designate must review and approve the request for deviation. Additional mandatory approvals are required from the Chief Accounting Officer when deviation affect technical accounting issues and/or Corporate Controller when deviations have an economic or disclosure impact on the financial statements.

Controls/Areas of Responsibility

The subsidiary or functional business area should retain documentation of the research, analysis, review, and communication for as long as the deviation is required. They must present the approved form, when there is an internal control testing engagement or internal audit.

A copy of the approved Request for Deviation form must be forwarded to the Policies and Procedures department where it is logged into a database with other deviations and kept on file. A number of similar request prompts a review of the documentation.

Contacts

Chief Accounting Officer

Corporate Controller

Policy and Procedures		
Procedure No. A04	Section: Introduction	Page 3 of 4
	Request to Deviate from Policies and Procedures	
Department Ownership	Issue/Effective Date:	Replaces previously issued

Exhibit

Request for Deviation from Company Approved Policies and Procedures

Subsidiary or functional business area		Location
Requester's name		Phone/e-mail
VP, General Manager		Date
Business Unit Controller or financial designate		Date
VP Internal Controls		Date
Chief Accounting Officer		Date

Attach signatures and comments from mandatory approvers.

Attach explanation and supporting documentation where appropriate.

Policy name and number	
Description of the deviation request	
Explain why compliance is not possible.	
Is the request temporary or permanent? If temporary, identify when compliance can be expected.	
Who are the stakeholders—other areas impacted?	
What is the risk of <u>not</u> complying?	
What is the cost to comply?	

Does this request impact: • Generally Accepted Accounting Principles? • Financial approval levels? • Separation of duties? • Local or regulatory statutes? If yes to any of the above, explain.	

	Policy and Procedures	
Procedure No. A04	Section: Introduction	Page 4 of 4
	Request to Deviate from Policies and Procedures	
Department Ownership	Issue/Effective Date:	Replaces previously issued

List and explain other considerations (costs, benefits, or risks) of issuing/not issuing.

When complete, as part of your internal controls program, retain a copy and forward to

Attention: Accounting and Finance Policy and Procedure Program Manager.

Signature _____   Date _____

Signature _____   Date _____

Signature _____   Date _____

Policy and Procedures		
Procedure No. A05	Section: Introduction	Page 1 of 3
Rescind Policies and Procedures		
Department Ownership	Issue/Effective Date:	Replaces previously issued

Prepared by: Approved by: Authorized by:
Date   Date   Date

Scope

The document applies to all IDÆAL LLP's legal entities, subsidiaries, and business units.

Policy

IDÆAL LLP's (Company) Accounting and Finance policies and procedures (PnP) are prepared and coordinated by the Chief Accounting Officer (CAO) or designated with support and counsel of the policy owner and related stakeholders. Only PnP issued by this organization with proper approval can be considered a Company policy and, as such, is expected to be followed by all employees.

It is the Company's policy that previously issued policies and correspondence that could be interpreted as Company policy should be formally withdrawn or rescinded by following the approved process (see Create, Issue, Revise Policies and Procedures).

Procedure

It is the policy/process owner's responsibility to ensure that inaccurate, previously issued, or outdated policies, procedures and correspondence be formally rescinded.

A process owner may rescind an existing policy or process with approval from related stakeholders (i.e., cross-functional participants in that process) and policy issuers (i.e., CAO).

A separate request to rescind outdated or inaccurate policies and procedures may be submitted using the attached exhibit and forwarded to the CAO, attention Policies and Procedures (form attached).

As part of document control, the Policy and Procedure department should maintain and issue the list of rescinded policies.

Previously issued policies and procedures must be retained in accordance with the Records Information Management policy and procedure.

Policy and Procedures		
Procedure No. A05	Section: Introduction	Page 2 of 3
Rescind Policies and Procedures		
Department Ownership	Issue/Effective Date:	Replaces previously issued

Control/Areas of Responsibility

The Policy and Procedure Program Manager should facilitate and control the process by maintaining the table of contents for those policies and procedures issued and rescinded.

Policies and procedures should be included within internal reviews and audits conducted as part of the routine Sarbanes-Oxley internal control testing and/or internal audit reviews.

Contacts

Chief Accounting Officer

Policy and Procedures		
Procedure No. A05	Section: Introduction	Page 3 of 3
	Rescind Policies and Procedures	
Department Ownership	Issue/Effective Date:	Replaces previously issued

Exhibit

Request to Rescind Policies and Procedures

Policy/Process Functional business area	Signature	Location
Requester's name		Phone/e-mail
VP, general manager, or functional head		Date
Business unit controller or financial designate		Date
Chief accounting officer		Date
Corporate controller		Date

Attach signatures and comments from mandatory approvers.

Attach explanation and supporting documentation as appropriate.

Policy name and number	
Brief description	
• Should a new or updated policy be issued? • If yes, when is it expected to be available? Identify who to contact.	
Does this request impact: • Generally Accepted Accounting Principles? • Financial approval levels? • Separation of duties? • Local or regulatory statutes? If yes to any of the above, explain.	
Which other functional areas should be notified? • Legal • Human Resources • Information Technology • Other: List	

When complete, as part of your internal controls program, retain a copy and forward to : Policies and Procedures.

POLICIES AND PROCEDURES

Policy and Procedures		
Procedure No. B01	Section: Accounting and Finance	Page 1 of 4
	Account Reconciliation	
Department Ownership	Issue/Effective Date:	Replaces previously issued

Prepared by:	Approved by:	Authorized by:
Date	Date	Date

Scope

The document applies to all IDÆAL LLP's legal entities, subsidiaries, and business units.

Policy

It is IDÆAL LLP's (Company) policy to reconcile every Balance Sheet (B/S) account with a closing balance greater than $5,000 USD on a monthly basis in accordance with the Accounting and Finance close schedule. B/S accounts with a closing balance less than $5,000 must be reconciled at least once a quarter. These analyses and reconciliations are to be prepared and reviewed by the appropriate divisional personnel, with all analysis subject to corporate review and audit.

Account reconciliations shall be forwarded for review and sign-off by the business area's respective financial manager or designate.

Underlying detail, in the form of a subledger or schedule, must support every B/S account balance, and such detail must be reconciled to the general ledger. Any unreconciled differences must be investigated and resolved, with adjustments made in a timely manner prior to the end of the quarter. Upon completion of the investigation, any remaining unsupported balance shall be written off.

Procedure

Corporate Accounting determines account ownership based on the area that has the most knowledge and control of the account Unless internal control considerations dictate otherwise the account owner is responsible for completing the account reconciliation. The B/S account balance is determined with the close of the books at each month-end.

Account Reconciliation

- The reconciliation begins with the current year-to-date closing balance as per the general ledger.

- Review the subledger or supporting schedule to summarize the components that correspond to the general ledger's balance. In some cases there may be more than one subledger that needs to be considered.

- Subtract the general ledger and subledger (or other supporting document) closing balances to determine the difference to be reconciled.

- List known adjustments that should be taken during the accounting period. Subtract the total of known adjustments from the difference to be reconciled.

	Policy and Procedures	
Procedure No. B01	Section: Accounting and Finance	Page 2 of 4
	Account Reconciliation	
Department Ownership	Issue/Effective Date:	Replaces previously issued

- The remaining balance is to be investigated and resolved.

- The reconciliation status is identified as either A, B, or C.

  - Circle **A** if there are no outstanding explanations required.

  - Circle **B** if there are known adjustments, and list those that will be taken during the current accounting period.

  - Circle **C** if there is a remaining balance that must be further investigated, and list the actions that will be taken during the following accounting period.

- Unreconciled items and amounts must be tracked, aged, and monitored for clearing.

- Each functional business area's controller or financial designate must review, agree, and sign off on the reconciliation.

- Reconciliations for accounts with closing balances greater than $100,000 USD must be submitted to Corporate Accounting for additional review at the end of each quarter.

- The reconciliation must be prepared using the standard format attached (see Exhibit) or as otherwise approved by the Corporate Controller.

- Account reconciliations must be completed no later than the fifth business day of the month.

Account Analysis

When summarizing the account activity, use the key components that represent the types of transactions flowing into the account. For example, Payroll Payable may have the following components: regular salaried full-time employees, regular hourly employees, temporary or partial period employees, reimbursements, and other. Components that make up an account may mirror the plan input, transaction sources, or areas that will aid in account analysis. It is not acceptable to simply summarize the debit and credit totals. For accounts that are reconciled for the first time, the opening balance must be reconciled.

Differences between the general ledger and subledgers or supporting documentation must be investigated and resolved in a timely, accurate manner. Recurring variances must be investigated and resolved at the root cause, as they may indicate a systemic issue.

- Out-of-balance situations may occur due to:

  1. Natural timing differences

  2. Misclassification (i.e., journal entry to the wrong account)

  3. Miscalculation (i.e., mathematical error in determining the amount of the journal entry that was to be recorded)

	Policy and Procedures	
Procedure No. B01	Section: Accounting and Finance	Page 3 of 4
	Account Reconciliation	
Department Ownership	Issue/Effective Date:	Replaces previously issued

4. Errors where an entry was omitted or recorded multiple times

5. Other unexplained or a combination of reasons that have not yet been identified

- Misclassifications, miscalculations, and errors of omission or duplication should be readily identified and corrected. Corrections should take place within the following month.

Any individual unreconciled differences greater than $5,000 USD occurring at quarter-end or year-end must be disclosed to the Chief Accounting Officer (CAO) (or a designate). Every effort must be made to understand and resolve such differences in the month the error occurs. If you are not sure if a difference is considered material, contact Corporate Financial Reporting to discuss and resolve the matter.

Levels of materiality are defined by the CAO and communicated. Each month the CAO receives a status of the reconciliation accounts identifying those accounts that have unreconciled values (i.e., exceed the materiality thresholds) as well as those that have long-term (level C) unexplained variances.

Control/Areas of Responsibility

The functional business area's controller or financial designate is responsible for ensuring that:

- B/S accounts are accurately reconciled on a timely basis.
- B/S accounts accurately reflect the recording of all business transactions.
- Assets are properly accounted for and expensed.
- Liabilities are properly reflected and accrued for.

Unreconciled amounts at the end of the quarter must be expensed. The regional controller or financial designate may approve write-offs up to $5,000, while all other write-off amounts must be approved by Corporate Accounting.

The Corporate Controller should assign a designate to monitor and track Account Reconciliations and report on the status of unreconciled items. Corporate Accounting should monitor and track the materiality and recurrence of unreconciled balances and review the status quarterly with the CAO.

Contact

Corporate Controller

Chief Accounting Officer

Policy and Procedures		
Procedure No. B01	Section: Accounting and Finance	Page 4 of 4
Account Reconciliation		
Department Ownership	Issue/Effective Date:	Replaces previously issued

Exhibit

Account Reconciliation for the Period Ending (Date) _____

Account Number	Account Name		
Owner of the account	Reconciliation prepared by		
Reconciliation status Circle one **A)** Balanced with no outstanding explanations **B)** Balanced with known adjustments to be taken **C)** Not balanced with investigative actions to be taken	**Actions** 1) _____ _____ 2) _____ _____ 3) _____ _____		
Reviewer's signature			Date
2nd-level signature			Date

Balance per Subledgers or Supporting Schedule			$xxx,xxx
Reconciling items (add or subtract known adjustments):	Month	$xx,xxx	
Total known adjustments to be taken			$xx,xxx
Unreconciled balance (aged and investigated)			$xx,xxx
Balance per general ledger			**$xxx,xxx**

In accordance with the policy, forward to Corporate Accounting with summary of supporting documentation.

<table>
<tr><td colspan="3" align="center">Policy and Procedures</td></tr>
<tr><td>Procedure No. B02</td><td align="center">Section: Accounting and Finance</td><td align="right">Page 1 of 3</td></tr>
<tr><td colspan="3" align="center">Accounting for Compensated Absences</td></tr>
<tr><td>Department Ownership</td><td align="center">Issue/Effective Date:</td><td>Replaces previously issued</td></tr>
</table>

Prepared by:	Approved by:	Authorized by:
Date	Date	Date

Scope/Background

Financial Accounting Standard (FAS) No. 43, "Accounting for Compensated Absences," requires employers to accrue a liability for employees' rights to receive compensation for future absences when certain conditions are met.

This FAS Statement applies to compensation for absences that are contingent on policies/events within the employer's or employee's control (e.g., paid vacation).

This FAS Statement does not apply to severance or termination pay, postretirement benefits, deferred compensation, stock or stock options issued to employees, or other long-term fringe benefits such as group insurance or long-term disability pay.

Liabilities are probably future sacrifices of economic benefits stemming from present legal, equitable, or constructive obligation to transfer assets (i.e., remuneration for time off) as a result of past transactions (i.e., employee service provided).

Policy

It is IDÆAL LLP's (Company) policy to accrue for employee absences, such as vacation, illness, and holidays, for which it is expected that employees will be paid in the period such absences are vested (i.e., the employer has an obligation to make payment even if an employee terminates).

It is the Company's policy to accrue a liability if all of the following conditions are met:

A. The Company's obligation relating to employees' rights to receive compensation for future absences is attributable to employees' services already rendered.

B. The obligation relates to rights that vest or accumulate.

C. Payment of the compensation is probable.

D. The amount can be reasonably estimated.

If an employer meets conditions A, B, and C and does not accrue a liability because condition D is not met, that fact shall be disclosed with financial statement reporting.

It is the Company's policy to use current pay rates, and the reserve will not be discounted for present value evaluation.

Refer to the Post Accounting for Retirement Benefits policy, which also uses these four conditions (A–D above) and the following procedure to accrue for the Company obligations other than pensions.

	Policy and Procedures	
Procedure No. B02	Section: Accounting and Finance	Page 2 of 3
	Accounting for Compensated Absences	
Department Ownership	Issue/Effective Date:	Replaces previously issued

For purposes of this document, **vested rights** refer to those for which the employer has an obligation to make payment even if an employee terminates; thus they are not contingent on an employee's future service.

For purposes of this document, **accumulate** refers to earned and unused rights to compensated absences which may be carried forward to one or more periods subsequent to that in which they are earned, even though there may be a limit to the amount that can be carried forward.

Procedure

An employee's right to future obligation is determined based on approved Human Resource (HR) policies and work practices, such as the vesting of vacation and personal time.

For example, if new employees receive two weeks paid vacation at the beginning of their second year, with no pro rata payment in the event of termination during the first year, the two weeks' vacation would be considered to be earned by work performed in the first year and an accrual for vacation pay would be required for new employees during their first year of service.

With reference to the Company's HR policies, only those benefits where the employee has earned the right to claim the benefit in the form of cash payout when terminated need to be reflected in the Compensated Absence closing balance.

Type of Absence	Comments regarding inclusion for Compensated Absences
Vacation	New employees are eligible to execute on earned vacation after the first year of service. At termination, the employee is eligible to receive the cash compensation equivalent of unused vacation. Annual unused vacation may be carried forward until a maximum is reached (i.e., equivalent of six weeks); then unused vacation is forfeited. Vacation is an earned expense and therefore a Company obligation from the first day of employment.
Personal Days	Employees are eligible to receive personal time off i.e., two to five days per year based on position and title. Unused personal days are forfeited at the end of each fiscal year. At termination, the employee is not eligible to receive the cash equivalent of unused personal days.
Paid Sick Leave	From the first day of employment, employees are eligible to receive paid sick leave at full pay for the first 10 days and then at 75% of regular payroll rates. Employees out sick for more than 30 days are placed on disability, with payment reimbursed via the company's disability insurance plan. At termination the employee is not eligible to receive the cash equivalent of unused sick leave. According to FAS No. 43, no accrual is required for compensated sick leave, because the sick leave does not "vest," and it is dependent on an unknown future event.
Other	From the first day of employment, employees are eligible to receive other types of paid absences, which include but are not limited to: jury duty, bereavement, military service. Time off is based on the situation and management discretion. In accordance with company HR policy, these rights do not "vest," and at termination the employee is not eligible to receive the cash equivalent; these amounts are considered when calculating the reserve.

Policy and Procedures		
Procedure No. B02	Section: Accounting and Finance	Page 3 of 3
	Accounting for Compensated Absences	
Department Ownership	Issue/Effective Date:	Replaces previously issued

At the end of each month, Payroll determines the amount of future benefit employees have earned during the period. This amount represents the amount the company is obligated to pay; however, the reserve may be adjusted to reflect anticipated forfeitures. Anticipated forfeitures are estimated based on the Company's historic performance and management discretion. The methodology must be documented and approved by the Chief Accounting Officer. The closing balance within the Compensated Absence liability account represents the Company's obligation to employees. The journal entry is prepared to "true up" the Compensated Absence liability closing balance amount.

Restructure and Reorganization

Accounting for compensated absences refers to continuing operations. See the Accounting for Restructuring and Reorganization policy and procedure for compensated absence costs incurred due to those topics.

Controls/Areas of Responsibility

In accordance with the Account Reconciliation policy, all balance sheet accounts must be reconciled. Once the reserve is established, there should be little movement from quarter to quarter, having to adjust only for employee use and movement in historic trends.

The methodology for calculating the compensated absence reserve must be reviewed and approved by the Chief Accounting Officer at least annually.

Contact

Payroll Manager
Chief Accounting Officer

	Policy and Procedures	
Procedure No. B03	Section: Accounting and Finance	Page 1 of 3
	Accounting for Goodwill, Patents, Trademarks, **and Other Intangible Assets**	
Department Ownership	Issue/Effective Date:	Replaces previously issued

Prepared by:
Date

Approved by:
Date

Authorized by:
Date

Scope

The document applies to all IDÆAL LLP's legal entities, subsidiaries, and business units.

Policy

It is IDÆAL LLP's (Company) policy to record goodwill and other intangible assets in accordance with U.S. Generally Accepted Accounting Principles (GAAP).

The Company recognizes the following categories as Intangible Assets: Goodwill, Patents and Trademarks, purchased technology, and purchased software.

Goodwill is determined by evaluating the excess of the cost of the acquired interest in an investee over the sum of the amounts assigned to identifiable assets less the liabilities assumed (see Accounting for Mergers and Acquisitions). Goodwill is evaluated for impairment on an annual basis under Financial Accounting Standard (FAS) No. 142, "Goodwill and Other Intangibles," and is not amortized.

Other long-lived intangible assets are recoded at their cost (which is usually determined by an independent valuation expert in conjunction with purchase accounting) and evaluated in accordance with the provisions of FAS No. 144, "Accounting for the Impairment or Disposal of Long-Lived Assets," when the carrying amount of the asset exceeds the fair value. Reversal of previously recognised losses is not permitted.

It is the Company's policy to capitalize all patent and trademark application costs over $1,000 and to amortize those costs on a straight-line basis over an estimated useful life of six years.

The Company may also purchase rights to use another company's technology or software. Costs related to purchased technology and purchased software should be amortized on a straight-line basis over the estimated useful life as determined by an outside service provider (generally between four and ten years).

Procedure

Goodwill

The value assigned to any Goodwill asset is determined based on the merger-and-acquisition analysis and approved by the Chief Accounting Officer (CAO). When a company is acquired, the assets and assumed liabilities are valued at fair market value.

If the fair value of the assets and liabilities exceed the allocated amount of the acquiring cost, the result is considered goodwill. Goodwill is subject to asset impairment testing.

	Policy and Procedures	
Procedure No. B03	Section: Accounting and Finance	Page 2 of 3
	Accounting for Goodwill, Patents, Trademarks, **and Other Intangible Assets**	
Department Ownership	Issue/Effective Date:	Replaces previously issued

If the fair value of the assets and liabilities are less than the allocated amount of the acquiring cost, the result is considered "negative" goodwill. The cost deficiency is allocated as a pro rata reduction to noncash and cash equivalent assets (e.g., inventory, property, plant and equipment). If the initially recorded amounts of these acquired assets are entirely eliminated, the excess should be recognized as an extraordinary gain on the Income Statement. The CAO must approve the accounting treatment.

Impairment Testing for Goodwill

As with the Property, Plant and Equipment procedure, Corporate Accounting or a qualified independent outside service provider performs an annual goodwill impairment assessment. Based on the results of the evaluation, the CAO determines if an impairment adjustment is necessary.

Patents, Trademarks and Other Intangible Assets

The value assigned to patents and trademarks are the application and outside legal costs associated with securing and registering the patents and trademarks. All costs should be tagged to a specific patent or trademark and accumulated in a Construction-in-Process (CIP) account until the patent/trademark is issued. The CIP account should be analyzed monthly and costs transferred to the appropriate asset account for patents issued during the month.

Costs that reflect the Company's Legal and other departments should not be included for capitalization and amortization. Maintenance fees should be expensed as incurred.

The value assigned to purchased software and purchased technology is determined at the time of acquisition using purchase accounting.

Impairment Testing for Patents, Trademarks, and Other Intangible Assets

An impairment loss shall be recognized only if the carrying amount of the long-lived asset is not recoverable and exceeds its fair market value. The carrying amount of a long-lived asset is not recoverable if it exceeds the sum of the undiscounted cash flows expected to result from the use and eventual disposition of the asset.

As with the Property, Plant and Equipment procedure, Corporate Accounting or a qualified independent outside service provider shall test long-lived assets for recoverability. Whenever events or changes in circumstances indicate that its carrying amount may not be recoverable and in accordance with FAS 144 "Accounting for the Impairment or Disposal of long lived Assets", are adjustments due to asset impairment may be required.

The following are examples of such events or changes in circumstances:

- Significant decrease in market price of a long-lived asset
- Significant changes in the extent or manner of use of long-lived asset

	Policy and Procedures	
Procedure No. B03	Section: Accounting and Finance	Page 3 of 3
	Accounting for Goodwill, Patents, Trademarks, and Other Intangible Assets	
Department Ownership	Issue/Effective Date:	Replaces previously issued

- A current expectation that "more likely than not" a long-lived asset will be sold or otherwise disposed of significantly before the end of its previously estimated useful life

Control/Areas of Responsibility

Corporate Accounting provides the necessary accounting data and financial information to ensure accurate and timely goodwill impairment testing. Corporate Accounting should prepare all accounting journal entries to establish, amortize, and adjust goodwill and intangible assets.

Corporate Accounting must approve additions, changes, or removal of any intangible assets or their carrying value.

The Legal department maintains the patent and trademark database.

Contacts

Chief Accounting Officer

Policy and Procedures		
Procedure No. B04	Section: Accounting and Finance	Page 1 of 3
	Accounting for Mergers and Acquisitions	
Department Ownership	Issue/Effective Date:	Replaces previously issued
Prepared by: Date	Approved by: Date	Authorized by: Date

Scope

The document applies to all IDÆAL LLP's legal entities, subsidiaries, and business units.

Policy

It is IDÆAL LLP's (Company's) policy to record and account for mergers and acquisitions in accordance with U.S. Generally Accepted Accounting Principles (GAAP).

All business combinations shall be accounted for using the purchase method as described in Financial Accounting Standard (FAS) No. 141, "Business Combinations." The purchase method records a business combination based on the values exchanged.

For all mergers and acquisitions, it is Company policy to perform a financial (as well as other appropriate functional area, e.g., technical, operational) due diligence.

Procedure

The following steps are performed when accounting for the merger or acquisition.

1. The acquiring entity shall be identified in all business combinations. The entity that distributes cash or other assets or incurs liabilities is generally the acquiring entity. As part of a potential business combination, the Company will either acquire a company's outstanding stock or specific assets.

2. The cash payment or the equivalent fair market value of the securities given up shall be used to measure the cost of an acquired entity. Independent appraisals should equally be used to determine the fair value of the assets being acquired. The full purchase price should be allocated to the net assets acquired, with any excess being charged to goodwill.

3. The purchase price of an entity acquired in a business combination includes direct costs, such as market analysis, legal and other searches, registration, and transaction costs. Indirect and general expenses incurred in conjunction with the acquisition should be expensed as incurred.

4. Restructuring and/or exit costs contemplated in connection with the business acquisition should be accounted for in accordance with Emerging Issues Task Force (EITF) No. 95-3, "Recognition of Liabilities in Connection with a Purchase Business Combination." In addition to the business case, an appropriate exit plan must be prepared in sufficient detail with the appropriate level of management authorization. See the Accounting for Restructuring and Reorganization policy and procedure.

	Policy and Procedures	
Procedure No. B04	Section: Accounting and Finance	Page 2 of 3
	Accounting for Mergers and Acquisitions	
Department Ownership	Issue/Effective Date:	Replaces previously issued

5. Additional consideration (i.e., cash or securities) required as part of the business combination agreement may be contingent on the achievement of future events, such as earnings levels. The acquiring entity shall record the fair value of the consideration issued or issuable as an additional cost of the acquired entity. The contingent consideration shall be recorded when the contingency is resolved and the consideration is issued or becomes issuable unless the outcome of the contingency is determinable beyond a reasonable doubt.

6. Post-acquisition accounting for long-lived assets and goodwill includes impairment testing. See the Accounting for Goodwill and Intangible Asset policy and procedure.

7. In some cases the sum of the amounts assigned to assets acquired and liabilities assumed will exceed the cost to acquire the entity. The excess shall generally be prorated to reduce the long-term assets.

8. The effective date of the acquisition is generally the date stipulated in the written acquisition agreement.

Other Acquisitions/Equity Interest Investments

The Company applies the equity method of accounting for those acquisitions where the Company has an ownership interest representing between 20 percent and 50 percent of the voting stock of the investee and has the ability to exercise significant influence. Under the equity method of accounting, investments are stated at initial cost and are adjusted for subsequent additional investments and the Company's proportionate share of income or losses and distributions. The Company records its share of the investees' earnings or losses in other income (expense) in the Consolidated Statement of Operations.

The Company applies the cost method of accounting for those investments where the Company has less than 20 percent ownership of the voting stock or is unable to exercise significant influence over the investee. Investments are accounted for under the cost method. Under the cost method, investments are carried at cost and adjusted only for the other-than-temporary declines in fair value or additional investments.

Controls/Areas of Responsibility

Senior executive for the following functional areas: Business Development, Engineering, Sales, Marketing, Logistics, Finance, Human Resources, and Legal must recommend and approve all business mergers and acquisitions.

The Chief Executive and the Board of Directors must approve all mergers and acquisitions.

Post-acquisition reviews and audits must be conducted to determine if the anticipated value has occurred. Failure to create value can occur at the many stages of a merger or acquisition,

Policy and Procedures		
Procedure No. B04	Section: Accounting and Finance	Page 3 of 3
Accounting for Mergers and Acquisitions		
Department Ownership	Issue/Effective Date:	Replaces previously issued

including strategic planning, deal structuring and negotiation, post-acquisition integration, and post-acquisition operations. Reviews of these areas shall be used to improve the process.

For all business combinations, the Chief Accounting Officer must review and approve the accounting treatment and journal entries that record business combinations.

Contacts

Chief Accounting Officer

	Policy and Procedures	
Procedure No. B05	Section: Accounting and Finance	Page 1 of 3
	Accounting for Post-Employment Benefits	
Policy Owner:	Issue/Effective Date:	Replaces previously issued

Prepared by: Approved by: Authorized by:
Date   Date   Date

Scope

This policy establishes the accounting treatment for anticipated benefits to former or inactive employees, their beneficiaries, and covered dependents. Post-employment refers to the period after employment but before retirement. The benefits may be paid as a result of a disability, layoff, death, or other event and may be paid immediately upon cessation of active employment or over a specified period of time.

Those benefits include but are not limited to salary continuation, supplemental unemployment benefits, severance benefits, disability-related benefits (including workers' compensation), job training and counseling, and continuation of benefits such as health care benefits and life insurance coverage.

Policy

It is IDÆAL LLP's (Company) policy to accrue for post-employment benefits in accordance with U.S. Generally Accepted Accounting Principles (GAAP).

Post-employment employee benefits and company obligations should be accrued when specific conditions are met for employees to receive compensation for future absences. The Statement of Financial Accounting Standards (SFAS) No. 43, "Accounting for Compensated Absences," instructs that "an employer shall accrue a liability for employees' compensation of future absences if *all* of the following conditions are met:

A. The employer's obligation relating to employees' rights to receive compensation for future absences is attributable to employees' services already rendered,

B. The obligation relates to rights that vest (i.e., the employer has an obligation to make payment) or accumulate (i.e., earned but unused rights may be carried forward),

C. Payment of the compensation is probable, and

D. The amount can be reasonably estimated

If an employer meets conditions (A), (B), and (C) and does not accrue a liability because condition (D) is not met, that fact shall be disclosed."

If the above conditions are not met, an estimated loss contingency shall be accrued as an expense and liability **if** both of the following conditions are met:

- Information is available prior to issuance of the financial statements indicating that it is probable that an asset has been impaired or a liability has been incurred.

<table>
<tr><td colspan="3" align="center">**Policy and Procedures**</td></tr>
<tr><td>Procedure No. B05</td><td align="center">Section: Accounting and Finance</td><td align="right">Page 2 of 3</td></tr>
<tr><td colspan="3" align="center">**Accounting for Post-Employment Benefits**</td></tr>
<tr><td>Policy Owner:</td><td align="center">Issue/Effective Date:</td><td align="right">Replaces previously issued</td></tr>
</table>

- The amount of the loss can be reasonably estimated. If the amount cannot be reasonably estimated, it must be disclosed as a note to the financial statements.

This policy does not apply to:

- Post-employment benefits provided through a pension or post-retirement benefit plan
- Individual deferred compensation arrangements
- Special or contractual termination benefits
- Stock compensation plans

Employee benefits for employees who are absent or on leave are not included as post-employment.

Procedure

Representatives from Human Resources Legal and Finance must approve all post-employment benefit plans and offerings. The financial impact should be considered within the business area's financial plan. **No offer should be communicated to the employee without HR, Legal, and Finance authorization.**

As soon as the post-employment benefit is known, the details should be evaluated according to the criteria listed above. If an accrual is required for post employment benefits it should be calculated and posted for the period in which the expense is incurred and the obligation is realized. Accruals should be prepared in accordance with the accrual policy.

Documentation to support the calculation and journal entry accrual must be maintained in accordance with the Journal Entries policy and procedure. Documentation must include but not be limited to:

- Name of each employee and related contact or identifying information
- Description of the type of post-employment benefit and related terms and conditions
- Approvals from the HR, Legal, and Finance departments
- Duration of the benefit, including anticipated start and stop dates
- Estimated value of the post-employment benefit, including assumptions as to the likelihood that the conditions will be met
- Present value of the estimated value of the post-employment benefit

HR shall forward or make available the list of approved post-employment benefit employees to payroll. As post-employment benefits come due and are released for payment, the Payroll department must confirm that the employee has been approved to receive the benefit.

Policy and Procedures		
Procedure No. B05	Section: Accounting and Finance	Page 3 of 3
Accounting for Post-Employment Benefits		
Policy Owner:	Issue/Effective Date:	Replaces previously issued

The accounting for post-employment benefits should include an initial journal entry to Payroll/ Salary expense and a Reserve for Post-Employment Benefits. The Reserve should be reduced as the employee begins to collect on the post-employment benefits.

Control/Areas of Responsibility

Payroll must be informed when there is a change to the employee's status, including changes to compensation and active status.

The business area HR, Legal, and Finance representatives must review and approve each proposal for post-employment benefits before submitting the proposal to Corporate HR and Finance for authorization and approval.

Accounts must be reconciled in accordance with the Account Reconciliation policy.

Contact

Finance
Human Resources
Legal

Policy and Procedures		
Procedure No. B06	Section: Accounting and Finance	Page 1 of 4
Accounting for Restructuring and Reorganization		
Department Ownership	Issue/Effective Date:	Replaces previously issued
Prepared by: Date	Approved by: Date	Authorized by: Date

Scope

This policy applies to all worldwide business units and subsidiaries and relates to restructuring and reorganization activities. Costs associated with an exit activity, including one-time employee termination benefits, costs incurred to terminate noncapital leases, and the cost to consolidate facilities or relocate employees, are covered by this policy.

Exit activities initiated in conjunction with an entity newly acquired in a business combination or related to the disposal of property, plant and equipment assets are governed by different accounting standards and covered in separate policies (refer to the policies and procedures for Business Combinations and Consolidation and Property, Plant and Equipment).

Policy

It is IDÆAL, LLP's (Company) policy to recognize a restructuring and reorganization liability in accordance with U.S. Generally Accepted Accounting Principles (GAAP). According to GAAP, a liability is incurred when there is a present obligation. A present obligation is considered to exist when a transaction or event occurs that leaves an entity little or no discretion to avoid the future transfer or use of assets to settle the liability. Corporate Accounting is responsible for ensuring all restructuring and reorganization activities are recognized and recorded in accordance with GAAP.

Background/Accounting Literature

Statement of Financial Accounting Standards (SFAS) No. 146, "Accounting for Costs Associated with Exit or Disposal Activities," applies to costs associated with an exit activity. It requires that a liability for costs associated with an exit activity must be recognized when the liability is incurred. The statement also establishes fair value as the objective for initial measurement of the liability. Typical costs associated with exit plans include but are not limited to:

- One-time termination benefits provided to current employees that are involuntarily terminated
- Contract termination costs
- Other associated costs

One-Time Termination Benefits

Termination benefits are benefits provided to current employees that are involuntarily terminated under the terms of a one-time benefit arrangement. A one-time benefit arrangement

	Policy and Procedures	
Procedure No. B06	Section: Accounting and Finance	Page 2 of 4
	Accounting for Restructuring and Reorganization	
Department Ownership	Issue/Effective Date:	Replaces previously issued

is established by a plan of termination that applies for a specified termination event or for a specified future period. The one-time benefit exists and a liability should be recognized as of the date the termination plan meets all of the following criteria and has been communicated to employees (which may also be referred to as the communication date):

- In accordance with the Authorization: Delegation of Authority policy an appropriate level of management approves and commits the enterprise to a restructure and reorganization plan as well as the related impact of termination.

- The plan specifically identifies the number of employees to be terminated, job classifications or functions, their locations, and the expected completion date. Note: specific individuals do not have to be identified.

- The plan establishes the terms of the benefit arrangement in sufficient detail to enable the employees to determine the type and amount of benefits that they will receive if they are involuntarily terminated.

- Actions required to complete the plan indicate that no significant changes to the plan are likely to occur or that the plan will be withdrawn. Contact Corporate Finance if you are not sure if you have a significant change.

Recognition and Measurement of Liability for One-Time Termination Benefits

The timing and measurement of a liability for one-time termination benefits depends on whether employees are required to render service until they are terminated in order to receive the termination benefits and, if so, whether employees will be retained to render service beyond the minimum retention period, which shall not exceed the legal notification period or 60 days in absence of legal notification.

- If employees are entitled to receive the termination benefits regardless of when they leave, the liability for termination benefits should be recognized and measured at its fair value as of at the communication date.

- If employees are required to render services until they are terminated in order to receive the termination benefits and will be retained to render service beyond the minimum retention period, a liability for the termination benefits shall be measured initially at the communication date based on the fair value of the liability as of the termination date. The liability shall be recognized ratably over the future service period.

  A change resulting from a revision to either the timing or amount of estimated cash flows over the future service period shall be measured using the credit-adjusted risk-free rate that was initially used to measure the liability initially. The cumulative effect of the change shall be recognized as an adjustment to the liability in the period of the change.

Policy and Procedures		
Procedure No. B06	Section: Accounting and Finance	Page 3 of 4
	Accounting for Restructuring and Reorganization	
Department Ownership	Issue/Effective Date:	Replaces previously issued

Contract Termination Costs

Contract termination costs include: (1) costs to terminate a contract (e.g., operating lease) before the end of its term or (2) costs that will continue to be incurred under the contract for its remaining term without economic benefit to the entity.

In accordance with the terms of the contract liability for costs to terminate a contract before the end of its term shall be recognized and measured at its fair value when the entity terminates the contract.

A liability for costs that will continue to be incurred under a contract for its remaining term without economic benefit to the entity shall be recognized and measured at its fair value when the entity ceases using the rights conveyed to it by the contract (i.e., the "cease use" date).

Other Associated Costs

Other costs associated with an exit or disposal activity include, but are not limited to, costs to consolidate or close facilities and relocate employees. A liability for other costs associated with an exit or disposal activity shall be recognized and measured at its fair value in the period in which the liability is incurred generally when goods and services associated with the activity are received.

Procedure

Restructuring and reorganization of opportunities may be part of corporate or local initiatives. When known, the business impact and cost benefit analysis shall be prepared to list and quantify the possible restructuring activities as part of the financial planning and/or forecasting process.

An exit plan shall be developed and approved by the business unit in conjunction with and approved by the following:

- Human Resources, which calculates termination benefits for severed employees.

- Corporate Services (e.g., Corporate Facilities, Real Estate and fixed asset management), which determines contract termination costs and, if applicable, the cost to shut down a facility and/or relocate employees. Existing leasehold improvements related to terminated leased facility are treated as an impaired asset and should be included in the provision.

- Legal, which provides advice and counsel on local as well as corporate impact and risk.

- Communications, which provides guidance as to how to communicate with employees and the public.

- Corporate Tax shall be notified inorder to identify the tax implications and if required, address local tax regulations. Corporate Tax as well as Intercompany Transactions must be notified of payments to/from Corporate on behalf of the international business units.

	Policy and Procedures	
Procedure No. B06	Section: Accounting and Finance	Page 4 of 4
	Accounting for Restructuring and Reorganization	
Department Ownership	Issue/Effective Date:	Replaces previously issued

- Corporate Treasury must be notified to update bank accounts and signature authorizations.

- Corporate Accounting reviews the exit plan to determine if the termination costs are calculated and classified in compliance with U.S. GAAP.

- Corporate Reporting determines the appropriate accounting disclosures.

In accordance with the Delegation of Authority and authorization schedule, and approvals from the Corporate business areas listed above, the business unit presents the exit plan including business justification and cost benefit analysis to the Executive and Senior Leadership Team and/or the Board of Directors.

When approved, Corporate Accounting establishes the restructuring and reorganization reserve within the Corporate Accounting records. The business units collect applicable restructuring and reorganization charges within a defined expense account. Corporate Accounting reviews the expense account monthly and reclassifies the appropriate charges as an offset to the reserve account.

Corporate Accounting is also responsible for reconciling the reserve on a monthly basis and for obtaining and maintaining documentation for all charges that hit the reserve. At the completion of the reorganization and restructuring, the reserve is closed.

Controls/Areas of Responsibility

The Business Unit is responsible for preparing the business impact analysis, restructuring, and reorganization costs and gaining necessary management approvals.

Corporate Accounting reconciles the reserve on a monthly basis in accordance with the Account Reconciliation policy and procedure.

Contact

Chief Accounting Officer

	Policy and Procedures	
Procedure No. B07	Section: Accounting and Finance	Page 1 of 5
	Accounting for Sales Compensation: **Expense, Accrual, Reconciliation**	
Department Ownership	Issue/Effective Date:	Replaces previously issued

Prepared by: Date	Approved by: Date	Authorized by: Date

Scope

This policy applies to the Company's customer account and sales managers.

Policy

It is IDÆAL LLP's (Company's) policy to compensate its sales representatives for the development and maintenance of the Company's business within assigned accounts or territories and in accordance with the Company's Incentive Compensation plan.

All revenue and nonrevenue incentives will be paid in accordance with the sales representative's individual compensation plan. Revenue-based incentives will be paid on revenue recognized in accordance with U.S. Generally Accepted Accounting Principles (GAAP).

Eligible employees must approve and sign their sales compensation plan and return it to the Human Resource (HR) Sales Commissions Administration no later than the end of first quarter or within 30 days of employment. If an approved, signed plan is not received, commissions may not be considered earned and therefore may be forfeited.

Procedure

Sales representatives and eligible customer account managers have a target earnings objective, made up of a base salary plus incentive compensation primarily earned from sales.

• Base salaries shall be paid in accordance with the Company's regular payroll cycle and represent compensation for maintaining relations with the Company's existing customers, the development of new business, short-term cover for other accounts not on their target account list, and the general performance of the job position's other responsibilities. Base salaries generally represent 20 percent of the sales representative's expected compensation, including commissions.

• Incentive compensation varies by employee, depending on the sales plan in which the employee participates. Incentive compensation details can be found in the employee's individual compensation statement.

Establishing Quotas

During the annual Financial Planning and Analysis schedule, Sales Finance develops revenue quotas and compensation targets on a global and geographic basis.

Policy and Procedures		
Procedure No. B07	Section: Accounting and Finance	Page 2 of 5
	Accounting for Sales Compensation: **Expense, Accrual, Reconciliation**	
Department Ownership	Issue/Effective Date:	Replaces previously issued

Quotas are established based on a set of planning indicators that consider the economic indicators and market potential of each region. The Company's Research, Development, and Engineering areas provide input regarding the release and availability of new products. The Company's financial pricing areas provide input regarding pricing and costing assumptions. The result of these considerations are evaluated by country and rolled up to the geography before consolidating at the Company level. Geographic sales and finance management discretion adjusts the geographic quota targets before an approved quota plan is rolled down to the geographies' eligible sales managers and representations.

A Sales Compensation Committee made up of Executive representatives from Research, Development, and Engineering; Finance; and Sales Operations and led by Sales approves the sales quotas by geography and oversees the implementation of the Sales Compensation plan. This committee meets monthly to review quota sales compensation attainment.

At the geography and regional level, sales compensation expense is calculated based on the formula described within the sales compensation plan. Sales compensation expense includes the basic salaries and incentive compensation. A fund for additional awards and bonuses may be determined and included as part of sales compensation and maintained at the Corporate Sales Operations only.

Geography/Territories

Multinational and geographic account activity shall be planned at a global level and local activities allocated using an intra-/inter area/regional split; the allocation must equal and not exceed 100%. By region, customer accounts are identified by the salesperson; with the salesperson serving as the primary customer relationship manager.

For all cross-territory/geography transactions, fee-splitting arrangements must be agreed upon, in writing and in advance. The allowable fee-splitting arrangements are 80/20, 70/30, 60/40, and 50/50. Any other fee-splitting arrangements require advance approval by Sales Executive Management.

In **no case** shall the commissions paid to managers and sales representatives **exceed 100%** as calculated from the sales compensation planning model.

Respect of Territory Boundaries

Sales representatives and their management are expected to respect the geographic boundaries identified as "territories." Sales outside their assigned territories result in performance credit not accruing to their target quota.

Territory changes normally become effective on the first day of the month following the month in which the Company notifies the sales representative of the change.

	Policy and Procedures	
Procedure No. B07	Section: Accounting and Finance	Page 3 of 5
	Accounting for Sales Compensation: **Expense, Accrual, Reconciliation**	
Department Ownership	Issue/Effective Date:	Replaces previously issued

Establishing Commissions

Commissions are calculated based on the net new contract value added during the period. Net new contract values are determined based on the value of new contracts less those contracts that have expired, less returns and adjustments due to contract changes and accounts receivable balances e.g., bad debt write-offs, short payments.

Commissions are not considered earned by the sales representative and payable by the Company until:

- The Company receives full payment of all amounts due from a customer during the initial 12-month period of a transaction document.

- All other requirements set out in the transaction documents have been fully satisfied and completed.

The Sales Compensation Committee at its sole discretion determines whether the requirements for payment of commissions for any transaction have been satisfied and its decision is final and binding on all affected parties. The Company will not pay commission for transactions in the following situations:

- Customer default or transaction termination

- Beta transactions and product trials

- Trials

- Product returns

The net new contract value quota is broken down into monthly expectations. Generally, the annual quota is spread out during the year smoothing the "rhythm of the business" provided by Financial Planning and Analysis. The "rhythm of the business" generally shows the dollar amount per contract growing quarter over quarter until the fourth quarter, which represents the Company's busiest sales volume quarter.

Unless specified by local laws and regulations, commissions owed to employees are paid in the last pay period of the month and 30 days after the transaction is deemed complete.

Based on transaction and activity reports, Sales administration is responsible for calculating the sales compensation paid to sales managers and representatives.

In accordance with the accrual policy, monthly accruals shall be calculated by Sales administration for sales commissions earned and not yet paid. The accrual must be reversed the following month.

Performance Measurement

Measurement of performance and quota attainment is based on the net new contract value generated from accepted orders. At least quarterly, the sales manager and sales representative formally assess quota attainment and performance management.

	Policy and Procedures	
Procedure No. B07	Section: Accounting and Finance	Page 4 of 5
	Accounting for Sales Compensation: **Expense, Accrual, Reconciliation**	
Department Ownership	Issue/Effective Date:	Replaces previously issued

Winner's Circle Award

Winner's Circle is an annual award to selected sales representatives, which executive management in its sole discretion may offer to a percentage of those eligible sales representatives and account managers who have achieved their sales quota. The details of this award are determined by the Sales Compensation Committee and may include gift certificates, trips, or cash bonuses.

Quota Changes

In order to balance performance and maximize sales for a geography, Sales executives may approve changes to an individual employee's quota if it does not affect the geographic area's quota. Changes must be submitted to Sales administration at least one week prior to the effective date.

Quotas shall be fully distributed to individual account managers with no quota held at the management level except where the manager holds a quota covering a period until a new sales employee is appointed. Quota changes must affect only future periods.

New Hire/Transfer into Positions with Incentive Plans

At their sole discretion, Sales management with Sales administration is responsible for account/territory assignment and quota creation for new hires or transfer employees. Quotas shall consider time and opportunity considerations.

Termination of Employment

In the event of an employee's employment terminates, sales incentive compensation should be paid in accordance with the payment terms of the employee's incentive compensation plan.

Termination of Plan

In the event an employee transfers to a position without an incentive plan or into a position with a different plan, the sales representative shall receive the eligible amounts earned from the previous position and is subject to the new commission plan in the new position.

Transaction Audits

In order to ensure that transactions are aligned with the Company's business objectives, the Company, in its sole discretion, reserves the right to review and audit any and all transactions periodically and without any advance notice.

Any executive who knowingly participates in a transaction that is designed to and/or does circumvent the provisions of the sales plan will be discharged.

Policy and Procedures		
Procedure No. B07	Section: Accounting and Finance	Page 5 of 5
	Accounting for Sales Compensation: **Expense, Accrual, Reconciliation**	
Department Ownership	Issue/Effective Date:	Replaces previously issued

Controls/Areas of Responsibility

HR administration responsible for sales compensation maintains the master data for all sales managers and representatives eligible to receive sales compensation. There must be no side agreements or contracts with employees.

Financial Planning and Analysis is responsible for approving and monitoring the:

- Sales Incentive Compensation plan
- Country and geography sales quotas
- Compensation expense targets

Sales administration is responsible for:

- Providing timely and accurate approval and processing of commission payments
- Monitoring and tracking changes to territory and account splits
- Conducting spot audits of commission payment calculations

Sales Management and the Area Controllers are responsible for the approval of Sales Compensation plans, quota changes, and mid-year account or territory changes and the sales compensation expense.

Sales compensation is processed through the Payroll department.

The employee is responsible for bringing any discrepancies, positive or negative, in writing to the attention of Sales administration within 30 days from the issue of the statement.

Under no circumstances must agreements outside the scope of this policy be honored. Any and all adjustments must be documented and approved by the Sales executives and the appropriate Area Controller.

Contacts

Corporate Controller

<table>
<tr><td colspan="3" align="center">Policy and Procedures</td></tr>
<tr><td>Procedure No. B08</td><td align="center">Section: Accounting and Finance</td><td align="right">Page 1 of 6</td></tr>
<tr><td colspan="3" align="center">Accounts Payable:
Request for Payment to Third Party Vendors</td></tr>
<tr><td>Department Ownership</td><td align="center">Issue/Effective Date:</td><td>Replaces previously issued</td></tr>
</table>

Prepared by: Date	Approved by: Date	Authorized by: Date

Scope

The document applies to all IDÆAL LLP's legal entities, subsidiaries, and business units and includes all requests for payment made by the party vendors.

Policy

It is IDÆAL LLP's (Company) policy to record and pay only valid and authorized invoices, which represent legitimate Company obligations. Accounting procedures are implemented to ensure the accuracy of amounts, coding of general ledger accounts, appropriate authorization, and timing of payments. The Accounts Payable (A/P) function is the sole area responsible for releasing checks and initiating requests for Automated Clearing House (ACH) payments to third-party vendors.

Corporate Treasury may issue wire transfers for third-party trade settlement with approval from A/P.

All amounts paid should be based on approved and valid vendor invoices and/or check requisitions supported by a valid/current Purchase Order (PO) and evidenced by receipt of goods and/or services.

Copied or resubmitted invoices shall be investigated and resolved in order to avoid duplicate payments. Payments shall be made from vendor invoices and not from vendor statements. Proper documentation shall be maintained to support statutory audit and regulatory requirements pertaining to paid vendor invoices.

Payments are to be made in accordance with stated terms in the vendor master agreement. The Company's standard terms are 45 days from date of invoice. Requests to accelerate or delay payments require the approval of the Corporate Controller.

It is Company's policy that all expenses should be captured to the greatest degree practical in the period that they are incurred.

Those amounts pertaining to invoices not processed by A/P for which an obligation exists within the accounting period must be accrued in accordance with the Accrual policy.

Procedure

Vendor Master Data

Vendor master data may be set up and maintained only by authorized employee(s) assigned the responsibility. A Master Data Supervisor is responsible for reviewing, approving, and recording all changes to the master vendor database. There must be appropriate separation of duties between

Policy and Procedures		
Procedure No. B08	Section: Accounting and Finance	Page 2 of 6
	Accounts Payable:	
	Request for Payment to Third Party Vendors	
Department Ownership	Issue/Effective Date:	Replaces previously issued

those who have access to vendor master data and those who are involved with procuring, receiving, or processing payments. The Purchasing and A/P departments are responsible for reviewing vendor activity reports in order to mitigate the risk of unauthorized or inaccurate vendor additions or editing.

Invoice Processing

Invoices from vendors shall be treated as legal documents representing a commitment to pay vendors who have delivered a product or rendered a service to the Company. A bona fide invoice is a financial liability that, if not recorded in a timely and accurate manner, can result in the misstatement of the Company's financial records (see the Accrual policy).

Prior to the processing of invoices, the appropriate documentation must be attached with the authorized signatures. Vendor invoices should include and not be limited to the following information:

- Vendor name, address, contact, vendor reference number, shipping terms, and payment terms
- Vendor information regarding where/how payment should be made (e.g., address, reference number)
- Company reference information such as PO number, contact name, address, or location where products and/or services are delivered
- For products and goods related invoices: A list of products by part number or other line item reference, including quantity, unit price, discounts, and sales or other value-added taxes
- For fixed-price service contracts: A list of services provided by task
- For variable price service contracts (e.g., consulting agreements and those quoted as time and materials), the following must be provided:
  - A list of services provided by task
  - For time related charges: Hours worked, role or level of consultant providing the service, and rate per hour
  - For materials related charges: Detail list for materials and/or expenses:
    - For parts and products: Detail list of parts and products:
    - For expenses, related charges include a level of detail to support the vendor's invoiced amount (i.e., larger-dollar items require greater detail): Examples:
      - Travel expenses must include dates, individuals' names, location, reason for travel, and other travel details.
      - Subcontractor expenses must include details to support hours worked and/or materials used.

All vendor invoices must be directly received into A/P for processing and are distributed to the appropriate A/P employee for validation and processing. If for some reason, invoices are received by the originating department, the invoices must be validated and forwarded to A/P for processing in a timely fashion (i.e. five business days). Monthly accruals must be recorded in accordance with the accrual policy.

A three-way or, in some circumstances, a two-way match shall be performed before an invoice is approved for payment. A three-way match includes matching the PO to the receipt confirmation to the vendor's invoice. Receipt confirmation validates the details of the goods and/or services received (e.g., description and quantity of goods or services acquired and unit price details to sum to the amount payable. **All** information (e.g., vendor name, address, description and quantity of goods or services acquired and amount to be paid) must be in agreement before the payment is approved for processing.

A three-way match may not be appropriate for the following types of invoices:

- POs are not required for utilities, tax payments, or royalty payments.

- Receiving or confirmation reports may not be required for membership fees or insurance.

- Vendor invoices may not occur for HR related benefit expenses.

- Legal and consulting invoices not requiring a PO must contain sufficient detail to indicate the particular work performed, the number of hours, and the related individuals.

For the above cases, a two-way match is acceptable as long as authorized signers as identified by the Authorization: Delegation of Authority and the Procurement policy and procedure approve the PO or vendor's invoice. A two-way match is between the PO and vendor's invoice or Company approval and confirmation of the receipt of goods or services and a vendor's invoice. If the vendor's invoice is not available, then a check request form (see Exhibit) and supporting documentation must be submitted.

Travel and expense forms completed in accordance with the Travel, Entertainment and Expense (T&E) policy and procedure are processed by the Travel and Expense department and paid through A/P.

Invoices received that do not meet the above objectives or are otherwise incomplete must be returned to the originating department or to the vendor for the outstanding issue to be resolved. A/P should maintain a log for these rejected invoices and monitor response for timely resolution.

Returns to Vendors

Employees who return purchases directly or who request a service or charge-back adjustment from the vendor must notify A/P immediately. A/P should pursue all credits after all supporting documentation is received from the employee or the vendor.

	Policy and Procedures	
Procedure No. B08	Section: Accounting and Finance	Page 4 of 6
	Accounts Payable:	
	Request for Payment to Third Party Vendors	
Department Ownership	Issue/Effective Date:	Replaces previously issued

Supporting documentation must include and is not limited to: Reference to the original PO number, the reason and description of the discrepancy where the company is seeking retribution, calculation in support of the amount being claimed and a contact name.

Payment Processing

Where applicable and as appropriate (e.g., subject to cash flow strategies and cost vs. benefit of vendor discounts) vendor discounts should be taken. The value of the vendor discount should be based on relative materiality of the invoice and the cost of money to the Company. In addition and as appropriate, the company's procurement representative may negotiate more favorable payment terms, longer vendor payment terms may be established.

A/P is responsible for all records forwarded to the department for processing as well as analysis and reports produced as part of the A/P subledger.

Distribution of Checks

A/P shall issue and distribute via external mail payments directly to vendors. With certain exceptions (e.g., tax payments and legal settlements) and with preapproval by the Corporate A/P manager, vendor checks may be distributed to Company employees. Under those circumstances, the employee must sign for receipt of the check and take responsibility for its distribution to the payee.

Note: Tax payments and legal settlement checks are often attached to and distributed with the related files.

Under no circumstance should checks for third-party vendors be made payable to Company employees.

Unclaimed Checks

Checks to vendors who do not cash the Company payment and who cannot be reached to resolve the issue must be treated as an unclaimed check. Every effort should be made to locate the recipients of unclaimed checks. These checks are tracked and reported to Corporate Accounting for processing under the escheat rules (see Escheat, Abandoned Property, and Unclaimed Checks policy and procedure).

Check Paper Stock and Signature Plate Controls

Corporate A/P may delegate the check preparation and issuance to an outsource service provider (e.g., XXX bank).

<table>
<tr><td colspan="3" align="center">Policy and Procedures</td></tr>
<tr><td>Procedure No. B08</td><td align="center">Section: Accounting and Finance</td><td align="right">Page 5 of 6</td></tr>
<tr><td colspan="3" align="center">Accounts Payable:
Request for Payment to Third Party Vendors</td></tr>
<tr><td>Department Ownership</td><td align="center">Issue/Effective Date:</td><td align="right">Replaces previously issued</td></tr>
</table>

A/P is responsible for accounting for all checks prepared and issued through A/P and the security of the i.e., check stock paper on which the checks are printed. This includes the related storage and use of electronic signature cards and plates. Only authorized A/P employees or authorized outsourced service providers shall access to the check paper stock and signature plates.

Wire and Other Electronic Transfers

Instead of checks, wire and other electronic transfers may be arranged through Corporate Treasury (or a regional treasury center). Requests for electronic transfers to third parties for vendor payments must be processed through A/P in accordance with the above.

Records Retention

A/P-related documentation, including support for the authorized payment and proof of payment, must be retained in accordance with the Records Information Management policy and procedure and records retention schedule.

Controls/Areas of Responsibility

Individuals within A/P must be independent of the purchasing and receiving function and control of the vendor master data. Situations arising where there may be an overlap of duties require additional review and mitigating controls to ensure integrity of the A/P process.

The A/P function or area shall review an aging analysis to ensure timely accurate payment to vendors. The A/P subledger is reconciled to the general ledger control account monthly. All past due outstanding invoices must be investigated and resolved in a timely manner by the appropriate individual.

Once verification for the goods or services received has been documented, only authorized Company employees (i.e., recognized budget holder) should release the invoice for payment. **Invoices must not be approved by administrative staff on behalf of the manager who signed the PO.**

All appropriate documentation supporting A/P and vendor payments must be retained and organized in an orderly manner and available to support tax, audit, and/or any other statutory requirements.

In accordance with the Accrual policy, potential accruals must be assessed and prepared by the originating department.

Contacts

Accounts Payable Manager

	Policy and Procedures	
Procedure No. B08	Section: Accounting and Finance	Page 6 of 6
	Accounts Payable:	
	Request for Payment to Third Party Vendors	
Department Ownership	Issue/Effective Date:	Replaces previously issued

Exhibit

Check Request Form

All information must be typed or printed. Illegible and incomplete requests will be returned.

Issue Check Payable to:			
Mailing Address:			
Reason for the Check Request			
Check Amount			
Vendor Number	Company Code		General Ledger Code
Vendor Federal ID or SS #			
Check Mailing Instructions			
Check Request Prepared by and Phone			
Check Requestor Signature and Date			

Check request must be approved based on the U.S. dollar limits defined below:

Title	US Dollar Limit	Print Name, Sign, and Date
Manager/Sr. Manager	Up to $ 5,000	
Director/Sr. Director	Up to $ 7,500	
VP Finance	Up to $ 25,000	
Sr. VP Finance	Up to $ 50,000	
Corporate Controller	Up to $100,000	
Chief Financial Officer	Over $100,000	

When complete with signed approvals, forward to A/P for processing.

Signature _____ Date _____

Signature _____ Date _____

	Policy and Procedures	
Procedure No. B09	Section: Accounting and Finance	Page 1 of 4
	Accounts Receivable: **Allowance for Doubtful Accounts**	
Department Ownership	Issue/Effective Date:	Replaces previously issued

Prepared by: Date	Approved by: Date	Authorized by: Date

Scope

This policy applies to all worldwide business units. Allowance for Doubtful Accounts refers to those amounts that are deemed uncollectible by the Collections department. See the Accounts Receivable: Third-Party Customer and Trade policy and procedure.

Definition

The Allowance for Doubtful Accounts is a valuation account used to reserve for the potential impairment of Accounts Receivable on the balance sheet.

The term bad debts is defined as those invoices and residual amounts that are unpaid due to bankruptcy, insolvency, cash flow, or other financial problems. Typically, these items may be referred to collection agencies or attorneys for collection action. Bad debts do not include items that are unpaid due to disputes due to product functionality, pricing, return issues, taxes, or other issues not related to the financial capacity of the obligor.

Policy

It is IDÆAL LLP's (Company) policy that Accounts Receivable (A/R) shall be recorded at face value and that an offsetting reserve account must be established for the estimation of uncollectible A/R (also known as doubtful accounts or bad debts).

The Allowance for Doubtful Accounts shall be used to estimate and write off those A/R balances that are not collectible. The account must not be used to reflect circumstances that are agreed to reduce the customer's invoice or sales price.

The reserve account shall be set at such a level so as to bring the closing balance of A/R to their estimated net realizable value in accordance with the procedure identified below.

Procedure

Invoices shall be aged as of the date the invoice is issued to the Customer and not when the invoice becomes due.

The Allowance method provides an expense for anticipated uncollectible receivables in advance of their write-off. The Allowance provides a general reserve without trying to match the Allowance to specific customer accounts.

	Policy and Procedures	
Procedure No. B09	Section: Accounting and Finance	Page 2 of 4
	Accounts Receivable: **Allowance for Doubtful Accounts**	
Department Ownership	Issue/Effective Date:	Replaces previously issued

The Allowance for Doubtful Accounts (Allowance) account shall be valued to cover receivables, which have been specifically identified as probable or highly probable not to be collected. The Allowance consists of three components that define the factors to be considered when evaluating the closing balance required in the Allowance:

1. General allowance—All open invoices with a payment due date greater than 180 days prior to the date for which the Allowance is calculated. This excludes all open invoices for which revenue recognition is held up for whatever reason and where revenue is to be recognized on the cash basis as well as any invoices that, at the discretion of the Collection department are deemed to have high risk of loss and are covered in the following reserves.

2. Specifically identified—All invoices, regardless of aging, where the customer has been designated as bankrupt (either voluntary or involuntary), is in receivership or has had its assets assigned for the benefit of creditors.

3. Specifically identified—Any other open or partially paid invoice(s), regardless of aging, which are deemed to have a low probability of collection. This will include invoices that have been assigned to commercial collection agencies, outside attorneys or other agents to effect collection or any invoice(s) identified by collections.

4. Other management considerations, including but not limited to:

   - Overall composition of the A/R aging

   - Prior history of A/R write-offs

   - Prior history of the Allowance in proportion to the overall receivable balance

   - Type of customer

   - Specific customer balance composition (i.e., unapplied cash, on account cash, credits)

   - Day-to-day knowledge of specific customer who may pose collection problems (input as a result of communication between the collectors, the clients, and the sales network)

   - Prior concessions granted to specific customers

   - Liquidation, receivership, or reorganization proceedings of a customer

The sum of the four classifications above is the amount that shall be provided for in the Allowance and represents the closing balance of the Allowance for Doubtful Accounts.

The desired closing balance is compared to the Allowance account's current balance, with a journal entry prepared to recognize the required increase or decrease to the Allowance and a corresponding increase or decrease to Bad Debt Expense.

	Policy and Procedures	
Procedure No. B09	Section: Accounting and Finance	Page 3 of 4
	Accounts Receivable:	
	Allowance for Doubtful Accounts	
Department Ownership	Issue/Effective Date:	Replaces previously issued

Write-Offs

Periodically, it may be necessary to write off amounts contained in the Allowance for Doubtful Accounts that are deemed to be uncollectible and for which all reasonable means of collection have been exhausted. In this instance, a written request containing the following information will be submitted to the Manager of the collections department.

- Customer name and address

- Account number

- Invoice/document number(s) to be written off

- Total amount

- Reason

- Required approval signature(s)

Authority to approve the write-off or the lowering of committed payments reflected in

A/R is as follows (aggregate amount per customer):

Up to $ U.S.	Finance Approval	Sales Approval
$ 1,000	Collections Manager	Sales Account Manager
$ 5,000	VP Finance	VP Business Unit Sales
$10,000	Sr. VP Finance	Sr. VP Business Unit Sales
Over $10,000	Corporate Controller	General Manager Business Unit

A/R write-offs remove the receivable from the customer's account and are written off to the Allowance for Doubtful Accounts.

Reporting

Monthly, the Collections department distributes a listing of customer accounts that have significant credit risk and that shall be considered for inclusion in the "specifically identified" portion of the Allowance calculation. This list is distributed to the sales account team.

Prior to the completion of the monthly close, Collections prepares a summary report for Finance that estimates the current funding requirement for the Allowance. At the end of each quarter, prior to the accounting close, a detailed analysis of the Allowance is prepared and submitted to Corporate Reporting and other members of the Finance Management team for review. This report is evaluated by Management to determine if additional adjustments to the monthly accrual of Bad Debt Expense and/or the Allowance for Doubtful Accounts are required.

	Policy and Procedures	
Procedure No. B09	Section: Accounting and Finance	Page 4 of 4
	Accounts Receivable: **Allowance for Doubtful Accounts**	
Department Ownership	Issue/Effective Date:	Replaces previously issued

Controls/Areas of Responsibility

Finance reviews and monitors the closing balance in the Allowance account. Comparative analysis is performed to test the adequacy for the coverage within the Allowance.

The Allowance of Doubtful Accounts is reconciled in accordance with the Account Reconciliation policy.

The Collections department is responsible for reporting and communicating "customers at risk" and those specifically identified as uncollectible to Credit Administration and Sales Account Management. The Collections manager is responsible for the review and approval of requests for write-offs.

Contacts

Accounts Receivable Manager

<table>
<tr><td colspan="3" align="center">Policy and Procedures</td></tr>
<tr><td>Procedure No. B10</td><td align="center">Section: Accounting and Finance</td><td align="right">Page 1 of 9</td></tr>
<tr><td colspan="3" align="center">Accounts Receivable: Third-Party Trade and Customer—
Credit, Collection, and Cash Applications</td></tr>
<tr><td>Department Ownership</td><td align="center">Issue/Effective Date:</td><td>Replaces previously issued</td></tr>
</table>

Prepared by:	Approved by:	Authorized by:
Date	Date	Date

Scope

This policy sets forth the guidelines by which IDEAL LLP manages the extension of credit limits and facilitates the collection and cash applications of payments for its direct sales, services, and indirect trade customers.

Policy

It is IDEAL LLP's (Company) policy to establish effective credit and collection standards that support The Company's goals to maximize sales while balancing the risk of bad debts from uncollected Accounts Receivable (A/R).

The A/R department has primary responsibility for extending credit, collection and applying cash collected to customer A/R balances.

- Assess the credit analysis for new and existing clients.

- Facilitate the collection of trade A/R.

- Inform customers of payment delinquency.

- Support sales by providing input about good and slow-paying customers.

- Cash applications applies the cash received to the outstanding Customer's A/R invoice balances

Corporate Treasury retains sole responsibility for determining if, when, and which accounts may become part of a securitization portfolio.

Procedure

A/R credit terms and conditions typically involve parameters for extending credit, payment terms and financial measures. A/R credit terms and conditions alternatives are assessed, evaluated and determined with input from Sales, Legal, Treasury and Finance.

Following are A/R procedures for the management and processing of Credit analysis and administration, Collections, and Cash applications.

Credit Analysis and Administration

Credit analysis is an important process to support the collectability requirement of revenue recognition (see the Revenue Recognition policy).

	Policy and Procedures	
Procedure No. B10	Section: Accounting and Finance	Page 2 of 9
	Accounts Receivable: Third-Party Trade and Customer—	
	Credit, Collection, and Cash Applications	
Department Ownership	Issue/Effective Date:	Replaces previously issued

The Credit Analysis and Administration function provides analysis and assessment for:

- New customers requesting first-time A/R credit limit and terms

- Existing customers

    - When the customer's account has been inactive for at least six months

    - As the customer's account is released from credit hold

    - With a sales order where the amount of the sales order exceeds the customer's approved A/R credit limit

Credit Administration performs the following which are then further described below:

A. Evaluate customer creditworthiness and establish credit limits.

B. Monitor customer accounts to determine the credit risk.

C. Inactivate or terminate credit limits by placing the customer on "credit hold."

D. Create and maintain customer credit management records.

A. *Evaluate Customer Creditworthiness and Establish Credit Limits*

Credit assessments should be performed **prior** to setting up a new customer within the A/R customer database or presenting the sales contract to an existing customer.

Requests from the Sales organization (e.g. Sales Account Manager) to establish credit for new customers shall identify a suggested credit limit and be accompanied by or reference the following documents:

- The customer's current financial statements or latest annual report

- If the customer is entitled to tax exemption, a copy of the customer's tax-exemption certificates for all ship-to locations

Credit Administration establishes the credit limit based on the financial assessment of the data supplied and with input from an outside credit reporting service (e.g., Dunn & Bradstreet). Customer credit files shall be maintained for all applications regardless of whether the application for credit is approved.

Subject to A/R credit assessment credit limits may be increased at the request of the Sales Account Manager as long as the customer is active and maintains a current and consistent payment history.

	Policy and Procedures	
Procedure No. B10	Section: Accounting and Finance	Page 3 of 9
	Accounts Receivable: Third-Party Trade and Customer—	
	Credit, Collection, and Cash Applications	
Department Ownership	Issue/Effective Date:	Replaces previously issued

Credit Administration must turn around requests for credit approval in a timely manner, generally by the end of the next business day. When assessing credit limits, ensure that all subsidiaries and variations on the customer's name are searched. When setting up customers in the customer master database, ensure that there is only one entry for the company regardless of the number and names of subsidiaries.

The Sales Representative and Credit and Collections Management shall keep each other informed about changes in the customer's sales, credit, or collection history and anticipated future conditions.

B. *Monitor the Customer Accounts to Determine the Credit Risk*

Sales, credit, and payment activity shall be monitored by the Credit and Collections function. On occasion and as deemed necessary, to extend credit to customers security in the form of an irrevocable confirmed letter of credit, standby letter of credit, or advanced payment may be required.

C. *Inactivate or Terminate Credit Limits by Placing the Customer on "Credit Hold"*

Credit hold refers to placing a customer's A/R account on hold, that is, not extending additional credit until the customer has paid overdue accounts, submitted a confirmed letter of credit or other suitable guarantee, and demonstrated a willingness and solvency to meet credit obligations.

The Credit and Collections function places a customer on Credit Hold when the customer has become delinquent or inconsistent with meeting A/R payment obligations or if the customer has other related legal or solvency issues that may preclude the Company from receiving or collection on the customer's obligation.

The Sales Account Manager must be notified when a customer is to be placed on credit hold. The Sales Account Manager shall facilitate resolution between the customer and Credit and Collections.

A customer's credit limit should be reassessed after six months of inactivity or if the customer's account becomes delinquent and requires subsequent legal action.

The customer's account may be reinstated once Credit Administration has reassessed the customer's credit profile and is satisfied that future customer payment obligations can be met.

D. *Create and Maintain Customer Credit Management Records*

Customer master data may be set up and maintained only by authorized employee(s) assigned the responsibility. A master data supervisor is responsible for reviewing, approving, and recording changes to the customer master database. There must be appropriate separation of duties between those who have access to customer master data and those who are involved

	Policy and Procedures	
Procedure No. B10	Section: Accounting and Finance	Page 4 of 9
	Accounts Receivable: Third-Party Trade and Customer— **Credit, Collection, and Cash Applications**	
Department Ownership	Issue/Effective Date:	Replaces previously issued

with the sales, distribution/delivery of products and/or services, or collections and cash applications of payments. The Sales Administration and Collections department are responsible to review Customer activity reports in order to mitigate the risk of unauthorized or inaccurate customer additions or editing.

Changes to this database must be requested by the Sales representative or A/R collector, and validated and approved by Credit Administration. As deemed necessary by Credit Administration changes to this database may require written approval from the customer.

A/R Collections

The Collections function reviews the Customer's A/R balances and invoices due. An A/R aging report is prepared and used for the following which are further described below:

A. Analyze and predict future cash flows

B. Present customer account balances, including current and overdue status

C. Determine the amount required within the allowance for doubtful accounts

D. Determine the internal measurements for days sales outstanding (DSO)

A. *Analyze and Predict Future Cash Flows*

The Collections department prepares monthly cash forecasts in anticipation of and forecasting of cash to be collected. This information is submitted to Corporate Treasury as input and for inclusion within the Statement of Cash Flow.

B. *Present Customer Account Balances, Including Current and Overdue Status*

The A/R aging report is based on the customer's unpaid invoices aged by the invoice date. Transactions between the invoice date and the due date (which may vary by customer according to sales terms and conditions) shall be considered current. The customer's due date (and other sales terms and conditions) is recorded within the customer master database as part of the Customer's A/R profile.

It is the collector's responsibility to resolve slow payment, short pays (i.e., customer deductions) and no payment issues. The collector notifies the Sales Account Manager to help resolve payment issues.

Methods of collection include but are not limited to the following:

- Collection calls should be professionally performed by the collectors and should be in accordance with State or regional regulations. The purpose of the collection call is not only to collect on overdue accounts receivable but also to resolve customer issues. A summary of the calls should be noted within the collections database.

Policy and Procedures		
Procedure No. B10	Section: Accounting and Finance	Page 5 of 9
Accounts Receivable: Third-Party Trade and Customer— Credit, Collection, and Cash Applications		
Department Ownership	Issue/Effective Date:	Replaces previously issued

- Calls and communication with the customer may include courtesy calls prior to the invoice due date and throughout the collection period.

- Dunning letters relating to overdue invoices may be sent at periodic intervals with progressive collection language and consequence.

- At appropriate times and at the discretion of the Collections Manager, each overdue account should be reviewed for potential submission to Legal or an outside collection agency.

When the Customer's A/R balances are close to reaching or exceeding approved credit limits, the collector notifies the Sales Account Manager and an evaluation is conducted to assess whether the Customer's credit limits may be increased.

On occasion and as necessary, the Collector is also responsible for initiating a request to adjust the Customer's outstanding A/R balance.

To reduce the amount owed to the Company, the collector may complete a Request for Customer Credit Adjustments form. The collector attaches backup from the customer to support the amount of the requested reduction and forwards it to the Collection supervisor and Sales for approval. Approval is required as per the following matrix. Approval for processing customer credits is as follows, with all requiring approval by Sales and Finance. Requests must reference the Company's sales order and invoice number and a new request must be opened for each customer sales order and/or invoice.

Up to $ U.S.	Finance Approval	Sales Approval
$ 1,000	Collections Manager	Sales Account Manager
$ 5,000	VP Finance	VP Business Unit Sales
$10,000	Sr. VP Finance	Sr. VP Business Unit Sales
Over $10,000	Corporate Controller	General Manager Business Unit

An account is considered overdue when the due date has past. Collection procedures begin prior to the account's becoming 30 days past due.

The customer may indicate and ask the collector to facilitate additional sales or cancellation of products. The collector should forward these requests to Sales Administration for processing.

Slow paying and non-paying Customers may be placed on a credit hold list. The credit hold list identifies that no new or additional credit may be issued to this customer until the outstanding A/R balances are paid down. Collections must notify the Sales Account Manager to assist with resolving the outstanding payment issues. The credit hold list is assessed at least monthly to ensure timely action is taken.

	Policy and Procedures	
Procedure No. B10	Section: Accounting and Finance	Page 6 of 9
	Accounts Receivable: Third-Party Trade and Customer— **Credit, Collection, and Cash Applications**	
Department Ownership	Issue/Effective Date:	Replaces previously issued

C. *Determine the amount required within the Allowance for Doubtful Accounts*

At least monthly, the collector reviews the aged A/R portfolio for accounts at risk. A risk account is one where the collector has doubts that the balance will be collected. Reasons to put an account on a high-risk list include but are not limited to:

- Notification of bankruptcy, with the collector immediately forwarding the information to the Sales Legal department.

- Cash flow issues as indicated by the customer, with broken payment promises or checks that have been returned due to insufficient funds, with the collector notifying the Sales account team.

With appropriate documentation the following individuals may approve A/R write-offs:

- Individual collectors may "clean up" small discrepancies and write-offs up to $50 USD per customer.

- All other write-offs should follow the above approval matrix for reducing the amount the customer owes.

For transactions where the write-off exceeds $1,000 USD, a detailed explanation as to the customer's circumstances and the collector's actions must be documented and maintained.

See the Allowance for Doubtful Accounts policy.

D. *Determine the Internal Measurements for Days Sales Outstanding (DSO)*

This internal measurement is reported to management monthly and represents the efficiency of the sales and collection process. The DSO calculation is determined based on the following formula. Trends may indicate that a change to the company's A/R terms and conditions is required. Refer to the key Financial Indicators for the DSO formula.

Cash Applications

Cash settlement for outstanding A/R accounts may be received from the following sources:

- Direct mail (i.e., mail received at the Company location)

- Bank lockboxes (i.e., customers are directed to send their remittances directly to the bank); this includes electronic funds transfer (EFT)

Payments received via direct mail are received in the Company's mail office. A mail officer opens the mail and logs in the following information into the mail register: date, sender's name and address, type of remittance (e.g., check), and amount. The mail together with the sender's envelope is then delivered to the cash application manager.

The cash application manager maintains a separate log, and once the payment is processed to the customer's A/R, the checks must be deposited to the bank daily. The following additional bank deposit reference information (e.g., date of deposit, branch deposited, and those checks that represent the deposit) is recorded in the direct mail log. Copies of the check and deposit slip are retained until the bank confirms the deposit with the bank statement and it is verified that the customer's account has been updated.

A cash application representative matches the payment received to the open invoices. The customer should have remitted a payment slip identifying which outstanding invoices the payment refers to. Any short payments or overpayments according to our records must be noted as part of the A/R cash application database and resolved with the customer by the Collections department.

Short payments generally occur when the customer believes a reduction to the outstanding A/R balance is due to them (e.g., due to merchandise returned). Our records may not have caught up with the internal processing of the A/R reduction memo.

An overpayment may occur due to customer error or inaccuracy in listing the invoices that are to be paid.

Bank lockboxes or other third-party A/R processing is a way for the company to outsource some of the cash application procedures. The customer remits their A/R payments to a bank or other company-approved service provider. The bank or service provider has real-time access to the company's A/R subledger. As the checks are opened and processed, they are matched to open invoices. As long as there is an exact match, the bank applies the payment to the invoice.

Those checks and invoice references that do not match are forwarded to the company for processing. The bank deposits the original check and photocopies or scans checks sent to the Company for further investigation or resolution.

Daily, the bank sends the company a system-generated report that identifies the date and each payer's name, address, and invoice references. This report serves in the same way as the company's deposit slip.

Receipt of this report is reconciled to the changes in A/R customer account balances.

EFTs are treated the same way as the bank lockbox, with funds going directly to the bank. Electronically, the payer lists the invoices and amounts to be paid and the list is electronically matched to the company's record for the customer's A/R balance.

	Policy and Procedures	
Procedure No. B10	Section: Accounting and Finance	Page 8 of 9
	Accounts Receivable: Third-Party Trade and Customer— **Credit, Collection, and Cash Applications**	
Department Ownership	Issue/Effective Date:	Replaces previously issued

Daily analysis and reconciliation occurs through the following:

- Deposits to bank statements

- A/R customer payments collected from the A/R listing matched to the deposits

- A/R subledger to the A/R ledger balance

Controls/Areas of Responsibility

- A credit analysis document must be retained for new and existing customers as long as the contract is active. Information must be retained in accordance with the records information management policy and procedure.

- The Sales account representative is the point of contact with the customer for sales transactions and no agreement should be made with the customer pertaining to credit limits or payment terms without the permission of the Credit Administration.

- The Collections function is the Company's primary point of contact with customers concerning the payment of outstanding A/R balances. The collectors are responsible for:

  - Communicating to management issues that affect the achievement of the collection goals

  - Applying appropriate and diligent collection activities and meeting the Company's DSO objectives

- A/R aging reports as well as a list of customers on credit hold and those with disputed deductions and overdue accounts are circulated to Sales and Finance managers weekly for resolution and action.

- In accordance with the Account Reconciliation policy, monthly reconciliations between the A/R subledger and the general ledger balances are performed, with the differences investigated.

- In order to ensure separation of duties, bank reconciliations and reconciliation of the A/R accounts are performed by general accounting and not the A/R function.

Contacts

Accounts Receivable

<table>
<tr><td colspan="3" align="center">**Policy and Procedures**</td></tr>
<tr><td>Procedure No. B10</td><td align="center">Section: Accounting and Finance</td><td align="right">Page 9 of 9</td></tr>
<tr><td colspan="3" align="center">**Accounts Receivable: Third-Party Trade and Customer—
Credit, Collection, and Cash Applications**</td></tr>
<tr><td>Department Ownership</td><td align="center">Issue/Effective Date:</td><td align="right">Replaces previously issued</td></tr>
</table>

Exhibit

Credit Analysis Checklist

Company Name	❏ Bloomberg (public companies)
	❏ D&B (public and private companies)
	❏ ADTP (Average days to pay)
	❏ EDGAR (http://yahoo.brand.edgar-online.com)
Site ID	❏ Internet—press releases, financials
Date of Report	❏ SEC.gov (10K fiscal yr) or 10Q Qtrly (public companies)
Credit Administrator	❏ RBC VP for Financials (last resort)

❏ **Balance Sheet**

	❏ Compare total liabilities $_____ to the customer's total assets $_____ The total liabilities should be less than the total assets amount.
	❏ The "current ratio" _____ can be located on the page titled "Ratios." If it is not there, then you can calculate it yourself by dividing the current liabilities into the current assets. The answer should be greater than "1" (one).
	❏ Compare shareholder equity $_____ to the net income (loss) $_____ found on the Cash Flow Summary page.
	❏ A positive number for shareholder equity $_____ and net income $_____ is good, while a negative number needs to be investigated further.
	❏ Verify that cash figures $_____ support the payment obligation for the new deal $_____.

❏ **Income Statement**

	❏ Verify that net sales or total revenue is stable and growing and not shrinking. Then compare it to the value of the deal. You are looking for a trend in revenue year after year. If the net income is a negative number, then you should raise a red flag and do further analysis.

❏ **Description Page**

	❏ Summarizes by giving a brief description of what type of company you are reviewing.

	❏ Verify the stock price today and confirm that it is not trading at a price close to what it was at its lowest point YTD.
	    ❏ Current stock price: _____ Low: _____
	    ❏ Date: _____ High: _____

The complete form is returned with the customer's credit file.

Policy and Procedures		
Procedure No. B11	Section: Accounting and Finance	Page 1 of 5
	Accruals	
Department Ownership	Issue/Effective Date:	Replaces previously issued
Prepared by: Date	Approved by: Date	Authorized by: Date

Scope/Background

This policy establishes the standards and procedures for ensuring that all monthly accruals are in compliance with management's objectives and U.S. Generally Accepted Accounting Principles (GAAP). See Financial Accounting Standard (FAS) No. 5, "Accounting for Contingencies," and FAS Interpretation No. 14, "Reasonable Estimation of the Amount of a Loss."

The purpose of monthly accruals is to record incurred expenses within the proper accounting period and to match expenses with related revenues. At month-end, accrual procedures ensure that expenses related to the month are properly included in the Company's financial statements. The accrual process shall be accomplished in a timely and accurate manner and must be in compliance with all applicable financial and accounting standards.

Policy

It is IDEAL LLP's (Company) policy to accrue all known incurred expenses over $1,000 and where the invoice has either not been received or processed through Accounts Payable (A/P) (see Accounts Payable policy and procedures) or where the expense has not otherwise been recorded.

Procedure

Accruals must be prepared when a Company obligation is "likely" to occur and can be "reasonably estimated."

"Likely to Occur"

According to Financial Accounting Standard (FAS) No. 5, a "likely to occur" condition exists when the "information available prior to issuance of the financial statements indicates that it is probable that an asset has been impaired or a liability has been incurred at the date of the financial statements."

Accruals shall be recorded when:

- The expense has been incurred; that is, the product or service has been received on or before the last day of the month and has not yet been paid. *Note:* Even though an expense may have originally been budgeted in the month, it does not qualify for accrual unless the product or service was actually received by the company.

- The Company has assumed the rights of ownership (i.e., title) and obligation in accordance with the terms and conditions of the agreement.

	Policy and Procedures	
Procedure No. B11	Section: Accounting and Finance	Page 2 of 5
	Accruals	
Department Ownership	Issue/Effective Date:	Replaces previously issued

- An existing condition or set of circumstances involving uncertainty may result in a future possible loss. If the anticipated loss is both probable and able to be estimated, then an accrual must be established.

Accruals include but are not limited to:

- Recurring and nonrecurring costs, expenses, or payments (e.g., rents, utilities)

- Purchase order and non–purchase order expenses or asset/inventory acquisitions

- Goods and services received and waiting for acceptance before payment may be authorized

- Procurement (P) Card and Travel, Entertainment and Expense-related items

- Contracts or contingencies that involve possible future loss

Each business unit's controller or financial designee maintains a list of known accounts where accruals are often required (e.g., outside service providers, advertising expense, royalty expense). Expenses shall be anticipated and the business unit's financial reporting statement reviewed prior to month end to ensure accurate and timely posting.

The following additional factors must be considered when recording accruals:

- Accruals shall represent the expense actually incurred, which may not necessarily match to the billing terms (e.g., deposits or retainer). If payment is due prior to performance, the amount shall be accrued/recorded within Prepaid Expenses.

- Services must be recorded and charged to expenses as appropriate as the services are performed.

- Taxes (e.g., Sales Tax) payable related to revenues must be recorded as a liability when the customer invoice is recorded.

- When applicable, payroll taxes withheld and other withholdings shall be recorded and charged to expense weekly.

- An accural is **not** required if the product is received on consignment and if title has not passed to the Company.

Reasonably Estimated

Accounting standards for assessing and estimating the amount to be accrued must be followed to ensure that only valid and authorized expenses:

- Are included for accrual consideration

- Relate to the current accounting period

- Are recorded to the appropriate accounts

	Policy and Procedures	
Procedure No. B11	Section: Accounting and Finance	Page 3 of 5
	Accruals	
Department Ownership	Issue/Effective Date:	Replaces previously issued

Actual expense amounts must be used if known. The accrued payable amount shall be determined from the vendor's invoice and verified against purchase orders/requisitions, contract terms, or other appropriate documents prior to recording the liability.

When actual values are not available, the estimated recorded value must be based on the most current available information. If the amount is unknown, an appropriate estimation methodology must be documented and, once approved by Corporate Accounting, must be used consistently.

Estimation methodologies commonly deployed include applying a(n):

- *Historic trend analysis.* This approach takes an average of the actual expense or amounts over the last three months and applies management's best estimate of current activity.

- *Variance to plan analysis.* This approach adjusts budgeted amounts with management's assessment that the item is likely to occur.

Events that give rise to loss contingencies that occur after the balance sheet date but before the financial statements are issued may require disclosure. If in doubt, contact Corporate Accounting or the Chief Accounting Officer.

Special Topics—Accrual consideration for the following costs and expenses:

A. Fixed-Price Contracts

B. Subcontractor Costs

C. Commissions

D. Restructuring

E. Unusual Entries

A. Fixed-Price Contracts

Loss contingency accruals are required to be recorded for projected future losses to be incurred on fixed-price engagements. The respective sales support team determines the likelihood and estimated amount of such loss accruals with the respective business unit controller.

B. Subcontractor Costs

All subcontractor costs (i.e., time and expenses), whether associated with earning revenue or incurring expenses for the current accounting period, must be captured and reported. Due to the timing associated with the processing of subcontractor expenses, accruals may need to be recorded to capture the subcontractor expenses incurred in the respective accounting period. The respective sales support team determines the likelihood and estimated amount of such loss accruals with the respective business unit controller.

Policy and Procedures

Procedure No. B11	Section: Accounting and Finance	Page 4 of 5
	Accruals	
Department Ownership	Issue/Effective Date:	Replaces previously issued

C. Commissions Guidance

For each component of the Sales Incentive plan, review actual results, actual payments, and model anticipated payments to determine the appropriate monthly commission accrual amount. See the Accounting for Sales Compensation policy.

D. Restructuring

See the Accounting for Restructuring and Reorganization policy. Under FAS No. 146, accruals for restructuring charges are made as follows:

• Employee terminations—One-time termination benefits to affected employees **can be accrued only when:**

1. The plan is committed

2. The number of employees, job classifications, locations, and completion dates are known

3. The benefits to be received are known by the employees (i.e., are either directly communicated or provided pursuant to a standard separation agreement), **and**

4. It is unlikely that changes to the plan will be made

This generally means that the accrual must be made in the period the employee is notified of the termination and the related benefit is committed.

E. Unusual Entries

Inform Corporate Accounting if unusual charges, accruals, adjustments, estimates, or other considerations (e.g., over-/underaccrued state) could impact the financial results for the current or future periods. Such items might include but are not limited to bonuses, consulting fees, legal fees, rent, and insurance.

Authorization and Approval

Accruals must be approved by the business unit Controllers or Corporate Accounting. Each journal entry must have supporting documentation, including the reason for the accrual and methodology as to how it was calculated. See the Journal Entries and Non-Routine Transactions policy.

For financial integrity and accuracy, documentation and records retention standards apply to all accrual journal entries. Documentation must include approved and appropriate backup to support the amount accrued (e.g., when the accrual amount is obtained from another area of the business, support must be provided). See the Records Information Management schedules to determine the record retention period.

Policy and Procedures		
Procedure No. B11	Section: Accounting and Finance	Page 5 of 5
	Accruals	
Department Ownership	Issue/Effective Date:	Replaces previously issued

The accrual balance must be reconciled each month and must be reversed at the beginning of the following month.

Controls/Areas of Responsibility

Each subsidiary and functional business area's controller is responsible for ensuring that all eligible expenses that have not been recorded via normal processing (e.g., Accounts Payable) are accrued.

All Balance Sheet account balances are reconciled monthly to the subledger detail or supporting analysis in accordance with the Account Reconciliation policy and procedure.

Contact

Corporate Controller
Chief Accounting Officer

Policy and Procedures		
Procedure No. B12	Section: Accounting and Finance	Page 1 of 4
Accounting and Audit-Related Complaints		
Department Ownership	Issue/Effective Date:	Replaces previously issued
Prepared by: Date	Approved by: Date	Authorized by: Date

Scope

The following policy and procedure supports and is subordinate to the Company's Compliance and Whistleblower policy and Code of Ethical Conduct. The Company's Compliance and Whistleblower procedures identify access phone numbers, e-mail, and other means for registering complaints.

Policy

It is IDEAL LLP's (Company) policy to ensure that complaints regarding accounting, internal controls, audit matters, or questionable financial practices are handled seriously, expeditiously, and in compliance with the Company's published policies and the Board of Directors' Audit and Compliance Committee objectives.

The objectives include receiving and processing input from:

- Investors, the Audit and Compliance Committee, and the Corporate Compliance Office

    - The Audit and Compliance Committee and the Corporate Compliance office need to know they are receiving input and submissions that have not been edited or tampered with in any manner.

    - The system shall be designed to offer 100 percent integrity and trust.

- Management

    - The process facilitates handling complaints consistently, based on Company established procedures and framework as defined in the investigation procedures and ensures the appropriate storage and retention of key documents.

    - The process is managed to meet cost, quality, timeliness, and confidentiality standards.

- Employees

    - The procedure encourages ethical conduct and includes communication, education, and discussion of the Corporate Code of Ethical Conduct as well as this policy.

    - The procedure facilitates disclosure by offering a convenient, confidential way for employees to raise concerns and a process for providing feedback and closure.

Policy and Procedures		
Procedure No. B12	Section: Accounting and Finance	Page 2 of 4
Accounting and Audit-Related Complaints		
Department Ownership	Issue/Effective Date:	Replaces previously issued

Background

In April 2003, the Securities and Exchange Commission (SEC) directed all SEC listed companies to have the Audit and Compliance Committee establish procedures for receipt, retention, and treatment of complaints regarding internal controls or auditing matters.

Procedure

Since the Audit and Compliance Committee is dependent on receiving information provided by management and internal and external auditors, it is imperative that the Audit and Compliance Committee cultivate open and effective channels of information.

The establishment of a formal procedure for receiving, retaining, and treating complaints shall serve to facilitate disclosures, encourage proper individual conduct, and alert the Audit and Compliance Committee and the Corporate Compliance office to potential problems before serious consequences occur.

The Corporate Compliance office tracks complaints logged in through the help line and monitors and reports on the forthcoming investigation. The help line is monitored by an outside service provider and respects a caller's right to remain anonymous. The help line service provider gathers information and details and reports to the Corporate Compliance office to further the internal investigation and resolve outstanding issues. The Corporate Compliance office reports their findings and resolution to the Audit and Compliance Committee of the Board of Directors.

A. Responsibilities of Audit and Compliance Committee with Respect to Specified Complaints

1. The Audit and Compliance Committee (Committee) shall provide direction and oversight for the receipt, retention, investigation, and act on complaints and concerns of employees regarding questionable accounting, internal accounting controls, and auditing matters, including those regarding the circumvention or attempted circumvention of internal accounting controls or that would otherwise constitute a violation of the Company's accounting policies i.e., an "accounting allegation".

2. At the discretion of the Committee, responsibilities created by these procedures may be delegated to any member of the Committee.

B. Procedures for Receiving Accounting Allegations

1. Any accounting allegation that is made to the help line or management (as detailed in F below), whether openly, confidentially, or anonymously, shall be promptly reported to the Corporate Compliance office, the Company's Internal Audit department and General Counsel.

	Policy and Procedures	
Procedure No. B12	Section: Accounting and Finance	Page 3 of 4
	Accounting and Audit-Related Complaints	
Department Ownership	Issue/Effective Date:	Replaces previously issued

    a. Allegations received via the help line are routed directly to the Corporate Compliance office. Internal Audit and General Counsel are promptly informed and investigative action: begin.

    b. Allegations received directly by management must be immediately reported to Internal Audit and logged with the help line service. Preliminary management fact finding may occur.

    c. The Corporate Compliance office shall promptly notify the chair of the Committee.

2. The Committee may, at their discretion, consult with any member of management, employees, or others whom they believe would have appropriate expertise or information to assist them.

3. The Committee may determine whether the whole Committee, a subcommittee, the Corporate Compliance office, the Company's Internal Audit department or General Counsel should investigate the accounting allegation, taking into account the considerations set forth in Section C.

If the Committee determines that management shall investigate the accounting allegation, the Committee notifies the Corporate Compliance office in writing of that conclusion. The Corporate Compliance office or Internal Audit shall be free in their discretion to engage outside auditors, counsel, or other experts to assist in the investigation and in the analysis of results.

C. Investigate Accounting Allegations

All allegations will be investigated and documented by the Corporate Compliance office or others as designated. In some cases, the Legal department may be requested to conduct an investigation under privilege, in which case a written request must be made and included in the file folder. The Corporate Compliance office coordinates closure, and final resolution is approved by the Committee.

D. Protection of Whistleblowers

Consistent with Company policies, the Corporate Compliance office shall not retaliate and shall not tolerate any retaliation by management or any other person or group, directly or indirectly, against anyone who, in good faith, makes an accounting allegation or provides assistance to the Corporate Compliance office, the Audit and Compliance Committee, management, or any other person or group, including any governmental, regulatory, or law enforcement body, investigating an accounting allegation.

The Corporate Compliance office shall not reveal the identity of any person who submits a good-faith accounting allegation, asking for anonymity, and shall not tolerate any effort made by another person or group, to ascertain the identity of such person.

Policy and Procedures		
Procedure No. B12	Section: Accounting and Finance	Page 4 of 4
Accounting and Audit-Related Complaints		
Department Ownership	Issue/Effective Date:	Replaces previously issued

E. Records

The Corporate Compliance office shall retain an electronic file of all records relating to any accounting allegation and to the investigation of any such accounting allegation.

F. Procedures for Making Complaints

Employees may report accounting allegations openly, confidentially or anonymously, either in writing or orally, to the Board of Directors or the Audit and Compliance Committee. Alternative reporting channels include the Company's General Counsel, the Corporate Compliance office, or the Vice President of Internal Audit.

The help line is intended to promote open communication without fear of retaliation. The toll-free help line is managed by an outside independent service provider and allows callers to report accounting issues without divulging their name.

A report is provided to the Corporate Compliance office; however, if a caller chooses to remain anonymous, the service provider's report reflects that fact.

Controls/Areas of Responsibility

Employees are made aware of this program through Internal Communications, with program materials strategically located throughout the Company.

Allegations may be raised through the internal line of command and/or by the employee directly to the Board of Directors, the Audit and Compliance Committee, or via the outside service provider. All allegations are logged and tracked by the Corporate Compliance office until they are resolved.

Contacts

Chief Financial Officer
Corporate Compliance Office
General Counsel
Internal Audit

	Policy and Procedures	
Procedure No. B13	Section: Accounting and Finance	Page 1 of 4
	Authorization: Delegation, SubDelegation of Authority	
Department Ownership	Issue/Effective Date:	Replaces previous issue

Prepared by:	Approved by:	Authorized by:
Date	Date	Date

Scope

By resolution of the Company's Board of Directors (BOD), the BOD delegates to the Chief Executive Officer (CEO) authority, including the authority to subdelegate and redelegate such authority to conduct activities necessary for the operational continuation of the business.

The purpose of this document is to:

- Identify expenditure authorizations in order to provide clear guidance over decision making and accountability company-wide

- Increase transparency of decision making to enhance operational efficiency

U.S. and international regulations require documented delegation of authority for public companies:

- Section 103 of the Sarbanes-Oxley Act requires external auditors to evaluate whether a company's internal control and procedures provide reasonable assurance that transactions are being made in accordance with authorizations as subdelegated to management and directors.

- Section 404 of the Sarbanes-Oxley Act, in order to support the effectiveness of the Company's internal control environment, requires that there be written documentation of the subdelegation chain and approval to execute a specific transaction.

- The U.S. Foreign Corrupt Practices Act of 1977 stipulates in its record-keeping and accounting provisions that access to a company's assets include management's authorization (i.e., written delegation and subdelegation authority).

Policy

In accordance with the BOD resolutions and with the delegations granted to the Chief Executive Officer (CEO); it is IDÆAL LLP's (Company) policy to establish and subdelegate authorization to specific functional areas of the business and to specific individuals for the purpose of making commitments and collecting and disbursing cash on behalf of the Company.

It is the Company's policy that authorization be delegated to those areas that are held responsible for the successful implementation of Company objectives. The Company assigns authorization levels based on the employee's level of responsibility. Commensurate authority is available to meet the needs of proper conduct for the business and therefore reflects the Company's strategic principles.

Policy and Procedures		
Procedure No. B13	Section: Accounting and Finance	Page 2 of 4
Authorization: Delegation, SubDelegation of Authority		
Department Ownership	Issue/Effective Date:	Replaces previous issue

Authorization must be in accordance with the Authorization Matrix. In a hierarchical corporate environment, authorization may be delegated following the reporting line of command and must be documented.

Delegation is restricted to full-time Company employees.

The CEO, Chief Operating Officer (COO), Chief Financial Officer (CFO), and General Counsel establish and delegate authorization limits.

The Company's executive management empowers, authorizes, and grants responsibility to specific corporate positions through the Company's formal policies and procedures. Each business unit's functional executive and their financial designate either directly approves every financial commitment made on behalf of the unit or document the delegated line of authority. **Functional authorizations must be aligned to the Authorization Matrix.**

Delegation of Authority

Delegation of Authority (DOA) is the formal written conveyance from one person to another of the authority to bind the Company to a legally enforceable obligation.

Each geographic and functional Business Area should document and align the subdelegation limits based on management responsibility. Note that business decisions require review and approval from a business manager or their financial controller or designate. DOA may be considered:

- Short term—each manager establishes protocols for delegation when they anticipate being absent due to illness, vacations, leaves, or extended business trips. Delegations are to be documented and distributed to the appropriate departments within the Business area.

- Long term—any delegation of a long-term nature must be approved by the CFO.

Special Areas with Worldwide Authority

In addition to the authorization levels identified within the matrix, the following transactions must comply with their related policies and procedures:

- **Accounting:** An accounting manager other than the originator must approve all journal entries.

- **Contracts:** The Worldwide Legal department (Legal) must approve all contracts and legal obligations made on behalf of the Company prior to their execution. Legal may subdelegate contract review of standard contracts to the functional business area. Alterations to Company standard contracts and agreements must be approved by Legal.

- **Investments and Project Expenses:** The Investment Committee must approve all purchases and sale/disposal of fixed assets as well as project related expenses where the project is greater than $10,000 USD.

Policy and Procedures		
Procedure No. B13	Section: Accounting and Finance	Page 3 of 4
Authorization: Delegation, SubDelegation of Authority		
Department Ownership	Issue/Effective Date:	Replaces previous issue

- **Information Services (IS)** must approve all purchases and sale/disposal of computer-related hardware, software, networks, and peripherals used for internal purposes.

- **Human Resources** must provide written approval prior to extending any financial commitments to employees (e.g., hiring, salary or wage increases, incentives, commissions, and bonuses).

- **Planning:** The Financial Planning and Analysis function coordinates the approval of the Company's plan and forecasts.

- **Product and Services Pricing** must be established according to preapproved guidelines and approved by the product/service business unit and the Senior Vice President Pricing.

- **Real Estate** commitments to purchase, lease, rent or sale/dispose of property on behalf of the Company must be approved by the headquarter Real Estate/Facilities function. Facility-related contracts (e.g., landscaping, cleaning, utilities) must be approved by Real Estate. The Treasurer must approve Real Estate financing arrangements.

- **Sales and/or Services Finance** must approve sales contracts and changes to sales terms and conditions, including delivery, shipment, payment, demo licenses, and future product discounts.

- **Tax:** Income, sales, and use or country equivalent, import/export, property, and other tax-related preparations and obligations must be approved or delegated by the Corporate Tax department.

- **Treasury** must approve any and all bank accounts and establishes signing authority for issuing checks and arranging for electronic transfers.

Planned Spending

Annually, the Company approves regional plans designed to achieve the Business Area's goals and objectives. Spending to the authorized plan limits requires approval as per the Authorization Matrix.

Under no circumstance shall local management authorize spending in excess of budget.

Roles and Responsibilities:

- Approval/Decisional authority. Employees who have requisite authority emanating from resolutions approved by the BOD through proper delegations of authority to make a decision to commit or bind the company to a legally enforceable obligation or benefit (transaction). Employees with approval/decisional authority should ensure that all requisition reviews of transactions have been completed and consider them prior to approving transactions.

- Authority/Signatory authority. Employees who have requisite authority to sign documents that commit or bind the Company to a legally enforceable obligation or benefit. Employees with signatory authority may not necessarily have approval/decisional authority; however, employees

	Policy and Procedures	
Procedure No. B13	Section: Accounting and Finance	Page 4 of 4
	Authorization: Delegation, SubDelegation of Authority	
Department Ownership	Issue/Effective Date:	Replaces previous issue

with approval authority have signatory authority. Any employee with signatory authority must ensure that all proposed transactions have received all requisite approvals prior to signing any documents that commit or bind the Company to transactions.

- Inform authority. Employees who must be informed about a transaction as early as practicable in the process and, in any event, prior to approval and execution. It is the responsibility of the employee with the approval/decisional authorities to ensure appropriate stakeholders in the organization are informed about transactions.

- Payment execution authority. Employees who have requisition authority emanating from their position in the organization to authorize release of payments for goods, services, and obligations entered into by the Company. Any employee authorized to execute payment must ensure that all requested transactions have received the appropriate documented reviews and approvals prior to the payment release. For most ordinary business expenditures, the payment execution authority and approval/decisional authority will be delegated to the same individual.

- Review authority. Employees responsible for reviewing proposed transactions and providing documented feedback within the reviewer's areas of functional or technical expertise to the approval/decisional authority employee, who in turn considers such feedback prior to approving the transactions.

Controls/Areas of Responsibility

- Each business area must have a documented list of financial delegation and approval limits that is aligned with the Company's Authorization Matrix.

- All financial commitments undertaken on the Company's behalf shall be in conformance with the Company's Code of Ethical Conduct and other company policies.

- The person granting financial authorization shall not be the same person who requests, purchases, or receives the product or service.

- All contracts and documented records require stewardship in accordance with the Records Information Management policy.

- A dedicated business planning and analysis group reviews and tracks results relative to achieving the Company's plan and reports variances as part of the monthly performance review package.

- Appropriate level of documentation and authorization signatures should accompany the request for spending and the subsequent set up in the accounting systems.

Contact

Chief Financial Officer

B13	Authorization: Delegation, SubDelegation of Authority
	**Authorization Matrix**

The Authorization Matrix is made up of the following sections:	
A	Annual Budget and Plans
B	Nonbudgeted Capital Projects and Lease Obligations
C	Human Resources
D	Legal
E	Acquisitions, Divestitures and Joint Ventures/Alliances
F	Procurement
G	Commercial Sales of Licensed Agreements, Product, Professional Services, Intellectual Property Asset Sharing Agreements
H	Treasury and Intercompany Matters

Definitions	
	Acquisition – acquiring or purchasing whether by asset purchase, stock purchase, merger, consolidation or other business combination or otherwise, of any business, line of business, product, product line, assets including intellectual property and other intangible assets, securities or any other ownership interest in any third-party or related entity.
	Agreements – encompass ALL one-time contracts and Master Agreements
	Divestitures – sale or disposition whether by asset purchase, stock purchase, merger, consolidation or other business combination or otherwise, of any business, line of business, product, product line, assets including intellectual property and other intangible assets, securities or any other ownership interest in any third party or related entity.
	Review – a) providing documented feedback within the reviewer's (or corporate committee's) area of functional or technical expertise to the employee (or corporate committee) with decisional authority who, in turn, should consider such feedback prior to approving a transaction; or b) that where review is conducted by the employee or committee with decisional authority over the transaction, considering of all of the facts and opinions gathered in the due diligence and review process and rendering a documented decision on whether to proceed with the proposed transaction as presented.
	Delegation of Authority (DOA) – formal written conveyance from one person to another of the authority to bind the company to a legally enforceable obligation.

Roles and Responsibilities	
A	**Approval/Decisional Authority** – employees who have requisite authority emanating from resolutions approved by the BOD through proper delegations of authority to make a decision to commit or bind the company to a legally enforceable obligation or benefit (transaction). Employees with approval/decisional authority should ensure all requisition reviews of transactions have been completed and consider them prior to approving transactions.
I	**Inform Authority** – employees who must be informed about a transaction as early as practicable in the process and, in any event, prior to approval and execution. It is the responsibility of the employee with the approval/decisional authorities to ensure appropriate stakeholders in the organization are informed about transactions.
R	**Review Authority** – employees responsible for reviewing proposed transactions and providing documented feedback within the reviewer's areas of functional or technical expertise to the approval/decisional authority employee who, in turn should consider such feedback prior to approving the transactions.

B13	Authorization: Delegation, SubDelegation of Authority
	Authorization Matrix
	Authority/Signatory Authority – employees who have requisite authority to sign documents which commit or bind the Company to a legally enforceable obligation or benefit. Employees with signatory authority may not necessarily have approval/decisional authority; however, employees with approval authority have signatory authority. Any employee with signatory authority must ensure that all proposed transactions have received all requisite approvals prior to signing any documents that commit or bind the Company to transactions.
	Payment Execution Authority – employees who have requisition authority emanating from his/her position in the organization to authorize release of payments for goods, services and obligations entered into by the company. Any employee authorized to execute payment must ensure that all requested transactions have received the appropriate documented reviews and approvals prior to the payment release. For most ordinary business expenditures, the payment execution authority and approval/decisional authority will be delegated to the same individual.
Areas with Worldwide Authority	

Accounting: An accounting manager other than the originator must approve all journal entries.

Contracts: The Worldwide Legal department (Legal) must approve all contracts and legal obligations made on behalf of the Company prior to their execution. Legal may subdelegate contract review of standard contracts to the functional business area. Alterations to Company standard contracts and agreements must be approved by Legal.

Investments and Project Expenses: The Investment Committee must approve all purchases and sale/disposal of fixed assets as well as project related expenses where the project is greater than $10,000 USD.

Information Services (IS) must approve all purchases and sale/disposal of computer-related hardware, software, networks, and peripherals used for internal purposes.

Human Resources must provide written approval prior to extending any financial commitments to employees (e.g., hiring, salary or wage increases, incentives, commissions, and bonuses).

Planning: The Financial Planning and Analysis function coordinates the approval of the Company's plan and forecasts.

Product and Services Pricing must be established according to preapproved guidelines and approved by the product/service business unit and the Senior Vice President Pricing.

Real Estate commitments to purchase, lease, rent or sale/dispose of property on behalf of the Company must be approved by the headquarter Real Estate/Facilities function. Facility-related contracts (e.g., landscaping, cleaning, utilities) must be approved by Real Estate. The Treasurer must approve Real Estate financing arrangements.

Sales and/or Services Finance must approve sales contracts and changes to sales terms and conditions, including delivery, shipment, payment, demo licenses, and future product discounts.

Tax: Income, sales, and use or country equivalent, import/export, property, and other tax-related preparations and obligations must be approved or delegated by the Corporate Tax department.

Treasury must approve any and all bank accounts and establishes signing authority for issuing checks and arranging for electronic transfers.

Authorization Matrix										
	U.S. Dollars	Authorization Levels - refers to a single transaction	BOD	CEO	COO	Human Resources	CFO	General Counsel	Business Unit Manager	Business Unit Finance Manager
A	Annual Budget and Plans		R	A	A	A	A	A	R	R
B	Nonbudgeted Capital Projects and Lease Obligations									
	Capital projects not approved as part of the annual budget - per project aggregate value	Over $10M	A	R	R	R	R	R	R	R
		$5M to $10M		A	R	R	R	R	R	R
		$2.5M to $5M			A	I	R	I	R	R
		$1M to $2.5M					A		R	R
		Up to $1M							A	A
	Capital and operating lease obligations	Over $10M	A	R	R	R	R	R	R	R
		$5M to $10M		A	R	R	R	R	R	R
		$2.5M to $5M			A		R	I	R	R
		$1M to $2.5M					A		R	R
		Up to $1M							A	A
B	Human Resources									
	Executive - individual employee plans: recruitment, hiring, severance	Any value	I	A	R	A	R	R		
	Nonexecutive - individual employee plans: recruitment, hiring, severance	Any value			I	A	A		A	A
	Restructuring and reorganization initiatives	Over $10M	A	R	R	R	R	R	R	R
		$5M to $10M		A	R	R	R	R	R	R
		$1M to $5M		I	A	R	A	I	R	R
		Up to $1M		I	A	R	A	I	R	R

Employee benefits, HR policy impact	Over $5M	R	R	R	R	R	A	A	R
Employee benefits, HR policy impact	Up to $5M	R	R	I	A	I	I	I	R
Executive - stock options or equity compensation programs	Any value			R	R	R	R	A	
Nonexecutive - stock options or equity compensation programs	Any value			R	R	R	I	A	
C Legal									
Product liability and class action claims, Corporate Secretary and SVP Public Relations needs to be informed of ALL.	Over $10M	R	R	R	R	R	R	A	R
	$5M to $10M	R	R	R	A	R	A	I	R
	Up to $5M	R	A	A	I	A	I	I	R
Nonmonetary, material settlement		R	R	R	A	R	A		R
Nonmonetary, nonmaterial settlement		R	A	A	I	A	I		R
Commercial litigation and claims including patent and intellectual property disputes, Corporate Secretary and SVP Public Relations needs to be informed of ALL except less than $5M	Over $10M	R	R	R	R	R	R	A	R
	$5M to $10M	R	R	R	A	R	A		R
	Up to $5M	R	A	A	I	A	I		R
Nonmonetary, material settlement		R	R	R	A	R	A		R
Nonmonetary, nonmaterial settlement		R	A	A	I	A	I		R
Labor and employment claims, Corporate Secretary and Public Relations needs to be informed	Over $10M	R	R	R	R	R	R	A	R
	$5M to $10M	R	R	R	A	R	A		R
	Up to $5M	R	A	A	I	A	I		R
Nonmonetary, material settlement		R	R	R	A	R	A		R
Nonmonetary, Nonmaterial settlement		R	A	A	I	A	I		R

	U.S. Dollars	Authorization Levels - refers to a single transaction	BOD	CEO	COO	Human Resources	CFO	General Counsel	Business Unit Manager	Business Unit Finance Manager
E	**Acquisitions, Divestitures, and Joint Ventures/Alliances**									
	Investment Committee: reviews ALL and is made up of the CEO, COO, Human Resources, CFO, general counsel, business unit management, business unit finance management									
	Any single acquisition or divestiture	Over $10M	A	R	R	R	R	R	R	R
	Acquisitions, divestitures, and joint ventures/alliances with a single or aggregate value	Up to $10M		A	A	A	A	A	R	R
F	**Procurement**									
	Purchase or lease of goods and services - VP Procurement must approve ALL	Over $5M	I	A	R	I	R	R	R	R
		Up to $5M			A		A	R	R	R
		Up to $500K					R	R	A	A
	Procurement (excludes: mergers, acquisitions, licensing agreements, royalties, intellectual property, technology									
	Professional services - external auditors	Annual contract	A							
G	**Sales**									
	Standard product pricing - list prices, discounts, terms and conditions	Any value		I	A		A		R	R
	Discount within standard range	Any value							A	A
	Discount exceeding standard range	Any value		I	A		A	A	R	R

	Activity	Value								
	Standard contract language	Any value	A				A		A	A
	Nonstandard contract language	Any value		I	A		A	A	R	R
	Commission plan			I	A	A	A	A	R	R
	Payment terms and concessions	Any value		I	A	A	A		R	R
	Licenses/asset-sharing agreements - outbound technology sharing	Any value		I	A		A	A	R	R
	Licenses/asset-sharing agreements - inbound technology sharing	Any value		I	A		A	A	R	R
H	**Treasury and Intercompany Matters - ALL must be approved by the Corporate Treasurer**									
	Cash and banking - opening, changing, closing accounts - movement of cash - investment of excess cash	Any value					I			
	Investment transactions	Over $10M		I			A	A		
		Up to $10M					I	R		
	Financing transactions including debt, issuance or retirement of debt, issuance or retirement of guarantees	Over $10M		I			A	A		
		Up to $10M					I	R		
	Transactions incorporating equity components	Any value	A			A	A	A		

	Policy and Procedures	
Procedure No. B14	Section: Accounting and Finance	Page 1 of 3
	Bank Reconciliation	
Department Ownership	Issue/Effective Date:	Replaces previously issued

Prepared by: Date	Approved by: Date	Authorized by: Date

Scope

This policy applies to all bank accounts maintained by the Company.

Policy

It is IDÆAL LLP's (Company) policy to take adequate steps to ensure the accuracy of the bank balances shown in the general ledger. Monthly, data from the cash receipts and disbursements journal shall be compared with the details reported on bank statements. Unmatched and mismatched data shall be used to reconcile the book and bank balances and the reconciliations shall be performed either manually by general accounting personnel (those not having access to cash or involvement in processing or recording transactions), or by computer when banks furnish statements in computer readable formats.

Procedures

Bank balances, as shown in bank statements, shall be reconciled monthly with the general ledger. Data from cash receipts and cash disbursements shall be compared on an item-by-item basis, with the details reported on the bank statement. Mismatches shall be listed for investigation.

Bank statements shall be received by Corporate Treasury (or a designate) and forwarded to the reconciliation preparer. In order to comply with segregation of duties principles, the reconciliation preparer must be someone who does not have access to preparing or issuing checks or preparing and depositing cash.

The format for monthly bank reconciliations shall be composed of two sections. See Exhibit for suggested format.

- The first section begins with the balance shown in the bank statement; the preparer adds or subtracts items that should have been included in the bank statement (e.g., deposits in transit, outstanding checks), resulting in an adjusted balance.

- The second section begins with the balance shown in the general ledger; the preparer adds or subtracts items that reflect transactions not recorded on the general ledger and identified on the bank statement (e.g., returned checks, bank charges).

The adjusted balance for each section must be equal. Research and determine the cause of any discrepancies between the two balances, such as recording errors, omissions, mispostings, and so on.

	Policy and Procedures	
Procedure No. B14	Section: Accounting and Finance	Page 2 of 3
	Bank Reconciliation	
Department Ownership	Issue/Effective Date:	Replaces previously issued

Summarize and draft any book reconciling items such as interest or bank charges, and prepare any necessary journal entries in accordance with management policy.

Review all outstanding checks over six months for disposition and flag as a possible abandoned property (see Escheat, Abandoned Property, and Unclaimed Checks policy and procedure).

Controls/Areas of Responsibility

All bank accounts must be reconciled monthly, with the reconciliations reviewed and approved by the Corporate Treasurer or delegate.

Journal entries for account fees, wire transfers, and other transactions are prepared by the Corporate Accounting staff person and approved by the Accounting Manager.

Contact

Corporate Controller
Corporate Treasury

	Policy and Procedures	
Procedure No. B14	Section: Accounting and Finance	Page 3 of 3
	Bank Reconciliation	
Department Ownership	Issue/Effective Date:	Replaces previously issued

Exhibit

Sample Bank Reconciliation Form

Bank Account/Name	
For the Month Ending	

Ending balance per bank statement	
Additions	
Deposits in transit (list individually)	
Deductions	
Outstanding checks (list individually)	
Adjusted balance (must equal the adjusted balance below)	

Ending balance per General Ledger	
Additions°	
Interest or other payments collected by the Bank on the Company's behalf that the Company has not recorded	
Deductions°	
Bank charges	
Wire transfer fees	
Returned deposits	
Interest or other payments made by the bank on the Company's behalf that the Company has not recorded	
Adjusted balance (must equal the adjusted balance above)	

°Journal entries are required for the items listed.

Prepared by/Date	
Reviewed by/Date	

Procedure No. B15	**Policy and Procedures**	Page 1 of 3
	Section: Accounting and Finance	
	Business Combinations, Consolidation and Foreign Entity Reporting	
Department Ownership	Issue/Effective Date:	Replaces previously issued

Prepared by:	Approved by:	Authorized by:
Date	Date	Date

Scope

For operational purposes, the Company is organized into four geographic regions: Europe, Middle East, and Africa (EMEA); Asia Pacific region (APJ); Caribbean, Central and South America (LA); and North America (NA). For purposes of financial and accounting consolidation, all Company business units, subsidiaries, and legal entities are assigned to one of these geographic areas.

Policy

It is IDŒAL LLP's (Company) policy to establish procedures and guidelines for the timely and accurate reporting of financial results of the Company's international subsidiaries and to consolidate each entity's financial results into a consolidated set of financial statements.

All non-majority-owned subsidiaries must be accounted for in accordance with the policy and procedure for Accounting for Business Combinations. Investments where the Company has minority ownership are accounted for using the equity method.

Procedure

Consolidation occurs at the Corporate (i.e., parent company) level using trial balance summaries provided by each country.

It is the responsibility of the geographical financial offices to maintain the accounting books and records of its operations. The geographic regional Finance Department is responsible for the set up of new offices, establishment of proper financial reporting practices, determination of the functional currency and initial monitoring of compliance with statutory filing and audit requirements.

Each location is provided a Reporting Package. The Reporting Package outlines the prescribed financial reporting format and data, which must be included with each month's financial reporting submission to Corporate Accounting. The Reporting Package includes the following documents:

- Chart of Accounts for those accounts to be submitted

- Trial balance with year to date account balances, year to date variance to the official plan, and forecasted fiscal year plan adjustments submitted in US dollars

- Receipts, cash disbursement records and bank reconciliation for all bank accounts

- Intercompany and intracompany transactions must be separately identified and follow the Intercompany Policy and Procedure

- Key statistical data and indicators for financial and operational performance

The Financial Statements for these subsidiaries are prepared and approved by the subsidiary's Controller or financial designate. The local Controller is responsible for submitting financial statements in accordance with U.S. Generally Accepted Accounting Principles (GAAP) or as otherwise approved by the Chief Accounting Officer. Corporate Accounting provides Accounting and Finance technical assistance and guidance as required.

Local books refers to the country's or subsidiary's local books and is generally stated in local currency. A local book trial balance is prepared in local currency and translated to U.S. GAAP and U.S. dollars.

Due to local regulations and income tax requirements, there may be differences between local reporting requirements and US GAAP. Any differences between local books and the amounts reported to Corporate must be reconciled and documented and approved by the Chief Accounting Officer.

Currency Transaction/Translation

Non-U.S. currency assets and liabilities of the Company's non-U.S. dollar subsidiaries are translated using the exchange rates in effect at the balance sheet date (i.e., balance sheet exchange rate). The Income Statement results from operations are translated using the average exchange rates prevailing throughout the period (i.e., Profit-and-Loss exchange rate). The effects of exchange rate fluctuations on translating foreign currency assets and liabilities into U.S. dollars are accumulated as part of the foreign currency translation adjustment in Stockholders' Equity.

As inter-company currency transactions are settled, the actual exchange gains and losses are included within Exchange Gains/Loss account on the Income Statement in the period in which they occur.

Country and Regional Financial Statements

Using U.S. GAAP and local books (prior to consolidation), Corporate Accounting measures each country's/region's financial performance and contribution. That is, individual country/regional performance is prior to the elimination of consolidation entries. Using a working paper technique, intercompany charges may be reclassified to the appropriate local book account for measurement purposes. However, all transactions that affect consolidation must remain within the intercompany accounts.

	Policy and Procedures	
Procedure No. B15	Section: Accounting and Finance	Page 3 of 3
	Business Combinations, Consolidation and Foreign Entity Reporting	
Department Ownership	Issue/Effective Date:	Replaces previously issued

Intercompany Accounts and Elimination Entries

Corporate Accounting reconciles and eliminates all Intercompany transactions. This includes subsidiary-to-subsidiary, parent-to-subsidiary and subsidiary-to-parent transactions. The Company classifies Intercompany transactions as those transactions which are expected to be settled and those transactions which are not expected to be settled. The intercompany transactions are eliminated during the consolidation process. See the Intercompany Transactions policy and procedure.

Tax Implications

Subsidiaries are responsible for accounting for income taxes using local statutory tax regulations and rates.

The Corporate Accounting department performs consolidation of each of the Company's subsidiaries and legal entities. Corporate accounting must ensure that all of the subsidiaries and legal entities have provided input via the Reporting Package and that their results are included within the consolidated financial statements.

Controls/Areas of Responsibility

Local Controllers or financial designates are responsible for the transactions within the local books, for identifying and making adjustments to ensure that local books comply with U.S. GAAP, and for identifying all intercompany transactions.

It is important that transactions are correctly coded such that they are properly identified for elimination during the consolidation process.

Corporate Accounting is responsible for reconciling the intercompany transactions and preparing the Consolidated Financial Statements.

Contact

Chief Accounting Officer
Corporate Controller

	Policy and Procedures	
Procedure No. B16	Section: Accounting and Finance	Page 1 of 3
	Business Licenses	
Department Ownership	Issue/Effective Date:	Replaces previously issued

Prepared by:	Approved by:	Authorized by:
Date	Date	Date

Scope

The document applies to all IDÆAL LLP's legal entities, subsidiaries, and business units.

Policy

When a corporation conducts business beyond the borders of its original state or country of incorporation, it is subject to the laws and regulations of the state or country in which it is conducting business. Accordingly, it must register to do business in that location.

It is IDÆAL LLP's (Company) policy to comply with all state and local regulations wherever the Company conducts business. Licenses, annual reports, and franchise tax reports applicable to the jurisdiction where the Company conducts business must be filed in a timely manner to avoid penalties and maintain the Company's "good standing status" as defined by the jurisdictions in which the company chooses to conduct business.

Accordingly, the Corporate Tax department provides this support and service for the U.S. jurisdictions. Within foreign countries, the local Business/Finance managers shall perform the filing function as required within their country and/or province, with a copy forwarded to the, regional tax offices and the financial designate within Corporate Tax.

Procedure

Offices and Company Establishments

At least annually, a Corporate Tax designate performs an analysis to determine if the list of required jurisdictions is complete and accurate. A list of current Company offices and locations input from Real Estate as is matched to the prior list to determine changes i.e., licenses for jurisdictions that are no longer required or for offices that have changed regions.

As a new office is established, Business and/or Finance managers shall be notified that a license or submission is required. If unsure as to the nature and timing of regulatory requirements, contact a local attorney for requirements.

The updated list is forwarded to Corporate Legal, the Chief Accounting Officer (CAO), and the Company's outside tax service providers to be validated as complete and accurate. Corporate Legal and the CAO validate the list and compare it to known Company entities, locations, and accounting submissions.

	Policy and Procedures	
Procedure No. B16	Section: Accounting and Finance	Page 2 of 3
	Business Licenses	
Department Ownership	Issue/Effective Date:	Replaces previously issued

Information

The information requested shall represent the Company's financial and/or operational position as at a point in time i.e., link to quarter-end or year-end submissions to Corporate. For external and internal auditability, related work papers and assumptions must be retained with each submission. In a peer-to-peer review, the information must be checked for accuracy and consistency. Corporate Tax approves the release of financial information for U.S.-based filings, and the country Controllers or financial designates approve the release for non-U.S.-based filings.

The information required may include but is not limited to:

- List of current Directors and Officers
- The capital stock (authorized and outstanding)
- Financial performance
- Location of Company office in that state, country, or province

Due Dates

Business licenses and annual reports are to be filed in accordance with the due dates of the jurisdiction e.g., quarterly, annually, or biennially.

Signature

Unless otherwise sub-delegated directed, an Officer of the Company must approve and sign the business licenses, franchise tax, and annual reports filings.

Fees

Fee amounts vary by locality and may be a flat or variable fee depending on such things as gross assets, issued shares, number of employees, and the value of real or personal property by location.

U.S.-Based Requirements

Corporate Tax, or a designated agent, coordinates the submission of required licenses and forms, in accordance with U.S.-based requirements. Corporate Tax maintains and monitors the list of required submissions.

	Policy and Procedures	
Procedure No. B16	Section: Accounting and Finance	Page 3 of 3
	Business Licenses	
Department Ownership	Issue/Effective Date:	Replaces previously issued

Non-U.S.-Based Requirements

The business and/or finance manager responsible for the jurisdiction coordinates the submission of required licenses and forms, in accordance with the local regulations. Corporate Tax is copied on the submission and maintains and monitors the list of required submissions.

Master List

A master list of the jurisdictions, the type of information required, and the business license fees are maintained by Corporate Tax. The lists include summary information for each license and shall include but are not limited to the scope of the business license, Company names on the license, date of last filing and license period.

Corporate Tax or the country Business/Finance Manager is responsible for ensuring compliance with tax filing requirements. Failure to comply may result in an inactive status for the entity and assessment of penalties for the Company.

The Legal department is responsible for notifying Corporate Tax of any new entities that must register new locations for any existing entity. Periodically (at least annually), the Legal department reviews the master list for accuracy and completeness.

Controls/Areas of Responsibility

Corporate Tax or a designated, approved service provider has the responsibility for completing the business licenses, annual reports, and franchise tax reports for U.S. jurisdictions.

Local Business and/or Finance Controllers or designates must address filing requirements in non-U.S.-based jurisdictions.

Contacts

Corporate Tax
Corporate Legal

Policy and Procedures		
Procedure No. B17	Section: Accounting and Finance	Page 1 of 7
	Cash and Banking	
Department Ownership	Issue/Effective Date:	Replaces all previously issued

Prepared by: Approved by: Authorized by:
Date Date Date

Scope

This document has been established to ensure effective and efficient internal controls pertaining to opening, maintaining, and closing bank accounts between IDÆAL LLP and its affiliated business units.

The policy is based on the Board of Directors' resolution (see the Authorization policy and procedure) authorizing the Corporate Treasurer as responsible for opening, maintaining, and closing bank accounts; assigning and changing authorized signatories; and designating the types of transactions that may be conducted within those banking relationships.

The following applies to all forms of cash deposits, payments (e.g. checks), and electronic payments (e.g., wire transfer/telegraphic transfer).

Policy

It is IDÆAL LLP's (Company) policy to ensure worldwide consistency in the area of cash and banking. The Company and its subsidiaries conduct general banking with financial institutions that meet the criteria identified below. Corporate Treasury must give its prior approval for Company employees to establish banking or financial institutional relationships.

Corporate Treasury shall be responsible for controlling the opening, closing, and maintenance of all company bank accounts. Compliance with the following procedures mitigates undue risk and reduces bank-related expenses.

Procedures

The following procedures provide an overview of:

A. Banking relations and the qualifications of those financial institutions

B. Opening and closing a bank account and conducting bank reviews

C. Approvals and documentation

D. Reporting

A. Banking Relations

The treasurer is the Company's primary representative in dealing with banks and/or financial institutions. The Treasurer is responsible for meeting with personnel of the company's primary banks

	Policy and Procedures	
Procedure No. B17	Section: Accounting and Finance	Page 2 of 7
	Cash and Banking	
Department Ownership	Issue/Effective Date:	Replaces all previously issued

at least quarterly to provide consistent financial information reporting and updates on the company's operations to bank officials. The Treasurer is responsible for promoting a positive working relationship between the Company and the banks. The Treasurer provides bank officials with a forecast of the Company's capital needs or financial service requirements in order for the bank officials to have adequate time to understand, approve and prepare for meeting the Company's investing and/or financing needs.

The Treasurer performs an ongoing credit assessment and evaluation of the bank's abilities to satisfy the needs of the company and makes appropriate changes whenever necessary. Criteria used in the evaluating banks may include:

- Size of Bank (i.e., appropriate size to meet company needs while being small enough to be responsive)

- Financial safety and capital structure

- Reputation

- Location

- Flexibility and lending philosophy/attitudes

- Operating efficiency and accuracy (e.g., computerization, employee training)

The Treasurer determines and documents an information profile on qualified banks with the above information including who at the bank has the relationship responsibility. Corporate Treasury maintains bank account files to include correspondence and official documents relating to the opening, closing and maintenance of all company and subsidiary bank accounts.

Qualifications of Financial Institutions

The Company and its subsidiaries conduct general banking activity with financial institutions that meet the following requirements:

- The bank, if based in the United States, is a member of the Federal Deposit Insurance Corporation (FDIC).

- The bank is among the top 50 U.S. banks or 200 banks worldwide ranked according to assets.

- The financial institution has a short-term rating of at least A1 by Standard and Poors and P1 by Moody's. If the financial institution does not have a short-term rating, the financial institution must have a long-term rating of at least A by Standard and Poors and A2 by Moodys.

- If the financial institution is a broker, their total capital must be in excess of $500 million and total capital of at least 10 percent in excess of the early warning level established by the Securities and Exchange Commission and the New York Stock Exchange.

	Policy and Procedures	
Procedure No. B17	Section: Accounting and Finance	Page 3 of 7
	Cash and Banking	
Department Ownership	Issue/Effective Date:	Replaces all previously issued

The Corporate Treasurer must approve all banks and financial institutions with whom the Company chooses to conduct business.

B. Opening a Bank Account

To open a bank account, a written request must be made to the Treasurer. The request must include but is not limited to the following:

- Bank name, address, bank contact, and phone number

- Purpose of account

- Anticipated monthly average bank balance

- Bank Account signatories must be limited to the Country and Regional Business Manager and their Financial counterparts and must be identified to Treasury and Legal prior to the bank account or signatory becoming active.

- The request must be reviewed and approved by the proper company personnel according to the following:

  1. Domestic U.S. regional bank account: Approval by Chief Financial Officer (CFO) or Chief Accounting Officer (CAO) and the Corporate Treasurer.

  2. Non-U.S. bank account: Approval by the Regional Treasury employee or the Regional Finance Director and Corporate Treasurer.

  3. Corporate bank account: Approval by CFO or CAO and Corporate Treasurer.

The request is reviewed by Corporate Treasury to determine that a clear need exists for a new bank account. If the need for a new bank account has been established, Treasury evaluates the request based on the qualifications noted above. Treasury either approves the requested bank or assists the requester to locate another bank that better meets Company objectives.

Once the bank account and the bank have been approved, Treasury prepares a bank account inventory form, which includes the following elements:

- Name of account

- Instructions regarding purpose of account and how it is to be operated

- Name of signatories and signing limits

- Instructions regarding use of facsimile signatures

- Address where all debit and credit advices and bank statements are to be sent

Policy and Procedures		
Procedure No. B17	Section: Accounting and Finance	Page 4 of 7
	Cash and Banking	
Department Ownership	Issue/Effective Date:	Replaces all previously issued

In addition to the Corporate Treasurer, the account letter must be signed by any two of the following:

- CFO

- Assistant Treasurer

- Corporate Secretary

- CAO

For Non-U.S. bank accounts, the account inventory form letter must be prepared and signed by the local Controller or Finance Manager and the Country Business Manager. A copy of the signed letter must be forwarded to Corporate Treasury.

Once the account has been opened, a Corporate Treasury employee or the local controller notifies the appropriate accounting personnel to activate the account in the general ledger.

It is the responsibility of Corporate Treasury to keep records as to the status of all Company bank accounts and to retain all relevant documents regarding the opening and maintenance of Company bank accounts.

Closing a Bank Account

To close a bank account, a written request must be made to the Corporate Treasurer. The following must be included in the request:

- Bank name, address, bank contact, and phone number

- Bank account number

- Disposition of closing bank balance and statement

- Approval by the proper Company personnel for:

   1. Domestic U.S. bank account: Approval by CFO or Corporate Treasurer

   2. Non-U.S bank account: Approval by Regional Treasury employee or Regional Finance Director, and Corporate Treasurer

   3. Corporate bank account: Approval by CFO or CAO and Corporate Treasurer

Upon receipt of the properly authorized form, Treasury prepares a bank account closing letter and notifies the bank where any remaining bank balance must be transferred. The letter must be signed by personnel as named above.

For foreign bank accounts, the account-closing letter must be prepared and signed by the local controller or finance manager and the Country Director. A copy of the signed letter must be forwarded to Corporate Treasury.

	Policy and Procedures	
Procedure No. B17	Section: Accounting and Finance	Page 5 of 7
	Cash and Banking	
Department Ownership	Issue/Effective Date:	Replaces all previously issued

Once the account has been closed, Corporate Treasury or the local Controller notifies the appropriate accounting personnel to deactivate the account in the general ledger.

Bank Account Review

At least annually, a Corporate Regional Treasury employee or local Controller reviews and report (using the Bank Inventory Form – exhibit) on the status of all bank accounts to determine that a business reason still exists for the continuation of the account. If it is determined that no reason exists for keeping an account open, then the account must be closed.

C. Approvals/Documentation

Bank Accounts

All bank accounts shall maintain the following characteristics:

- No one person should have single signing authority

- At least one Corporate Officer must have signing authority on the account

Bank Credit

The Corporate Treasurer must approve all bank loans, lines of credit, overdraft facilities, letter-of-credit arrangements, or other financing requirements prior to their inception.

Wire Transfer

Wire transfers must be initiated through Accounts Payable and documented with a Wire Transfer Request form and appropriate financial approvals. Vendor payment requests and sales tax payments are examples of wire transfer requests.

Wire transfers to Company subsidiaries must be initiated from the subsidiary to Corporate Treasury with a forecasted Statement of Cash Flows and an approved Wire Transfer form.

Other wire transfer requests, including but not limited to stock dividends and legal settlements, shall be requested through Corporate Treasury directly.

D. Reporting

The Treasurer maintains the master Bank account inventory list and the names of all U.S. and Non-U.S. financial institutions the company and its subsidiaries are authorized to conduct banking activity with. This list is validated at least quarterly and provided to the CFO and appropriate staff. The report contains:

- Short- and long-term credit rating of Standard and Poors and Moodys

- Worldwide ranking by total assets for approved U.S. and international banks

- If a broker, amount of total capital and early warning level calculation

	Policy and Procedures	
Procedure No. B17	Section: Accounting and Finance	Page 6 of 7
	Cash and Banking	
Department Ownership	Issue/Effective Date:	Replaces all previously issued

Controls/Areas of Responsibility

The Cash Manager reports to the Corporate Treasurer and is responsible for:

- Funds management, which is made up of monitoring the daily cash position, controlling cash balances on deposit at financial institutions, and moving funds from concentration accounts or other accounts to where they are needed.

- Liquidity management, which is made up of short-term borrowing and investing.

- Forecasting, which includes projecting future cash shortages and surpluses and monitoring the accuracy of prior projections.

The Corporate Treasurer is responsible for:

- Banking system administration which is made up of managing bank relationships, including compensation for banking services, conducting analytical reviews and feasibility studies of banking services.

- Inventory of banks

Contacts

Corporate Treasurer

	Policy and Procedures	
Procedure No. B17	Section: Accounting and Finance	Page 7 of 7
	Cash and Banking	
Department Ownership	Issue/Effective Date:	Replaces all previously issued

Bank Account Inventory Form

Date: _____

Reporting Unit _____   Prepared by: _____

Please complete one bank account inventory form for each bank account used by your unit. Repetitive information such as bank addresses, account names, or other similar information need only be indicated on one form if the same for all accounts.

Bank Name	Bank Address	
Contact Name	Telephone	Fax

Account Name	Account Number	
Interest Bearing: Yes / No	Currency:	
Purpose of Account:		

Authorized Signers/Signatures:

Name:	Title	Joint Signatory Yes / No	Authorization Limit Up to
Name:	Title	Joint Signatory Yes / No	Authorization Limit Up to
Name:	Title	Joint Signatory Yes / No	Authorization Limit Up to

Indicate if signing authorities require individual or joint signatories and authorization limits.

Reporting Unit Authorization	Reporting Unit Finance
Date	Date

Corporate Treasury Approval:	Treasury Comments
Date	

Forward the completed form to the corporate Treasurer.

<table>
<tr><td colspan="3" align="center">**Policy and Procedures**</td></tr>
<tr><td>Procedure No. B18</td><td align="center">Section: Accounting and Finance</td><td align="right">Page 1 of 3</td></tr>
<tr><td colspan="3" align="center">**Communication with Financial Community**</td></tr>
<tr><td>Department Ownership</td><td align="center">Issue/Effective Date:</td><td align="right">Replaces previously issued</td></tr>
<tr><td>Prepared by:
Date</td><td>Approved by:
Date</td><td>Authorized by:
Date</td></tr>
</table>

Scope/Background

The objective of this policy is to eliminate the unauthorized communication of material, non-public information about the Company to shareholders and market professionals. See the Material Non-Public Information and Insider Trading policy and procedure. This objective is consistent with the Fair Disclosure Regulation (FD) as communicate by the Securities Exchange Commission (SEC), which became effective October 23, 2000.

This policy is intended to restrict Company employees within the worldwide organization, except for authorized individuals (identified below), from talking to financial or industry market professionals about the various Company business.

Authorized individuals are in two categories: those who do not need approval to discuss the Company businesses with stock market and financial investment professionals (refer to the **A** list below) and those who may be authorized in advance for specific content and for a limited duration (the **B** list).

Policy

It is IDEAL LLP's (Company) policy that only authorized individuals communicate with Wall Street analysts and other market and/or financial investment professionals.

The Company's officers, executives, and selected senior managers and their designees (i.e., authorized individuals) must not knowingly disclose any material, nonpublic information to buy-side and sell-side market and/or financial investment analysts and portfolio managers (collectively known as market professionals).

Material information shall be defined as information that may cause a significant move in the market price of Company securities, within a limited period of time (i.e., 24 hours).

Procedure

It is recommended that every telephone call or face-to-face discussion between an authorized individual and a market professional be documented and the content noted. Documentation may be in the form of meeting notes, calendar entries, telephone logs, or taped conversations. These notes must be filed within 24 hours with the Company's Investor Relations (IR) department, where they will be retained for up to one year.

In the event of an unintentional disclosure, the individual must immediately notify Investor Relations. If IR, in discussions with the General Counsel, confirms that the disclosure is material, it will issue a news release or, if required, the General Counsel will file a Form 8-K with the SEC.

Policy and Procedures		
Procedure No. B18	Section: Accounting and Finance	Page 2 of 3
Communication with Financial Community		
Department Ownership	Issue/Effective Date:	Replaces previously issued

Exempt from this policy are routine business conversations with Company partners (e.g., media and outside consultants) who have a fiduciary responsibility, or who are bound by confidentiality agreements and therefore restricted by insider trading rules.

All authorized individuals as designated by the General Counsel as well as all employees shall observe quarterly "quiet periods." Discussion of all material nonpublic information during these periods is strictly forbidden.

Quiet periods generally begin two weeks prior to the end of each fiscal quarter and will extend to the point at which the Company conducts its quarterly conference call. Additional quiet periods may be required from time to time and are communicated to authorized individuals and employees as appropriate.

Conferences, quarterly conference calls, breakout sessions, and one-on-one meetings with market professionals are permitted under this policy. However, in these and other public forums where there is a script, the Company's General Counsel or Deputy General Counsel must review and approve the script in advance. In the case of sell-side conferences, at a minimum, the presentation (slides and text) should be posted within 24 hours to the IR Web site.

Scheduled teleconferences must be publicly announced in advance with access information for the live event as well as access to replays or transcripts.

Press releases announcing that an authorized individual will be speaking at a conference or meetings with buy-side clients of a sell-side firm on specific dates must be issued in advance of the event.

Review of market professional models, projections, or industry reports should be provided only by authorized individuals and must be restricted to historical data and the correction of egregious errors. Under no circumstances will private guidance be given with respect to financials for any current or future period.

Authorization

Selected Company employees (as identified below) have authority to speak to market professionals on behalf of the Company and in regard to its various businesses:

List A	List B
President and Chief Executive Officer	Company employees and members of the Board of Directors who would be authorized in advance for specific content and for a limited duration.
General Counsel and Secretary	
Deputy General Counsel	
Chief Financial Officer	
Vice President, Investor Relations	

Policy and Procedures		
Procedure No. B18	Section: Accounting and Finance	Page 3 of 3
Communication with Financial Community		
Department Ownership	Issue/Effective Date:	Replaces previously issued

Controls/Areas of Responsibility

It is the responsibility of every Company employee to uphold the provisions of this policy.

It is IR's responsibility to administer this policy and procedure.

IR reviews telephone and meeting records at least on a quarterly basis to ensure that authorized individuals are submitting notes regularly.

IR maintains a calendar of scheduled conferences and meetings at which an authorized individual may present; this serves as a guideline for the issuance of new releases concerning the events.

Contact

Chief Accounting Officer
Investor Relations

Policy and Procedures		
Procedure No. B19	Section: Accounting and Finance	Page 1 of 4
Escheat, Abandoned Property, Unclaimed Checks: **U.S., Canada, and Where Local Regulations Require**		
Department Ownership	Issue/Effective Date:	Replaces previously issued

Prepared by:

Date

Approved by:

Date

Authorized by:

Date

Scope

Escheat refers to the reversion of property to the state or county, as provided by state law, when the property is abandoned or remains unclaimed, generally five years or as defined by local regulation.

If the property owner's address is unknown or is in a Non-U.S. country other than Canada, the unclaimed property is reported to the state where the corporation is incorporated (e.g., Delaware). For those lost owners with a last known address that is in a state that does not have an applicable statute for the type of property being reported, the unclaimed property should be reported to the state of incorporation. If the owner's last known address is in a state with an applicable statute, then the unclaimed property should be reported to the Unclaimed Property department within that state.

Policy

IDÆAL LLP (Company), which includes all non-U.S. and U.S subsidiaries, is a Delaware Corporation and, as such, it must abide by, report, and remit abandoned property to the state of Delaware or the applicable jurisdiction as required by regulation.

Unclaimed property must be remitted to the jurisdiction where the transaction beneficiary resides. Unless otherwise stipulated by local laws, the following jurisdictions should be used:

- The "Remit to" address is used for Accounts Payable (A/P) uncashed checks.

- The employee's home address is used for employee uncashed checks.

- The "Bill to" address is used for Accounts Receivable (A/R) unclaimed adjustments.

It is the Company's policy to comply with escheat-related laws and regulations where and as applicable. Canada has and other countries may have similar laws to the United States. Non-U.S. locations should adhere to statutory requirements for managing abandoned property with local transactions and processes documented. Corporate Finance must be notified when/where these regulations are enacted and require the Company to comply.

Procedure

For the Company, the most common form of unclaimed property refers to the following transactions processed through:

- Accounts Payable (A/P) i.e., vendor checks not cashed or unclaimed

- Payroll i.e., employee payroll checks not cashed or unclaimed

- Accounts Receivable (A/R) i.e., overpayments, refunds, or open credits, which cannot be applied to open receivables

Aggregate amounts by vendor, employee, or customer in excess of $20 USD per transaction are subject to these procedures. Unclaimed amounts less than $20 USD shall be written off.

Unclaimed checks paid to vendors or employees shall be identified through monthly bank reconciliations. After 180 days, the unclaimed property is set up as a liability, while every effort is made to contact the owner. Reasonable efforts must be made to locate owners when the account first becomes inactive or the check remains uncashed. Graduated investigative efforts depending on amount and duration may include such additional search activities as telephone calls and registered mail.

Unclaimed A/R deductions are determined from the monthly aging report, which must identify unapplied adjustments separately. After 180 days, to the extent no right of offset exists, these unapplied adjustments must be isolated in the liability account, while they are to be further investigated and resolved.

A/P, Payroll, and A/R should monitor and track unclaimed property. At least quarterly, the Company shall list and report the following information to the financial designate responsible for filing escheat reports (currently located within A/R Collections) and provide the following information:

- Type of unclaimed property (e.g., A/P vendor or payroll check, A/R adjustment).

- Full name (first, middle, and last name; list all information that would help with identification).

- Federal employer identification, Social Security number, or other similar tracking information as provided.

- Company or Corporate titles must be entered exactly as adopted.

- Vendor, customer, and associate identification numbers or other related references must be noted.

- Individual transactions shall be identified with company code, date, and other related reference information such as purchase or sales order numbers if known.

- List the complete address, including zip code or mail code.

- If a single item has two or more owners, the names and addresses of both must be shown, along with the relationship.

- Date of last contact and description (e.g., deposited check, telephone call, or e-mail).

- Amount due refers to the total cash value due of the item, including all interest earned on deposits and without the deduction of any service charges, withholding, and escheat fees and/or charges.

<table>
<tr><td colspan="3" align="center">**Policy and Procedures**</td></tr>
</table>

Procedure No. B19	Section: Accounting and Finance	Page 3 of 4
	**Escheat, Abandoned Property, Unclaimed Checks: U.S., Canada, and Where Local Regulations Require**	
Department Ownership	Issue/Effective Date:	Replaces previously issued

List individual transaction amounts separately and convert to U.S. dollars at the applicable Balance Sheet conversion rate (refer to Source and Use of Exchange Rates policy and procedure).

- Summarize actions taken to locate property owner.

For U.S. state jurisdictions, an outsource service provider (i.e., company that specializes in reporting and filing) reviews the report and files the required reports, and if/when required, they should coordinate responses for the inquiries and audits.

The financial designate responsible for collecting and monitoring the information must assess the Company's corporate liability and provide the necessary accounting journal entry.

The amount must be directed to the Reserve for Escheat account. Once the property qualifies as unclaimed (e.g., after 180 days). The closing balance amount must be monitored periodically and reconciled monthly in accordance with the Account Reconciliation policy.

A representative from Corporate Tax (or a designate) monitors the reserve account for completeness and accuracy. A list/spreadsheet of those jurisdictions where escheat rules apply is updated, along with the amounts owed to those jurisdictions. According to the jurisdictional schedules, forms and remittances are prepared and processed through A/P.

As a result of research and investigation, owners of abandoned property may be located prior to the forwarding of settlement to the jurisdiction. When this occurs, the recipient's information and amount due must be adjusted within the Escheat Reserve account. If account ownership is discovered after the Escheat settlement has been forwarded to the jurisdiction, the owner must be directed to the jurisdiction to reclaim their property.

Accounting and Journal Entry example

An expense and liability is incurred due to the normal course of business operations.

Dr	Expense	100	
Cr	Accounts Payable		100
	Prepared at the time the expense is incurred		

The liability is paid in accordance with the Accounts Payable policy and practice.

Dr	Accounts Payable	100	
Cr	Cash		100
	Prepared at the time the check is prepared		

<table>
<tr><td colspan="3" align="center">Policy and Procedures</td></tr>
<tr><td>Procedure No. B19</td><td align="center">Section: Accounting and Finance</td><td align="right">Page 4 of 4</td></tr>
<tr><td colspan="3" align="center">Escheat, Abandoned Property, Unclaimed Checks:
U.S., Canada, and Where Local Regulations Require</td></tr>
<tr><td>Department Ownership</td><td align="center">Issue/Effective Date:</td><td align="right">Replaces previously issued</td></tr>
</table>

Because the check has not been cashed, the item remains an unreconciled (i.e., outstanding) item within the Bank Reconciliation.

The Reserve for Escheat is monitored monthly, with additions to the reserve calculated at least each quarter.

Dr	Cash	100	
Cr	Reserve for Escheat		100
	Prepared at the time the property is deemed abandoned		

Payment to the regulatory agency should be made in accordance with the statutory requirements.

Dr	Reserve for Escheat	100	
Cr	Cash		100
	Prepared at the time the unclaimed property is forwarded to the regulatory agency		

Controls/Areas of Responsibility

The Corporate Tax department is responsible for the research, assessment and control of the amount required in the Escheat Reserve account, settlement to appropriate jurisdictions and reconciliation of the account.

Under no circumstances should the unclaimed property be written off in order to avoid classification as abandoned property.

Separate liability accounts should be maintained and reconciled for unclaimed A/P, Payroll, and A/R property.

A/P request vendor statements to validate outstanding balances and investigate unreconciled differences.

The A/R collections functions use a variety of techniques, including credit balance reports to validate unclaimed adjustments and investigate unreconciled differences.

Contacts

Corporate Tax
Accounts Payable
Accounts Receivable Collections
Payroll

Policy and Procedures		
Procedure No. B20	Section: Accounting and Finance	Page 1 of 3
Finance Code of Ethical Conduct		
Department Ownership	Issue/Effective Date:	Replaces previously issued
Prepared by: Date	Approved by: Date	Authorized by: Date

Scope

The following Code is adapted from the Financial Executives International (FEI) http://www.fei .org/eweb/Dynamicpage.aspx?webcode=fei_Home Financial Code of Conduct.

Policy

It is IDÆAL LLP's (Company) policy to have each Accounting and Finance employee read, understand, and sign the Finance Code of Ethical Conduct (Code) and submit it to the Corporate Controller (or a designate).

The Code requires an annual attestation by all Accounting and Finance employees and is in addition to the Corporate Code of Ethical Conduct.

Procedure

During the first quarter of the fiscal year, the Chief Financial Officer announces this annual program, by inviting all to participate and attest to the code by a specified date (usually the end of first quarter).

The Code is posted on the Company's intranet site with an e-mail link to a program manager responsible for ensuring all Code attestations have been received and any employee questions or issues are addressed. Once participants read the Code, they are asked to accept or reject the Code. Their response is sent via e-mail to address provided and the responses are captured, monitored and tracked, with a copy of their response forwarded to the employee's e-mail.

The e-mail address is monitored and matched to a list of Accounting and Finance employees. The manager in charge of the program follows up with those who did not complete the attestation or those who had questions or issues which require resolution.

Progress reports are prepared and distributed to the employee's manager with the purpose of following up with those who have not signed the Code. Consequences for not signing the Code in a timely manner may vary from a negative rating on their performance management evaluation up to and including termination.

At the beginning of the fourth quarter, a report from Human Resources is requested that lists the current Accounting and Finance employees. All new employees who have not been made aware of the Code by their managers are asked to attest to the Code prior to the fiscal year-end.

Policy and Procedures		
Procedure No. B20	Section: Accounting and Finance	Page 2 of 3
	Finance Code of Ethical Conduct	
Department Ownership	Issue/Effective Date:	Replaces previously issued

Annually, training and discussion material is made available to Accounting and Finance managers to facilitate awareness and discussion with their employees during staff/department meetings. At least quarterly, additional ethics-related awareness materials and/or training is made generally available to all employees.

Controls/Areas of Responsibility

It is the responsibility of employees with direct reports who have accounting and/or financial job activities to ensure that each complies with this policy and with the Finance Code of Ethical Conduct. Managers should:

- Ensure that new employees entering the department understand and sign the Finance Code of Ethical Conduct.

- Assess each employee's performance based on this code, with results and feedback included as part of the annual performance management evaluation process.

Contact

Chief Financial Officer

	Policy and Procedures	
Procedure No. B20	Section: Accounting and Finance	Page 3 of 3
	Finance Code of Ethical Conduct	
Department Ownership	Issue/Effective Date:	Replaces previously issued

Finance Code of Ethical Conduct

In my role as an Accounting and Finance professional of the _____ business area within IDÆAL LLP, I recognize that Accounting and Finance professionals hold an important and elevated role in corporate governance. I am uniquely capable and empowered to ensure that stakeholders' interests are appropriately balanced, protected, and preserved.

Accordingly, the Finance Code of Ethical Conduct (Code), in addition to the Corporate Code of Ethical Conduct and related business practice policies and procedures, provide principles to which financial professionals are expected to adhere and advocate. The Code embodies rules regarding individual and peer responsibilities, as well as responsibilities to the company, the public, and other stakeholders.

I certify to you that I adhere to and advocate the following principles and responsibilities governing my professional and ethical conduct.

To the best of my knowledge and ability:

1. I act with honesty and integrity, avoiding actual or apparent conflicts of interest in personal and professional relationships.

2. I provide constituents with information that is accurate, complete, objective, relevant, timely, and understandable.

3. I comply with applicable rules and regulations of federal, state, provincial, and local governments and other appropriate private and public regulatory agencies.

4. I act in good faith, responsibly, with due care, competence, and diligence, without misrepresenting material facts or allowing my independent judgment to be subordinated.

5. I respect the confidentiality of information acquired in the course of my work except when authorized or otherwise legally obligated to disclose. Confidential information acquired in the course of my work is not used for personal advantage (e.g., Insider Trading policy).

6. I share knowledge and maintain skills important and relevant to my constituents' needs.

7. I proactively promote ethical behavior as a responsible partner among peers in my work environment and community.

8. I ensure responsible use of and control over all assets and resources employed or entrusted to me.

9. I will report known or suspected violations of this Code in accordance with all applicable rules of procedure (see the Compliance and Ethics Help Line policy and procedures).

10. I will be accountable for adhering to this Code.

Name (print) _____ Date _____

Signature _____ E-mail address _____

Internal Use Only

<table>
<tr><td></td><td colspan="2" align="center">**Policy and Procedures**</td></tr>
<tr><td>Procedure No. B21</td><td align="center">Section: Accounting and Finance</td><td align="right">Page 1 of 5</td></tr>
<tr><td></td><td colspan="2" align="center">**Key Financial Indicators**</td></tr>
<tr><td>Department Ownership</td><td align="center">Issue/Effective Date:</td><td align="right">Replaces previously issued</td></tr>
</table>

Prepared by:	Approved by:	Authorized by:
Date	Date	Date

Scope

According to the Statement of Financial Accounting Concepts (SFAC), the objectives of financial reporting are to provide:

1. Information useful in making informed business and economic decisions

2. Understandable information capable of predicting financial performance

3. Relevant information about economic resources and transactions, and the events and circumstances that change them

The Company provides financial information to external and internal users. For external users, reviewing the financial indicators serves as an approach toward analyzing historic transactions and predicting future trends. For internal users, financial indicators serve as an objective tool in measuring actual to forecasted performance. Most frequently determined using consolidated reports, these measurements may be requested for individual business areas.

Policy

Unless otherwise noted, all data must reflect U.S. Generally Accepted Accounting Principles (GAAP).

It is IDEAL LLP's (Company) policy to provide guidance for the consistent calculation of key financial indicators, when these indicators are used for internal and external communication and internal management reporting and decision making.

Procedures

Following are the calculations that should be used when measurements are used for external reporting, published results and internal reporting and decision making.

Measurements used for External Reporting and Published Results

The Company has identified the following ratios and calculation methodology to be included with published results and corporate communications. Results should be communicated only with the express permission of Investor Relations (see Communication with Financial Community policy).

Policy and Procedures		
Procedure No. B21	Section: Accounting and Finance	Page 2 of 5
	Key Financial Indicators	
Department Ownership	Issue/Effective Date:	Replaces previously issued

Published results refer to those items that are published and available to the public (e.g., 10K, 10Q, Annual Report, press release). To calculate the external reporting financial indicators, use the data as it is classified and consolidated within the published results.

Period-over-Period Growth Margins

Expressed as a percentage (e.g., quarter-over-quarter increase/decrease in Revenue)

Current period results minus previous period results divided by previous period results

$$\frac{\text{Current period} - \text{Previous period}}{\text{Previous period}}$$

Operating Expenses (OPEX) is the sum of Net Research, Development and Engineering plus Selling, General and Administration (SG&A). OPEX may be reported as a percent of net Revenue

OPEX as percent of net revenue

$$\frac{\text{OPEX for the period}}{\text{Net Revenue for the period}}$$

Days Sales Outstanding (DSO) for Accounts Receivable (A/R)

Current end-of-quarter net A/R balance divided by net revenue for the quarter multiplied by 91 days

$$\frac{\text{End-of-quarter net A/R}}{\text{Net Revenue for the quarter}} \times 91$$

Inventory Turnover

Current quarter Cost of Sales multiplied by 4 divided by current end-of-period Inventory

$$\frac{\text{Cost of Sales for the quarter} \times 4}{\text{End-of-period inventory}}$$

Working Capital as a Percent of Revenue

Total Current Assets minus Total Current Liabilities divided by net revenue for the quarter multiplied by 4

$$\frac{\text{Total Current Assets} - \text{Total Current Liabilities}}{\text{Net Revenue for the quarter} \times 4}$$

Return on Assets

Net Income for the quarter multiplied by 4 divided by the average of Total assets

$$\frac{\text{Net Income for the quarter} \times 4}{(\text{Beginning-of-quarter Total assets} + \text{End-of-quarter Total Assets}) / 2}$$

Return on Equity

Net Income for the quarter multiplied by 4 divided by the average of total Shareholders' Equity (S/E)

$$\frac{\text{Net Income for the quarter} \times 4}{(\text{Beginning-of quarter Total S/E} + \text{End-of-quarter S/E}) / 2}$$

	Policy and Procedures	
Procedure No. B21	Section: Accounting and Finance	Page 3 of 5
	Key Financial Indicators	
Department Ownership	Issue/Effective Date:	Replaces previously issued

Debt to Cash

Current portion of Long-term debt plus the long-term portion of Long-term Debt divided by the sum of Cash and Marketable Investments

$$\frac{\text{Current} + \text{Long-term portion of Long-term Debt}}{\text{Cash} + \text{Marketable Investments}}$$

Debt to Working Capital

Long-term Debt divided by Total Current Assets minus Total Current Liabilities

$$\frac{\text{Long-term Debt}}{\text{Total Current Assets} - \text{Total Current Liabilities}}$$

Other published results may include the following:

Profitability	Financial Strength
• Gross margin	• Quick ratio
• Operating margin	• Current ratio
• Profit margin	• Long-term Debt/Equity
	• Total Debt to Equity
Management Effectiveness	**Share-Related Items and Valuation Ratios**
• Return on Equity	• Market Capital
• Return on Assets	• Shares Outstanding
• Return on Investment	• Price to Earnings
	• Price to Sales
	• Price to Book
	• Price to Cash Flow
Financial Snapshot	**Per-Share Data**
• Revenue	• Earnings per Share
• Total Net Income	• Sales per Share
• Earnings per Share	• Book Value per Share
• Earnings before Interest, Tax, Depreciation, and Amortization (EBITDA)	• Cash Flow per Share
• Long-term Debt	

Measurements used for Internal Reporting and decision making

The Company has identified the following ratios and calculation methodology to be included for internal reporting to management. To calculate the internal reporting financial indicators, use the data as it is classified and consolidated in the business unit/country trial balance.

	Policy and Procedures	
Procedure No. B21	Section: Accounting and Finance	Page 4 of 5
	Key Financial Indicators	
Department Ownership	Issue/Effective Date:	Replaces previously issued

Accounting and Finance areas use key financial indicators during the monthly analysis and reconciliation of the financial results. As a tool, the financial indicators may point to specific areas that require attention and action.

Indicator	Calculation
Gross Margin percent of revenue using standard costs	Revenue for the quarter minus Cost of Sales at standard cost for the quarter divided by Net Revenue for the quarter
Gross Margin percent of revenue using total costs (standard plus variance)	Revenue for the quarter minus Cost of Sales at standard cost plus the Cost of sales Variance for the quarter divided by Net Revenue for the quarter
Operating Income as a percent of Net Revenue	Operating Income for the quarter divided by Net Revenue for the quarter
Net Income before Tax as a percent of Net Revenue	Net Income before Tax for the quarter divided by Net Revenue for the quarter
Current Ratio	Current Assets divided by Current Liabilities
Working Capital	Current Assets minus Current Liabilities
Return on Equity (ROE)	Net Income for the quarter times 4 divided by the average of Beginning- and End-of-quarter Shareholders' Equity
Return on Assets (ROA)	Net Income for the quarter times 4 divided by the average of Beginning- and End-of-quarter Total Assets
Return on Net Assets (RONA)	Last 4 quarters Earnings before Interest and Tax divided by average of last 4 quarters of Short- and Long-term Debt
Days Sales Outstanding (DSO)	Quarter-end Net Accounts Receivables divided by quarterly Net Sales divided by 91 days
Inventory Turns	Cost of Sales for the quarter times 4 divided by the quarter-end Net Inventory
Days Payable Outstanding (DPO)	Quarter-end Accounts Payable divided by quarterly purchases divided by 91 days
Expense to Revenue	Selling plus Marketing Expense for the quarter divided by Net Revenue for the quarter
Productivity	Quarter-end head count divided by quarter-end revenue times 4 (Note: Revenue per person includes full-time equivalents)
Earnings per Share (EPS) on a pro forma basis	Net Earnings adjusted for restructuring and one-time charges divided by the diluted weighted average Common Shares Outstanding

Policy and Procedures		
Procedure No. B21	Section: Accounting and Finance	Page 5 of 5
	Key Financial Indicators	
Department Ownership	Issue/Effective Date:	Replaces previously issued

Controls/Areas of Responsibility

Financial Reporting is responsible for issuing the published results. In order to increase the usefulness of financial statements, the Company presents financial information in a comparable format. Key financial indicators are calculated and published along with the corporate results to satisfy reporting requirements for external users.

Monthly, each country/business unit submits a management reporting package, which includes the area's trial balance and financial indicators for internal reporting.

Contacts

Financial Planning and Analysis
Financial Reporting

Policy and Procedures		
Procedure No. B22	Section: Accounting and Finance	Page 1 of 3
	Financial Planning and Analysis	
Department Ownership	Issue/Effective Date:	Replaces previously issued

Prepared by:	Approved by:	Authorized by:
Date	Date	Date

Scope

The policy and procedure applies to all legal entities, subsidiaries, and business units.

Policy

It is IDÆAL LLP's (Company) policy that each subsidiary and functional business area participates in and produces an Annual Plan (Plan) in accordance with the Plan Guidance which is updated annually and issued prior to the planning cycle. Each geographical and business area shall monitor and report on their planned performance by submitting key results (metrics) and financial indicators quarterly. See Key Financial Indicators policy and procedure.

It is Company policy that the Geographic and Business Areas are measured on meeting their planned targets.

Procedure

The Financial Planning and Analysis (FP&A) department:

A. Consolidates and prepares the planning guidance

B. Deploys the rollout of the planning guidance to the business units and country representatives

C. Monitors plan attainment and makes adjustments to the plan forecasts

A. Plan Guidance

The Planning Guidance is prepared using current economic indicators and historic performance or achievement trends. FP&A and Executive Leadership gather input from a variety of sources to establish corporate goals and prepare the plan guidance. The following segments are identified during this strategic process:

1. Market intelligence and discovery—examines the Company's position to market conditions and competitive pressures.

2. Objectives and initiatives—a summary of the Company's goals, objectives, and initiatives as they are cascaded to each of the business units. This segment examines the business unit's positioning in supporting the attainment of the Company's goals, objectives, and initiatives.

3. Product development and product lifecycle management

Internal Use Only

Policy and Procedures		
Procedure No. B22	Section: Accounting and Finance	Page 2 of 3
Financial Planning and Analysis		
Department Ownership	Issue/Effective Date:	Replaces previously issued

4. Product pricing and product placement

5. Marketing plan/strategy—examines the various approaches and investments the business unit requires to achieve attaining the objectives and initiatives

6. Selling, general and administration expenses

7. Other income and deductions

8. Income Tax Provisions

In accordance with the FP&A schedule, generally in late November (to be ready for the beginning of the year in January), each subsidiary and functional business area submits the completed Plan templates and presents their proposed Plan assumptions. An iterative process follows to consolidate and align the Plan submissions. The CEO, Chief Financial Officer (CFO) the remaining Senior Executive Staff evaluate the plans and prioritize the opportunities. Several iterations may be required to balance each subsidiary's and business area's opportunities and allocate limited Corporate resources.

B. Rollout

The Corporate FP&A department distributes the annual planning guidelines, assumptions, and calendar via the CEO staff meeting. The information is cascaded through the organization to business unit management and operational and financial staff.

The next steps include:

9. Organization structure and staffing reviews—examines the head count, skill resources required, and the method the business unit will use to secure these resources.

10. Functional Plan input—examines the cumulative business unit plan with narrative, P&L, and selected Balance Sheet accounts. These inputs are consolidated to form the Company's annual financial plan. An iterative process may be required if the sum of the business unit's objectives do not equal the Company's goals and objectives.

Each subsidiary and functional business area uses historic results and trends to determine the future resources required to meet the planned goals and objectives. The Plan is evaluated in relation to other business areas and for alignment with Company strategies and direction.

> Example: A Product Group must determine their head count and operating plan requirements in order to deliver key product launches identified on their product road map. Their operating plan requirements must be represented (aligned) with the Manufacturing and Operations Plan. Human Resources must represent the Product Group's head count and staffing requirements within their Plan and Worldwide Sales must represent the bookings, revenue, and expense with the product release.

Policy and Procedures		
Procedure No. B22	Section: Accounting and Finance	Page 3 of 3
	Financial Planning and Analysis	
Department Ownership	Issue/Effective Date:	Replaces previously issued

Final Plan numbers and/or targets are presented to each business unit manager. The December plan meeting agrees on allocations and cross-functional transfers. Generally in December, each business unit's and the Company's consolidated plan for the following year is approved.

Plans prepared from Non-U.S. currencies are reported in U.S. dollars and converted using the appropriate exchange rates.

C. Monitor and Update

Variance of the actual achievements versus the plan assumptions is monitored monthly. Revising the forecast and actions to achieve the forecast are developed monthly to limit the exposure of not attaining the planned results. The final steps include:

11. Financial Plan Budget reviews—monthly and quarterly reviews to monitor and track the issues and actions taken by each business unit to achieve the Company's goals and objectives.

12. Execution Plan (i.e., measurement metrics and recommit)—each quarter, the business unit will be asked to forecast and recommit their contribution to attaining the Company's annual plan.

Each quarter is treated as a separate fiscal period e.g., if a business unit were to underspend their planned operating expense in first quarter, the amount would not be carried forward to the next quarter. However, when the sales bookings reach the "stretch plan" levels, additional planned spending may be requested and approved to further achieve the "stretch plan" targets. A stretch plan refers to a challenge to improve the achievement of the stated goals (e.g., increase revenue, decrease costs).

During the year, transfer of Plan budgets between departments may be arranged through the "Plan Transfer Form." This form requires the reciprocal approval from the business unit owners and should be submitted to FP&A.

Controls/Areas of Responsibility

Each Business Area's Controller must ensure compliance with this policy and FP&A planning instruction.

FP&A serves as the project manager for this annual activity. Variance to plan is monitored on a monthly basis.

To improve the planning process, Plan effectiveness, e.g., forecast accuracy is evaluated.

Contacts

Corporate Financial Planning and Analysis

Procedure No. B23	**Policy and Procedures** Section: Accounting and Finance	Page 1 of 19
	Property, Plant and Equipment: Fixed Assets, Long-Lived Assets, Tangible Assets	
Department Ownership	Issue/Effective Date:	Replaces previously issued

Prepared by:	Approved by:	Authorized by:
Date	Date	Date

Scope

This policy and procedure applies to all business units worldwide.

The Company takes a conservative (more restrictive) interpretation of U.S. Generally Accepted Accounting Principles (GAAP) in defining the scope of what is eligible to be capitalized and how those assets will be depreciated.

Property, Plant and Equipment Index

	Policy and Procedures	
Procedure No. B23	Section: Accounting and Finance	Page 2 of 19
	Property, Plant and Equipment: Fixed Assets, Long-Lived Assets, Tangible Assets	
Department Ownership	Issue/Effective Date:	Replaces previously issued

A. Policy

It is IDÆAL LLP's (Company) policy to define Property, Plant and Equipment (PP&E, also referred to as Long Lived Assets or Fixed Assets) in accordance with U.S. GAAP, which states that property, plant and equipment assets:

1. Are to be held for use in the normal course of business and not held for investment

2. Have an expected economic useful life of more than one year or will not be converted into cash within the operating cycle

3. Are to be tangible in nature and have physical substance

Items that qualify as assets that do not meet these characteristics may be classified as "Other Assets" or "Intangible Assets."

In addition, the Company has established the following standard for capitalizing PP&E Assets:

4. An acquisition cost greater than $5,000 USD per item or less for non-U.S. business units as regulated by local laws and approved by Corporate Finance and Corporate Tax.

Assets begin depreciating in the month they are acquired or placed into service, whichever is later. Assets waiting to be placed into service are held in a Construction-in-Progress (CIP) account.

PP&E Assets owned by the company are depreciated over the asset's anticipated useful life. Leased assets must be evaluated by Corporate Treasury and accounted for in accordance with the Capital and Operating Leases policy and procedure.

It is the Company's policy to depreciate PP&E Assets assuming a straight-line methodology and zero salvage or residual value. The Company has established asset categories and determined the depreciable life schedule based on the typical term the asset is in use. If the asset's economic life is estimated to be different than the amount of time shown, use the lesser life span and notify the Chief Accounting Officer.

Depreciable Life Schedule

Property, Plant and Equipment Asset Category	Depreciable Life
Land	Not applicable
Buildings	25 years
Leasehold Improvements	Lesser of 5 years or life of lease
Transportation Equipment (e.g., Auto and Trucks)	3 years

Policy and Procedures		
Procedure No. B23	Section: Accounting and Finance	Page 3 of 19
	Property, Plant and Equipment: Fixed Assets, **Long-Lived Assets, Tangible Assets**	
Department Ownership	Issue/Effective Date:	Replaces previously issued

Property, Plant and Equipment Asset Category	Depreciable Life
Computer Software, Internally Developed, Commercial Licenses, Enterprise Software	5 years
Computer Hardware	5 years
Furniture, Office Equipment, Trade Show Booths	5 years
Audiovisual	5 years
Art and Printing	5 years
Construction in Progress	Not applicable

Financial Authorization and Approval

In order to acquire, modify, or dispose of PP&E Assets, local business unit and financial management authorization is required. In order to provide appropriate financial control over the expenditure of funds, a system of approvals based on organization level and dollar amount has been established. Financial authorization and approval are in accordance with the Procurement policy and procedure and the Company's Delegation of Authorization policy and procedure.

B. Asset Categories

Following is a description of each of the asset categories with a list of those items that should/ should not be included when determining the amount to be capitalized. The General Characteristics category applies to all asset categories; therefore, to apply this section, refer to General Characteristics, and then refer to the specific asset category.

1. General Characteristics

Each PP&E Asset must be recorded in an approved database according to its category. The asset category reflects the type of asset that is acquired, not the business area that is acquiring or approving the asset. In other words, if the Information Systems (IS) function is acquiring office furniture, the office furniture is categorized as furniture and fixtures.

The following guidance applies to all asset categories:

Costs included for capitalization:

- Contract price from supplier or vendor, less available sales discounts, plus applicable freight and federal, state, sales, or local taxes

- External costs directly related to the setup, assembly, installation, or testing of the asset to enable it to be ready for use and placed into service

	Policy and Procedures	
Procedure No. B23	Section: Accounting and Finance	Page 4 of 19
	Property, Plant and Equipment: Fixed Assets, Long-Lived Assets, Tangible Assets	
Department Ownership	Issue/Effective Date:	Replaces previously issued

Costs excluded for capitalization and must be expensed in the period incurred:

- Additional, excess, or redundant parts are considered routine repair whether acquired with the asset or subsequent to the installation of the asset. If purchased in bulk, these may be considered Prepaid Expenses.

- Costs to move or rearrange the asset once it has been installed.

- Feasibility studies, market studies, and comparable bid analysis required prior to acquiring the asset.

- Items that do not qualify as PP&E Assets (e.g., less than $5,000 USD or as otherwise stated or assets with an estimated economic life of less than one year).

- Ongoing maintenance and routine repairs including recurring activities such as cleaning, servicing, repair, replacement, and minor parts.

- Removal costs associated with replacing PP&E Assets.

- Training and travel costs for employees to acquire operational knowledge and skill related to the use of the PP&E Asset.

Approval to acquire, modify, or dispose of the asset

An approved Purchase Order (PO) is required for all asset acquisitions and modifications.

Authorization to replace or dispose of the asset requires business unit approval with corresponding documentation forwarded to the area providing fixed asset accounting support. Documentation should include the following for each asset: type of asset, date originally purchased or acquired, asset description, vendor, and acquisition cost, if known.

In order to take advantage of the Company's purchasing power in the global marketplace, it is the Company's policy that certain business areas are responsible for establishing, maintaining and enforcing purchasing guidelines. Refer to Section D1 for a list of the areas responsible for approving the acquisition, modification, or disposal of these assets.

Requests to review and approve capital acquisitions or disposition must be in accordance with the authorization policy and matrix.

2. Land

Company-owned Land is used in the normal course of operating the business. Land is not depreciated.

When the Company owns land and buildings, the value of the land should be segregated and classified separately from the value of the building. Land improvements must be recorded within the Building asset category.

	Policy and Procedures	
Procedure No. B23	Section: Accounting and Finance	Page 5 of 19
	Property, Plant and Equipment: Fixed Assets, Long-Lived Assets, Tangible Assets	
Department Ownership	Issue/Effective Date:	Replaces previously issued

In addition to those items listed in B1, costs that may be capitalized are:

- Real Estate commissions and closing costs

- Title searches and land surveys

- At the time the land is acquired, costs related to preparing the land for its particular use such as clearing and grading when such improvements have an indefinite life

In addition to those items listed in B1, costs that must be expensed are:

- Interest and finance charges once the land is placed in service

- Legal and advisory fees

- Market or economic development surveys

- Property taxes and insurance

3. *Building*

The Building asset category is made up of Buildings, Building Improvements, and Land Improvements.

Buildings are company-owned structures used to house the Company's development, sales, distribution, administration, and support activities.

Building Improvements refer to structural additions and permanently attached fixtures and other items that cannot be removed without damaging the building property (e.g., customization for built-in lighting and wiring, heating, and plumbing).

Note: Similar improvements to leased buildings and rented spaces are considered leasehold improvements.

Land Improvements refer to investments made to the land that are separate from the building (e.g., driveways, sidewalks or pathways, sewers, and parking spaces).

In addition to those items listed in B1, costs that may be capitalized are:

- Remodeling, renovation, and reconditioning

- Excavation for the specific building

- Building permits and architectural fees

In addition to those items listed in B1, costs that must be expensed are:

- Interest and finance charges once the building is placed in service

- Legal and advisory fees

	Policy and Procedures	
Procedure No. B23	Section: Accounting and Finance	Page 6 of 19
	Property, Plant and Equipment: Fixed Assets, **Long-Lived Assets, Tangible Assets**	
Department Ownership	Issue/Effective Date:	Replaces previously issued

- Ongoing building expenses such as utilities, security, or facilities management

- Property taxes and insurance

- Routine building repair, supplies, and maintenance, such as painting and plumbing, regardless of dollar amount

- Ongoing land maintenance and upkeep (e.g., gardening, landscaping and seasonal clearing)

4. *Leasehold Improvements*

Leasehold improvements are permanently attached fixtures and other items that cannot be removed without cutting into walls, ceilings or floors or otherwise damaging the leased property or asset. Generally, these are constructed or installed at the leased location prior to taking possession or opening the facility for operations. Examples of leasehold improvements are:

- Ceiling lights or wiring

- Air conditioning or heating systems

- Electrical or telephone cables

- Flooring and wall coverings

- Construction of office and meeting spaces

As part of setting up a leased location, other items may be acquired (e.g., furniture and fixtures, computers). **Each item** must meet the criteria for a PP&E asset or be expensed. If it is possible to segregate the assets by categories, they should be classified in the appropriate asset category. Additional items that generally accompany the leasehold setup should be evaluated as PP&E Assets or expensed. Examples of leasehold improvements are:

- Lighting and fixtures that cannot be removed at the end of the lease

- Reception area

- Training center

In addition to those items listed in B1, costs that may be capitalized are:

- Architectural design and blueprints

- Building permits and inspection fees

- External construction and contracting fees

- Major upgrades and renovations

<table>
<tr><td colspan="3" align="center">Policy and Procedures</td></tr>
</table>

Procedure No. B23	Section: Accounting and Finance	Page 7 of 19

**Property, Plant and Equipment: Fixed Assets,
Long-Lived Assets, Tangible Assets**

Department Ownership	Issue/Effective Date:	Replaces previously issued

In addition to those items listed in B1, costs that must be expensed are:

- Business licenses and insurance

- Costs to remove debris and unwanted items

- Legal or advisory fees

- Office supplies and services

- Prepaid Rent expensed as it becomes due; refer to the Capital, Operating Leases, and Real Estate Rental Property policy and procedure

5. Manufacturing, Research and Development Equipment

Investments in manufacturing, research and development includes Machinery and Equipment and Tooling and Fixtures.

Machinery and Equipment (M&E)

M&E refers to machinery and equipment used for research and development (R&D), manufacturing and production, quality assurance, and packaging and distribution (e.g., production machines, conveyor belts, storage bins, forklifts, and trolleys). M&E includes R&D equipment purchased to support the R&D function. Note: Autos and trucks assigned to manufacturing or distribution should be classified as Autos and Trucks.

In addition to those items listed in B1, costs that may be capitalized are:

- Third-party labor costs to assemble, install, or otherwise bring equipment into service

- Travel expenses **directly** related to the installation and testing of the asset

In addition to those items listed in B1, costs that must be expensed are:

- An allocation of in-house labor costs to assemble, install, or otherwise bring the equipment into service

- Inventory and materials used in R&D

- Machine trial costs related to installation and testing

- Materials, parts, and supplies added after the hardware is placed into service

- Internal labor costs to set up, install, integrate, and test the hardware to the system

- Maintenance, technical, and operational support

- Office services and supplies

Procedure No. B23	**Policy and Procedures** Section: Accounting and Finance	Page 8 of 19
	Property, Plant and Equipment: Fixed Assets, **Long-Lived Assets, Tangible Assets**	
Department Ownership	Issue/Effective Date:	Replaces previously issued

Tooling and Fixtures

Tooling requirements are identified during the new product development phase. An example of tooling is the metal mold used to pour housing for products. Tooling and tooling modifications may be provided to third-party manufacturers who support the Company's manufacturing process. The equipment and tooling is owned by the Company and must be tracked in the Fixed-Asset database.

Fixtures refer to those molds and customized attachments to the machines or tools that enable and support the production environment. Fixtures may be used for either assembly or testing of products and are used throughout the product life cycle, including engineering, product development, manufacturing, quality, and customer service.

It is Company policy to expense all fixtures under $5,000. Fixture costs in excess of $5,000 must be approved by the investment committee process and transferred into production.

6. Transportation Equipment

Transportation equipment refers to autos and trucks purchased to support specific business activities. Autos and trucks may be assigned to specific employees or locations and should be capitalized.

Autos and Trucks are generally leased, and if leased, an assessment must be made to determine if the lease is a capital lease. See Section C, Capital Leases.

See comments in Section B1 for costs that may be included for capitalization.

In addition to those items listed in B1, costs that must be expensed are:

- Insurance and safety checks

- Registration and license plates

- Repairs, parts, and maintenance, regardless of dollar amount

It is the Department Manager's responsibility to safeguard assets and to ensure the asset is returned to the Company in good working order when the employee is transferred to a different work assignment or is terminated.

7. Computer Software, Internally Developed and Commercial Licenses (for Internal Use)

Computer software utilized for internal use by the Company may be developed internally and/or acquired externally through commercial licensing.

	Policy and Procedures	
Procedure No. B23	Section: Accounting and Finance	Page 9 of 19
	Property, Plant and Equipment: Fixed Assets, **Long-Lived Assets, Tangible Assets**	
Department Ownership	Issue/Effective Date:	Replaces previously issued

Computer software for internal use includes:

- Enterprise software—global or regional applications such as SAP, Oracle, and Microsoft Office

- PC Desktop and other applications acquired for local use

Externally acquired licensed software

In addition to those items listed in B1, costs that may be capitalized for externally licensed software are:

- Initial License Charges (ILC) or fees—an upfront payment treated as a down payment or prepayment.

- One-Time Charge (OTC) license fees—a license fee that does not need to be renewed (e.g., perpetual). This license charge may be capitalized if maintenance is not included in the fee and the product may not be returned, that is, if there is no remaining vendor obligation.

In addition to those items listed in B1, costs that must be expensed for externally licensed software are:

- Monthly license fees—monthly, quarterly, or annual license fees related to the use of the product. If appropriate, these charges may be treated as Prepaid Expenses (see the Prepaid Assets/Expenses policy and procedure.

- Level 1, 2, or 3 license maintenance support

- Costs related to vendor selection and software evaluation

- Internal labor costs to set up, install, or integrate the software into the system

- Training and travel costs for employees to acquire operational knowledge and skill related to the use of the PP&E Asset

Internally Developed

Statement of Position (SOP) 98-1, "Accounting for the Costs of Computer Software Developed or Obtained for Internal Use," provides guidance for the types of costs that may be capitalized and must be expensed. In addition, questions should be directed to the Chief Accounting Officer (CAO) or designate.

In addition to those items listed in B1, costs that may be capitalized for internally developed or modified software are:

- Application development stage—includes coding and testing activities

Policy and Procedures		
Procedure No. B23	Section: Accounting and Finance	Page 10 of 19
Property, Plant and Equipment: Fixed Assets, Long-Lived Assets, Tangible Assets		
Department Ownership	Issue/Effective Date:	Replaces previously issued

- Direct costs of materials and services consumed in developing or obtaining internal use computer software

- Payroll and payroll-related costs for employees who are **directly** assigned to the development of the software if such costs are incremental to normal run rate

- Installation of the software including **direct** personnel only

- Travel costs related to installation

- Parallel test processing

In addition to those items listed in B1, costs that must be expensed for internally developed or modified software are:

- Preliminary project stage which includes:

  - Viability studies

  - Analysis and architecture assessment, evaluation, analysis, and selection

  - Vendor selection

- Post-Implementation stage which includes:

  - Data conversion and integration of the software with the system

  - Application maintenance and operational support

  - Training and travel costs for employees to acquire operational knowledge and skill related to the use of the PP&E Asset

Note: Software licenses that must be renewed on a periodic basis (e.g., annually or biannually) are to be recorded as a prepaid expense, with the monthly expense allocated over the term of the license.

8. Computer Hardware

Computer Hardware refers to:

- Mainframes, midrange (e.g., Dell, AS/400, Unix) or servers and their related:

  - Disk access storage devices (DASD), added memory

  - Operating System Software

  - Production printers

  - Networking assets such as cabling, routers, switches

Policy and Procedures		
Procedure No. B23	Section: Accounting and Finance	Page 11 of 19
Property, Plant and Equipment: Fixed Assets, Long-Lived Assets, Tangible Assets		
Department Ownership	Issue/Effective Date:	Replaces previously issued

- PC desktop and laptop computers and related connected peripherals such as scanners and printers when acquired as a system

Because of the technology obsolescence factor, it is customary to prepare a "lease versus buy" analysis when acquiring computer hardware. See Section C, Capital Leases.

See comments in Section B1 for costs that may be included for capitalization.

In addition to those items listed in B1, costs that must be expensed include:

- Materials, parts, and supplies added after the hardware is placed into service

- Internal labor costs to set up, install, integrate, and test the hardware to the system

- Maintenance, technical, and operational support

- Office services and supplies

Computer hardware and software asset, depreciation began as it is placed into service and not held (e.g., as Construction in Progress) until the long-range project is complete.

Laptop computers begin depreciating as soon as they are received by the Information Technology (IT) function as it is presumed to be placed into service.

9. *Furniture, Office Equipment, and Trade Show Booths*

Furniture refers to the broad definition of assets purchased to outfit offices, training centers, reception areas, and other common support spaces (e.g., desks, chairs, credenzas, lighting, window coverings, and bookcases).

See comments in Section B1 for costs that may be included for capitalization.

In addition to those items listed in B1, costs that must be expensed are:

- Rental of office furniture and fixtures

- Routine furniture repair, parts, supplies, and maintenance such as:

  - Replacement of Plexiglas and fabric dividers

  - Additional electrical outlets

  - Office supplies

Office equipment refers to noncomputer office electronics (e.g., faxes, postal meters, and copiers) owned by the Company.

	Policy and Procedures	
Procedure No. B23	Section: Accounting and Finance	Page 12 of 19
	Property, Plant and Equipment: Fixed Assets, Long-Lived Assets, Tangible Assets	
Department Ownership	Issue/Effective Date:	Replaces previously issued

Office equipment may be leased, and if leased, an assessment must be made to determine if the lease is a capital lease. See Section C, Capital Leases.

See comments in Section B1 for costs that may be included for capitalization.

In addition to those items listed in B1, costs that must be expensed are:

- Rental of office equipment

- Office supplies

Trade Show Booths refers to those assets that are required to be constructed, acquired, or developed for special events and shows.

See comments in Section B1 for costs that may be included or must be excluded for capitalization.

10. *Audiovisual Equipment*

Audiovisual Equipment refers to those assets purchased to support audiovisual activities including but not limited to voice communication equipment, conference center recording and editing equipment, and imagining equipment.

See comments in Section B1 for costs that may be included or must be excluded for capitalization.

11. *Artwork*

Artwork and printing refers to those qualifying assets purchased as decoration for Company office space. This category should not include those items purchased as investments.

See comments in Section B1 for costs that may be included for capitalization.

In addition to those items listed in B1, costs that must be expensed are:

- Insurance, repairs, and maintenance, regardless of dollar amount

12. *Construction in Progress (CIP) or Under Construction*

CIP is used to accumulate costs related to PP&E Assets prior to the asset being placed into service and the beginning of depreciation. CIP projects are generally used for internal use software either obtained or internally developed and leasehold or building improvements. When the asset is placed into service, the accumulated cost is transferred from CIP to its proper asset category and depreciation begins.

See comments in Section B1 and related PP&E Asset categories for costs that may be included for capitalization.

Policy and Procedures		
Procedure No. B23	Section: Accounting and Finance	Page 13 of 19
Property, Plant and Equipment: Fixed Assets, Long-Lived Assets, Tangible Assets		
Department Ownership	Issue/Effective Date:	Replaces previously issued

In addition to those items listed in B1 and related PP&E Asset categories, costs that must be expensed are:

- CIP or clearing accounts must not be used to accumulate charges that would normally be expensed. Assets that are received and placed into service must not be held in a CIP or other clearing account. Depreciation begins when the unit is placed in service even if the total project spending has not been completed or if vendor invoices have not been received and processed.

C. Capital Lease

In accordance with Statement of Financial Accounting Standard (SFAS) No. 13, "Accounting for Leases," leases must be capitalized as a PP&E Asset if they meet any **one** of the following criteria:

1. Ownership of the asset is transferred.

2. Lease term is 75 percent or more of the economic life of the asset.

3. The present value of the lease payments is equal to at least 90 percent of the price to purchase the asset.

4. There is a bargain purchase price at the end of the lease.

If **none** of the above four conditions are met, the lease is considered an operating lease with the lease payments expensed as they are incurred. Corporate Finance shall review all lease agreements to determine the appropriate accounting treatment.

Regardless of whether the lease is considered a capital or operating lease, Corporate Treasury must review and approve all proposed leases and lease renewals with annual payments in excess of $12,000 (except for real estate and automobile leases). This process will help to ensure that the Company receives the most competitive financing rates available when leasing assets.

See the Capital, Operating Leases, and Real Estate Rental Property policy and procedure.

D. Special Topics

Following is a brief description of special topics that apply to the acquisition, modification, and disposal of PP&E Assets.

	Policy and Procedures	
Procedure No. B23	Section: Accounting and Finance	Page 14 of 19
	Property, Plant and Equipment: Fixed Assets, Long-Lived Assets, Tangible Assets	
Department Ownership	Issue/Effective Date:	Replaces previously issued

1. Purchasing Responsibilities

In order to take advantage of the Company's purchasing power in the global marketplace, it is the Company's policy that certain business areas are responsible for establishing, maintaining, and enforcing purchasing guidelines.

- Real Estate is responsible for investments in Land, and Land Improvements, Buildings and Building Improvements, and Leasehold Improvements.

- Corporate Facilities is responsible for establishing guidelines for investments in furniture and office equipment.

- Information Technology (IT) is responsible for establishing guidelines for investments in telephone and communication equipment and computer equipment.

- Research and Development (R&D) is responsible for investments in Machinery and Equipment for R&D.

- The Chief Information Officer (CIO) is responsible for investments in Computer Hardware, Software, and Networking systems. The scope of this includes all desktop and workstation investments in hardware, software, and network interfaces.

- Treasury is responsible for reviewing all leases and determining whether a lease should be treated (for accounting purposes) as a capital or operating lease. Airplane, auto, and truck leases are negotiated and approved by Corporate Treasury.

The purpose of assigning worldwide purchasing responsibilities is to ensure a consistent approach for selecting vendors who provide the best terms, conditions, and product to meet Company standards and requirements.

2. Bulk Purchases

Unless the individual assets qualify as PP&E Assets according to GAAP and the Company standard (see Section A, Policy Statement), purchases acquired in bulk must be expensed. The capitalization limit of $5,000 refers to a specific item, not the overall purchase order or project spending.

> Example: If 10 items are purchased, each with a purchase price of $750, each should be expensed. Even though the total purchase order is $7,500 and exceeds the $5,000 minimum, the items should **not** be capitalized.

Exceptions:

a. When individual parts are ordered and constructed into a whole (e.g., workstation or cube space). Example: Individual cubes or workstations are constructed from parts; if the sum of the parts exceeds the $5,000 threshold, then the parts may be capitalized.

	Policy and Procedures	
Procedure No. B23	Section: Accounting and Finance	Page 15 of 19
	Property, Plant and Equipment: Fixed Assets, **Long-Lived Assets, Tangible Assets**	
Department Ownership	Issue/Effective Date:	Replaces previously issued

b. When individual items are purchased in bulk as part of a project. Example: 300 telephones costing a total of $30,000 to outfit a new office location may be capitalized.

3. Accounting for Repairs, Renovations, and Upgrades

Costs incurred subsequent to the purchase and installation of the asset are considered repairs, renovations, or upgrades.

- Repairs related to "wear and tear," are defined as recurring expenses related to maintaining the asset in normal operating condition, and are expensed in the period incurred.

- Renovations are defined as nonrecurring extraordinary items that extend the operational use and performance of the asset and may be capitalized.

- Upgrades are additions to the assets or replacements of components that have superior performance capabilities and may be capitalized.

Example: Repair, Renovation and Upgrade

Repair - When an entire roof requires replacement, the cost to replace the roof may be capitalized. This cost is considered a major repair and improves the value of the asset or its economic life.

Renovation - When a portion of the roof requires repair, these costs are expensed. This cost, however significant, is considered part of the recurring normal repair and maintenance and should be expensed.

Upgrade - When an upgrade occurs, the asset value and remaining life extended over the revised asset life.

If the upgrade, refurbishment or renovation **extends the life of the asset,** then the costs are capitalized and a new depreciable term begins. The remaining net book value is added to the cost of the upgrade and the total is allocated over a new term.

Assume a straight line depreciation and with zero residual value. The initial investment in the roof was $12,000 and a six year life. 24 months have passsed, therefore, there is $4,800 accumulated depreciation and a net book value of ($12,000 − 4,800) $7,200.

At month 24, an upgrade occurs with the company incurring costs of $6,300. The asset now has a value of ($7,200 + 6,300) $13,500.

- For this example, the useful life after renovation is 60 months. The remaining net book value of $7,200 (12,000 − 4,800) is added to the renovation costs of $6,300 to give a total asset value of $13,500.

If we assume the upgrade extends the roof's life to 60 months from now, the $13,500 is depreciated over 60 months with monthly depreciation expense of $225.

Policy and Procedures		
Procedure No. B23	Section: Accounting and Finance	Page 16 of 19
Property, Plant and Equipment: Fixed Assets,		
Long-Lived Assets, Tangible Assets		
Department Ownership	Issue/Effective Date:	Replaces previously issued

If we assume the upgrade does not extend the roof's life, then the costs are capitalized over the remaining useful life (60 months – 24) 36 months with $175 added to the roof's original $200 a month depreciation.

4. Accounting for Disposal or Replacement

Assets remain on the Balance Sheet and in the Fixed-Asset (or PP&E Asset) ledger as long as the asset is still in use, even if the asset is fully depreciated. When the Company no longer owns the asset and the Company has transferred its rights and responsibilities of ownership, the cost of the asset and the related accumulated depreciation (also known as net book value) must be removed from the fixed-asset register. The remaining net book value plus cost of disposal less proceeds (salvage or resale value) determines whether a net Gain or Loss on Disposal is to be recorded on the Income Statement.

It is the Department Manager's responsibility to notify the fixed asset manager when an asset is disposed of or is no longer in use and to provide any additional costs or proceeds associated with the disposal of the asset.

5. Depreciation and Income Tax

Depreciation is the accounting treatment that recognizes the consumption of the asset and is recurring monthly until the asset is fully depreciated or retired and disposed.

Depreciation is determined based on the cost to acquire the asset and as defined by the asset category. PP&E Assets begin depreciating at the time the asset is placed into service. If at the time the asset is placed into service, the final asset cost is not known or the vendor's invoice has not been processed, then the asset value should be estimated and accrued along with the anticipated depreciation expense. Once the actual amounts are known the accruals must be reversed and the actual amounts recorded.

For ease in monitoring and tracking deprecation, only full month depreciation expenses are to be recorded.

Depreciation that is allowable for determining income tax is different than depreciation that is used to determine accounting net income. The difference between the two methods is generally considered temporary timing differences. The Corporate Tax Department works with finance and the functional business areas to ensure the PP&E (or Fixed-Asset) <u>accounting ledger</u> can be reconciled to the PP&E (or Fixed-Asset) <u>tax ledger</u>.

6. Asset Retirement Obligation

Assets shall be recorded and retired in accordance with U.S. GAAP, Financial Accounting Standard (FAS) No. 143, "Accounting for Asset Retirement Obligations." FAS No. 143 refers to

	Policy and Procedures	
Procedure No. B23	Section: Accounting and Finance	Page 17 of 19
	Property, Plant and Equipment: Fixed Assets, **Long-Lived Assets, Tangible Assets**	
Department Ownership	Issue/Effective Date:	Replaces previously issued

the costs or obligations associated with disposing of qualified assets at the end of their useful life to the Company.

FAS No. 143 requires that the fair value of a liability for an asset retirement obligation be recognized in the period in which the obligation occurs (i.e., at the time the contract is signed) and requires the Company to pay for additional costs (e.g., renovation, guaranteed residual) associated with retiring or disposing of the asset. The associated asset retirement costs are capitalized as part of the carrying amount of the long-lived asset.

7. Impairment

According to SFAS No. 144, "Accounting for the Impairment of Long-Lived Assets," impairment of a PP&E Asset occurs when the asset's carrying amount is not expected to be recoverable over its remaining useful life. Recoverability is determined by comparing the carrying amount of the asset to net future undiscounted cash flows that the asset was expected to generate. If such cash flow did not equal or exceed the carrying value, impairment is recognized equal to the amount by which the carrying amount exceeded the discounted value of expected cash flow (fair value).

Corporate Finance or a qualified independent outside service provider shall test PP&E Assets for recoverability whenever events or changes in circumstances indicate that its carrying amount may not be recoverable. Circumstances that may indicate the carrying amount of an asset or asset group is impaired include:

- A current expectation that, more likely than not, the PP&E Asset will be sold or otherwise disposed of before the end of its previously estimated useful life.

- A significant adverse change in the extent or manner in which the asset is being used.

- A significant decrease in the market or selling price.

- An accumulation of costs significantly in excess of the amount originally expected for the acquisition or construction of the PP&E Asset.

E. Procedure

A. The annual planning cycle determines and approves requests for capital and operating budget requirements. The department or business area requesting the asset is responsible for making application and gaining all financial and operational approvals.

- A Return on Investment (ROI) analysis may be submitted as support for the investment. The analysis compares the costs associated with acquiring and maintaining the asset versus the savings and benefits to the company utilizing the asset.

<table>
<tr><td colspan="3" align="center">**Policy and Procedures**</td></tr>
<tr><td>Procedure No. B23</td><td align="center">Section: Accounting and Finance</td><td align="right">Page 18 of 19</td></tr>
<tr><td colspan="3" align="center">**Property, Plant and Equipment: Fixed Assets,
Long-Lived Assets, Tangible Assets**</td></tr>
<tr><td>Department Ownership</td><td align="center">Issue/Effective Date:</td><td align="right">Replaces previously issued</td></tr>
</table>

- A "Make versus Buy" analysis may be submitted to justify the spending limit. This analysis compares the time and costs associated with making or customizing the asset using a combination of internal and external materials and labor versus buying a finished product.

B. As the requesting business area is ready to begin a PP&E the project, business approvals and related supporting documentation are prepared and approved. **Prior to beginning the project,** the approvals are forwarded to Purchasing, where they are reviewed and a Capital-Asset project number is assigned. Because of its complexity, a capital project is monitored and tracked separately from other procurement purchase orders. Once all the approvals are in place, an approved purchase order is prepared and forwarded to the vendor. An approved Purchase Order is prepared and forwarded to the vendor.

The requesting business area verifies receipt of the asset. Sometimes, due to delay in receiving and processing vendors' invoices, assets are placed into service prior to their being set up in the PP&E Asset ledger. The business area's Finance area must initiate an accrual of the PP&E Asset and depreciation expense to correspond to the date the asset is placed into service.

C. The asset is recorded on the PP&E (or Fixed Asset) ledger, and monthly depreciation begins when the asset is placed into service.

D. Once the asset is no longer required for use in business activities, the asset may be retired and disposed of by sale, trade-in, exchange, or abandonment. The business area responsible for the asset approves, arranges for the asset disposal and notifies Fixed Assets accounting to remove the asset from the ledger and recognize any corresponding accounting gains and/or losses.

F. Controls/Areas of Responsibility

Depreciable Lives

The estimated lives are based on historical experience with similar assets as well as taking into consideration anticipated technological or other changes. If technological changes occur more rapidly or slowly than anticipated, or in a different form, useful lives may need to be updated accordingly. Asset useful life shall be reviewed annually or as events or circumstances are indicated. Factors that could trigger an impairment review include significant changes in the manner of our use of the acquired asset, changes in historical or projected operating performance and cash flows and significant negative economic trends. The Chief Accounting Officer establishes monitors and the depreciable life of each asset category.

Purchasing and Financial Authorization

The Corporate Controller sets and defines financial authorization levels and limits used for the purchase of PP&E Assets. Subsidiaries and functional business area controllers or financial

Policy and Procedures		
Procedure No. B23	Section: Accounting and Finance	Page 19 of 19
Property, Plant and Equipment: Fixed Assets, Long-Lived Assets, Tangible Assets		
Department Ownership	Issue/Effective Date:	Replaces previously issued

designates must approve all local purchases of PP&E Assets and are responsible for securing additional financial and other approval.

Safeguarding the Asset

From the time the asset is received and accepted by the Company until it is disposed of, the asset must be safeguarded from damage and theft. Safeguarding the asset occurs at each stage of the asset's life, including when the asset is received, assigned, and used in the normal course of business operations. Evaluating and setting up controls to limit the risk of damage or theft of the asset reside locally with the Safety and Security team, Business Practices, and Internal Controls.

It is the department manager's responsibility to ensure the asset is returned to the Company in good working order when the employee is transferred to a different work assignment or is terminated.

Finance Responsibility

Each subsidiary and functional business area's controller or financial designate is responsible for the assets contained within the PP&E Asset ledger. Their responsibility includes but is not limited to:

- Maintaining the accuracy and reliability of the accounting records. Documentation must be kept to support asset acquisition, journal entries, and asset disposal. See the Records Information Management policy and procedure.

- Reconciling the subledger to the ledger balances in accordance with the account reconciliation policy and procedures.

- Maintaining records to support depreciation and amortization expense for the accounting and tax books (where appropriate).

Corporate Finance must approve any and all additions, deletions, or changes to the asset category, classification and/or Depreciable Life Schedule. The documentation shall include the reason for the request, with references to the related U.S. GAAP Accounting literature, alternatives to be considered, and a comparative and impact analysis of the requested change on prior and future results.

Once implemented, Corporate Finance verifies that the change has occurred as anticipated. Corporate Finance should maintain a change control log to monitor and keep track of all change requests.

G. Contacts

Chief Accounting Officer
Fixed Asset Manager

Policy and Procedures		
Procedure No. B24	Section: Accounting and Finance	Page 1 of 3
	Foreign Currency Risk Management	
Department Ownership	Issue/Effective Date:	Replaces Previously Issued

Prepared by:
Date

Approved by:
Date

Authorized by:
Date

Scope

IDÆAL LLP (Company) is a U.S.-based company with legal entities in many countries. The Company uses U.S. dollars as its functional currency. As such, the Company is exposed to foreign currency exchange risk when it sells products to non–U.S. dollar subsidiaries or nonrelated customers in their local currencies. Currency exposures are also created through the purchase of goods or services from third-party vendors in currencies other than U.S. dollars.

The Company has determined that it should manage selective foreign currency exchange risks. The objective is to lock in a portion of the exchange rate risk. The importance of local currency exchange risk management increases as non-U.S. operations continue to grow.

Policy

It is the Company's policy to minimize non-U.S. (foreign) currency risk by practicing hedging techniques to the extent practicable. *Hedging* refers to an investment made in order to reduce the risk of adverse price movements in a security, by taking an offsetting position in a related security in another currency.

It is the Company's policy to hedge with the purpose of minimizing:

1. Foreign exchange losses due to selective balance sheet exposures (i.e., monetary assets and liabilities)

2. The risk that currency movement will adversely impact U.S. dollar cash flows through the end of the outlook period

The Corporate Treasurer or his/her designee (the Risk Manager) centrally manages all hedging operations.

Transactions that qualify for hedging include cross-currency transactions, monetary assets such as current assets and current liabilities, and intercompany accounts receivable/payable.

Transactions that do not qualify for hedging include financial statement translation exposure and non-cash flow (economic) exposures.

In all cases, hedge transactions must be used to cover the risks associated with exposures, which are known or reasonably expected to occur.

Under no circumstances is it appropriate or authorized to enter into a contract for the purchase or sale of currency that is speculative in nature, including but not limited to leveraged derivatives.

Policy and Procedures		
Procedure No. B24	Section: Accounting and Finance	Page 2 of 3
	Foreign Currency Risk Management	
Department Ownership	Issue/Effective Date:	Replaces Previously Issued

Procedure

The Company conducts business in a number of worldwide markets, each with its local currency.

The Treasurer or the Risk Manager reviews budgeted foreign currency exposures during the planning and forecast process and during the fiscal year as movement occurs. The Treasurer obtains concurrence from the Chief Financial Officer (CFO) on the strategic and tactical elements of currency risk management and reports to the CFO at least quarterly on results of the selective performance measures.

Based on the following reports, the Risk Manager determines the Company's hedging requirements:

1. 12- to 18-month Rolling Forecast of Non-U.S. Exchange (FX) Hedged Exposures

2. FX Hedge Effectiveness Report—compares the performance of actual hedging activities to the benchmarks over the past quarter and year-to-date

3. Counterparty Credit Risk Report—details the credit risk exposure of each non-U.S. exchange counterparty

Matched to specific transactions or portfolio balances, hedging contracts are generally up to 18 months and may be adjusted as forecasted exposures are determined to have changed. A hedging contract may be put in place when the underlying exposure is likely to occur, and the contract does not exceed the underlying or forecasted exposure.

Although there is a wide array of hedge instruments, the Company first looks to internal netting of offsetting exposures, then to external vehicles such as forward contracts and intercompany and third-party borrowings.

For Accounts Receivable/Accounts Payable trade execution and processing the following process shall be followed:

- The Risk Manager is responsible for maintaining all related analyses and documentation. Transaction must be identified with related exposures and approved hedging strategies prior to execution.

- For hedge transactions in excess of $50,000, the Risk Manager obtains two competing price quotes from approved counterparties. Each transaction must be entered into the Corporate Treasury trade database.

- An authorized verbal confirmer, other than the Risk Manager, verifies every transaction with the counterparty, including payment instructions.

- The Cash Manager is responsible for obtaining written confirmations of the payment from the Risk Manager and the bank counterparty within 24 hours of the trade date.

Policy and Procedures		
Procedure No. B24	Section: Accounting and Finance	Page 3 of 3
Foreign Currency Risk Management		
Department Ownership	Issue/Effective Date:	Replaces Previously Issued

The Treasurer and one other designated Treasury employee approves each hedge transaction. The Risk Manager is responsible for the execution of each hedging transaction and its conformance to this policy. The use of derivative financial instruments may expose the Company to counterparty credit risk. As such, the Treasurer maintains a list of approved counterparties and their respective credit limits for financial instrument transactions.

Clearing Intercompany Transactions

Intercompany transactions are recognized at the contract exchange rate with the related exchange transaction gains or losses recognized within the local accounting records and consolidated in the U.S. Corporate accounting records.

Monthly, the international subsidiaries are required to make payments toward their Intercompany Accounts Payable. The invoices to be paid are identified, and with confirmation of the cash transfer, Intercompany Accounts Receivable updates the subsidiary's Intercompany Account Payable balance.

Requests for exception to Hedging Practice

The Chief Accounting Officer (CAO) must verify that a foreign currency hedge can be accorded special accounting ("hedge accounting") treatment as set forth in Financial Accounting Standard No. 133/138 (as amended), "Accounting for Derivative Instruments and Hedging Activities." Transactions that cannot be accorded hedge treatment are not permitted unless previously approved by the Treasurer and CFO.

Controls/Areas of Responsibility

Authorities and Limits

The list of approved counterparties with their respective credit limits is maintained and updated by the Corporate Cash Manager.

Cash Payments

The Risk Manager maintains a schedule of maturities, which is used to ensure timely settlement of transactions, and initiate all related cash payments or receipts.

Accounting

Corporate financial accounting creates and maintains accounting journal entries and reports related to the foreign currency exchange risk management program.

Contacts

Corporate Treasury

Policy and Procedures		
Procedure No. B25	Section: Accounting and Finance	Page 1 of 2
Funding and Financing Risk Management		
Department Ownership:	Issue/Effective Date:	Replaces Previously Issued

Prepared by:	Approved by:	Authorized by:
Date	Date	Date

Scope

It is IDÆAL LLP's (Company) vision to provide a financial "environment" that enables long-term, high-quality revenue and earnings growth and increases value to stakeholders. In an effort to fulfill this vision, the Company may issue short, long-term debt and/or other securities on an as-needed basis. This policy refers to all forms of debt and equity securities and applies to all legal entities.

Policy

It is the Company's policy that funding and financial risk be coordinated by and is the sole responsibility of Corporate Treasury. Except as approved by the Corporate Treasurer, it is the Company's policy that no subsidiary may enter into debt or leases or otherwise pledge, assign, commit, or use Company resources as collateral for securing debt.

The accounting treatment shall be in accordance with U.S. Generally Accepted Accounting Principles (GAAP) and financial reporting regulations.

Procedure

As part of the annual planning process, cash flow analysis provides information as to the short- and long-term requirements for capital. Determining the funding and financing arrangements to meet the various Company needs is the responsibility of Corporate Treasury.

The Chief Financial Officer, Executive Leadership review and approve the annual Funding and Financing plan and delegates execution to the Corporate Treasurer. At least quarterly, the Corporate Treasurer provides progress reports to the CFO.

Funding and financing objectives include:

- Implementing a funding and financing program to serve the Company's vision and approved projects, consistent with an optimal capital structure as approved by the Chief Financial Officer (CFO)

- Complying with all rules and regulations governing all borrowing, including but not limited to bank guarantees, letters of credit, and issuance of debt and equity

- Promptly repaying when due the principal and interest on all debt and dividends on Company shares issued and outstanding

- Ensuring that the Company's excess liquidity is invested in safe, liquid, and secure investment that earns competitive market rates of return

Policy and Procedures		
Procedure No. B25	Section: Accounting and Finance	Page 2 of 2
Funding and Financing Risk Management		
Department Ownership:	Issue/Effective Date:	Replaces Previously Issued

- Exploring and implementing innovative structuring ideas when they are prudent and consistent with the above statements

Funding and financing may come from a variety of internal or external sources.

- Internal funding sources are identified within Cash Flow From Operations (CFFO).

- External funding sources include reaching out to all forms of global private and public investors.

The Treasurer, with concurrence of the CFO, determines prospective financing products and considers such elements as:

- Interest rate risk

- Counterparty credit risks

- Refinancing risks

- Covenant risks/risk of default

- Early termination risks

- Tax implications

- Earnings dilution

The Corporate Treasurer executes the funding and financing plan according to the approved schedule. ensuring that there is an appropriate mix of internal/external sources and uses of funds.

Funding and financing contracts must be reviewed and approved by Corporate Legal prior to entering into an arrangement.

External disclosures in quarterly and annual submissions to the Securities and Exchange Commission require that contracts and commitments be analyzed and evaluated at least quarterly.

Controls/Areas of Responsibility

The Corporate Treasurer has the ability to execute transactions as authorized by the CFO and the Executive Leadership and submits progress reports at least quarterly.

The Corporate Treasurer monitors funding and financing transactions through the use of the monthly and rolling CFFO.

Contacts

Corporate Treasury

	Policy and Procedures	
Procedure No. B26	Section: Accounting and Finance	Page 1 of 6
	Hiring and Use of External Auditors	
Department Ownership	Issue/Effective Date:	Replaces previously issued

Prepared by: Approved by: Authorized by:
Date   Date   Date

Scope/Background

The Company engages an independent audit firm (i.e., external auditors) each year to audit its financial records, provide an opinion on the financial results, and attest and report on the effectiveness of the Company's internal control structure.

The independence of such firms has recently come under scrutiny by the public as well as regulators such as the Securities and Exchange Commission (SEC) and the New York Stock Exchange (NYSE). In addition, the U.S. Congress has enacted legislation to improve the corporate governance of publicly traded companies.

Policy

In order to ensure that the Company's External Auditors (currently fill in the name of your External Auditors) remain independent under applicable regulations; it is IDÆAL LLP's (Company) policy that **no one is authorized to:**

A. **Hire or extend a hiring offer to a candidate** from the external auditor's firm within the "cooling off" period limitation of one year.

B. **Engage the services** of the external auditors without the prior approval of the Audit and Compliance Committee of the Board of Directors.

This policy applies to all Company subsidiaries and entities.

Procedure

A. *Hire or extend a hiring offer to a Candidate*

Regardless of position, a potential candidate should not be approached if the potential candidate is: a) still an employee of the External Auditing firm, even if the employee is not working at our Company or b) was an employee of the External Auditing firm within the last twelve months.

Approval is required from the Chief Financial Officer, the External Auditor's lead audit partner and the Audit Committee of the Board of Directors (BOD) if discussions are to take place prior to the one-year cooling-off period.

Policy and Procedures		
Procedure No. B26	Section: Accounting and Finance	Page 2 of 6
	Hiring and Use of External Auditors	
Department Ownership	Issue/Effective Date:	Replaces previously issued

Cooling-Off Period

Section 206 of the Sarbanes-Oxley Act establishes a one-year cooling-off period before a member of the audit engagement team may accept employment in certain designated positions (i.e., financial reporting oversight roles).

All other standard Human Resources (HR) recruiting and hiring policies and procedures apply.

B. *Engage the Services of the External Auditing Firm*

The Audit and Compliance Committee of the Board of Directors is solely responsible for determining the type of nonaudit and audit work (and relevant fee limits) that may be provided by the external auditors to the Company or any of its subsidiaries.

Each person seeking to engage the external auditors must complete the attached questionnaire (see Exhibit) regarding the requested engagement and submit such questionnaire to the CFO or a designee. The CFO reviews the questionnaire and, in accordance with the overall Audit and Compliance Committee preapproval process, decides whether or not to approve the engagement of the external auditors. No employee may engage the designated external audit firm to perform services without the express written approval of the CFO or a designee.

Prohibited Services

Under Section 201 of the Sarbanes-Oxley Act, the following activities may not be performed by the External Auditors (including any affiliates of such firm):

- Bookkeeping services

- Financial system design and implementation

- Appraisal or valuation services, fairness opinions, or contribution-in-kind reports

- Actuarial services

- Internal Audit outsourcing

- Management functions or Human Resources

- Investment banking services

- Legal services and expert services unrelated to the audit

The CFO will not approve requests to use the External Auditors for the above services.

The Audit and Compliance Committee of the BOD has adopted a policy that requires the preapproval of audit and nonaudit services rendered by the external auditors.

	Policy and Procedures	
Procedure No. B26	Section: Accounting and Finance	Page 3 of 6
	Hiring and Use of External Auditors	
Department Ownership	Issue/Effective Date:	Replaces previously issued

- For audit services, the external auditing firm shall provide an audit services plan during the third quarter of each fiscal year outlining the scope of the audit services proposed to be performed for the fiscal year and the related fees.

- For nonaudit services, the CFO shall submit to the Audit and Compliance Committee for approval, from time to time during the fiscal year, the list of nonaudit services that it recommends the Audit and Compliance Committee engage the external auditing firm to provide for the current and subsequent fiscal years.

The CFO and the external auditing firm each confirm to the Audit and Compliance Committee that each nonaudit service on the list is permissible under all applicable legal requirements. The Audit and Compliance Committee review and approve both the list of permissible nonaudit services and the budget for such services. The Audit and Compliance Committee delegates to the CFO the authority to amend or modify the list of approved permissible nonaudit services and fees. The CFO reports action taken to the Audit and Compliance Committee at a subsequent Audit and Compliance Committee meeting.

The Company has identified certain nonaudit services where it may be appropriate and beneficial for the Company to engage its external auditors or to have them participate in the bidding process. The services are as follows:

- Statutory audits

- Pension audits

- Certain tax services (see Tax Services section below)

- Due diligence

Approval from the Company's CFO is **required** for the engagement of the external auditors in **all the above circumstances**. The External Auditors—Nonaudit Services form (see Exhibit) must be used to request for services from the external auditors.

Tax Services

In respect of tax services, the CFO has determined the following:

- Tax advisors, preparers other than the external auditors may be engaged with the approval of the Senior Vice President Tax. The Company generally recommends that legal entities use advisors other than the external auditors to perform tax services.

- Our external auditors would be limited to their work in connection with the determination of the accuracy of the tax provision and balance sheet tax accounts on the Company's interim and year-end consolidated financial statements.

	Policy and Procedures	
Procedure No. B26	Section: Accounting and Finance	Page 4 of 6
	Hiring and Use of External Auditors	
Department Ownership	Issue/Effective Date:	Replaces previously issued

- The external auditors may **not** provide any tax service that relates to appraisals, valuations, or legal work.

- Global tax compliance is an outsource decision managed by Corporate Tax. These services would include ongoing day-to-day tax compliance, advice, and assistance as well as corporate or expatriate tax questions that require immediate answers. The Corporate Tax Department determines which firm is to be used as the primary provider of this category of services.

Controls/Areas of Responsibility

The types of services provided by the external auditors shall be reviewed and approved by the CFO at least quarterly.

The Audit and Compliance Committee must approve **all** engagements with the external auditors.

Corporate Tax maintains a list of qualified tax advisors and preparers engaged by the Company's legal entities.

Contacts

Chief Financial Officer

	Policy and Procedures	
Procedure No. B26	Section: Accounting and Finance	Page 5 of 6
	Hiring and Use of External Auditors	
Department Ownership	Issue/Effective Date:	Replaces previously issued

Exhibit

External Auditors—Nonaudit Services

ASSIGNMENT/ENGAGEMENT_____

Summary or description of engagement (include the anticipated scope of work)
_____
_____

1. In your view, will this assignment/engagement impact the audit effectiveness or the quality and timeliness of the quarterly or annual financial reporting?

    Yes ☐   No ☐

    Explain: _____
    _____

2. Will this assignment/engagement be performed by specialists (e.g., information technology) who will also provide support during the year-end audit?

    Yes ☐   No ☐

3. Will this assignment/engagement be performed by audit personnel of external auditors?

    Yes ☐   No ☐

    If yes, will it enhance their knowledge of the company's business and operations?

    Yes ☐   No ☐

4. In your view, will the performances of the assignment/engagement by an individual who may also work on the year-end audit affect his/her objectivity in the year-end audit?

    Yes ☐   No ☐

    Explain: _____
    _____

5. On this assignment/engagement, will external auditors be assuming a managerial role or creating a mutual or conflicting interest with Company management?

    Yes ☐   No ☐

    Explain: _____
    _____

6. In the course of this assignment/engagement, will the external auditors' personnel be generating information that will be "audited" by external auditors as part of the year-end audit?

    Yes ☐   No ☐

	Policy and Procedures	
Procedure No. B26	Section: Accounting and Finance	Page 6 of 6
	Hiring and Use of External Auditors	
Department Ownership	Issue/Effective Date:	Replaces previously issued

7. Does this assignment/engagement need to be started and completed expeditiously?

  Yes [ ]   No [ ]

8. In your view, does external auditors possess unique expertise/experience to provide services needed to perform this assignment/engagement?

  Yes [ ]   No [ ]

9. Indicate the proposed/estimated fee for this assignment/engagement:

  $_____

10. Indicate the basis for determining the fee for this assignment/engagement:

  [ ] Fixed for project

  [ ] Hourly or "time and materials"

  [ ] Other. If so, explain: _____

Prepared by: _____ Date:_____

Reviewed by: _____ Date:_____

* Approved by: _____ Date:_____

* Approval limits are as defined within the procurement section of the authorization matrix.

Recommendation/Rationale:

_____

_____

_____

Once completed this form must be forwarded for assessment and approval to the Corporate Controller and Chief Accounting Officer prior to submission to the Chief Financial Officer.

Corporate Controller Signature

_____ Date:_____

Chief Accounting Officer Signature

_____ Date:_____

Chief Financial Officer Signature

_____ Date:_____

Completed forms are to be returned by the CAO

Policy and Procedures		
Procedure No. B27	Section: Accounting and Finance	Page 1 of 5
	Income Tax Preparation and Reporting	
Department Ownership	Issue/Effective Date:	Replaces previously issued
Prepared by: Date	Approved by: Date	Authorized by: Date

Scope

This policy applies to all worldwide operations, whether the subsidiary is consolidated or is accounted for on the equity method. The financial accounting for income taxes must follow the balance sheet approach in accordance with the Financial Accounting Standards (FAS) Instruction No. 109, "Accounting for Income Taxes."

This scope of this policy includes income tax planning, tax return filings, financial reporting, and addressing Income Tax controversies for consolidated and local Income Taxes.

Policy

It is IDÆAL LLP's (Company) policy that the Corporate Tax department prepares the U.S. consolidated corporate Income Tax return and related filings. For non-U.S. Income Tax preparation and filings, Corporate Tax has approved a third-party Income Tax preparation service. Each country's Business Manager and Controller are responsible for working with the provider to meet local requirements and regulations.

Corporate Tax calculates the corporate provision and consolidates the U.S. and non-U.S. information for financial statement presentation and related Income Tax disclosures.

Corporate Tax defends (or arranges for the defense of) the Company's position relating to Income Tax inquiries and audits.

Procedure

Income Tax Preparation and reporting procedures include:

A. Analysis of the Company's accounts and financial statements

B. Reconciliation between the accounting records (i.e., "book") and Income Tax preparation records (i.e., "tax") differences including permanent and timing differences

C. Determination of the Income Tax expense and related disclosures for external financial reporting

D. Preparation and filing of Income Tax returns

E. Evaluation of inquiries, audits, and Tax controversy

Policy and Procedures		
Procedure No. B27	Section: Accounting and Finance	Page 2 of 5
	Income Tax Preparation and Reporting	
Department Ownership	Issue/Effective Date:	Replaces previously issued

A. *Analysis of the Company's Accounts and Financial Statements*

Planning, estimating, and calculating the Income Tax expense and obligations includes an analysis of the Company's books and records.

The local country trial balance is reviewed and analyzed to identify potential book (i.e., according to U.S. Generally Accepted Accounting Principles (GAAP) account balances) and tax (i.e., according to local Income Tax laws and regulation) differences. In addition, the following reviews are conducted to identify changes that may impact Income Tax calculations and reporting:

- The Company's accounting policies and procedures

- New financial accounts

- Certain accounts based on their known or anticipated activity (e.g., deferred revenue, royalty, depreciation).

In conjunction with the annual planning process, the projected Income Tax expense and related obligations are estimated.

Monthly/Quarterly Reporting

Each month, the Income Tax expense is accrued based on the Company's planned effective tax rate.

For non-U.S. countries, transactions are captured on local books according to local regulations. A local trial balance may be maintained to support local Income Tax preparation and submission. Each month, the Company's subsidiaries submit a trial balance based on U.S. GAAP. In order to address Financial Accounting Standard (FAS) No. 109, "Accounting for Income Taxes," each country identifies those accounts which require FAS 109 consideration.

For U.S. operations, the Corporate Tax department maintains a file to adjust for book and tax differences.

Each quarter, the effective Income Tax expense rate is updated (i.e., the budgeted amount is forecasted based on the actual year-to-date and project performance), and the year-to-date accrued amount is compared to the forecasted full year expense.

Corporate Tax prepares and approves external and internal reporting disclosures related to income tax accounting (eg., 10-K, 10-Qs, bank covenants). Corporate Tax engages the external auditors, as required.

B. *Book/Tax Differences for Income Tax calculation and reporting*

Book/Tax differences may be permanent or temporary in nature.

	Policy and Procedures	
Procedure No. B27	Section: Accounting and Finance	Page 3 of 5
	Income Tax Preparation and Reporting	
Department Ownership	Issue/Effective Date:	Replaces previously issued

Permanent Differences

Permanent differences relate to those items that are not eligible or relevant for future taxable or deductible amounts and incentive tax credits. Permanent differences may be classified as:

- Book revenues/gains that will never be taxable due to statutory exclusion. Example: Municipal bond interest

- Book expenses/losses that will never be deductible for Income Tax purposes. Examples: Fines, nondeductible meals and entertainment, expense

- Items taxable or deductible for tax purposes but not included in financial statements. Examples: Stock option deduction, transfer pricing adjustments

Timing Differences

Timing differences refer to differences (sometimes accumulating over more than one year) between the tax basis of an asset or liability and its reported amount in financial statements. Temporary differences may be classified as:

- Revenue and Expenses currently recognized for book purposes but not yet for tax purposes. Examples: Accounts Receivable installment payment options, Allowance for Doubtful Accounts, Compensation accruals (vacation, bonus, commission), Contingency accruals (legal, environmental), Depreciation from fixed assets, treatment of Goodwill and Intangible assets

- Revenues currently recognized for tax purposes but not yet recognized for book purposes. Examples: Deferred Revenue, Royalties

- Tax carryforward items are timing adjustments to be recognized in a future period. Examples: Foreign Tax Credits in worldwide taxation regimes that allow credits for foreign taxes paid, Net Operating Losses

Deferred Taxes

Once the book/tax differences have been identified, the determination of the balances in the ending deferred tax accounts must be calculated. Deferred tax accounts must be classified between short-term and long-term assets or liabilities. Each subsidiary shall make every effort to properly categorize their deferred taxes appropriately. Corporate Tax should review, evaluate, and approve the deferred account tax balances.

C. Determination of the Income Tax Expense and disclosures for Financial Reporting

The Income Tax provision calculation has two components: the current Income Tax expense and the deferred Income Tax provision.

	Policy and Procedures	
Procedure No. B27	Section: Accounting and Finance	Page 4 of 5
	Income Tax Preparation and Reporting	
Department Ownership	Issue/Effective Date:	Replaces previously issued

Current Income Tax Expense

The current Income Tax expense and provision is calculated from the Company's pretax profit/loss, taking into account permanent and timing differences. The net of these items is multiplied by the current local statutory tax rate. This result is further adjusted by incentive tax credits available to the company (Example: eligible Research and Development tax credits).

Deferred Income Tax Provision

The deferred Income Tax provision is calculated by the difference between the beginning deferred tax payables/receivables and the ending deferred tax payables/receivables for "temporary" differences, which impact net profit before tax.

Interim Period Income Tax Accounting

At the end of each interim period (i.e., end of quarter), the Company reviews the effective tax rate, reflective of the expected full fiscal year Income Tax effect. The effective tax rate reflects year-to-date company results, anticipated tax credits, and foreign tax rates. Interim period calculations shall be in accordance with U.S. GAAP FAS No. 109, "Accounting for Income Taxes"; Accounting Planning Board (APB) No. 28, "Interim Financial Reporting"; and Financial Accounting Standards Board Interpretation (FIN) No. 18, "Accounting for Income Taxes in Interim Periods."

Non-U.S. countries provide input to Corporate Tax based on the quarterly instruction letter issued by corporate tax department.

Disclosures

In accordance with Securities and Exchange Commission (SEC) and other regulatory reporting requirements, certain disclosures for Income Tax expense and provisions must be disclosed. Corporate Tax must review and approve tax-related disclosures made in conjunction with the release of financial statements and other regulatory submissions.

D. Preparation and Filing of Income Tax Returns

Corporate Tax prepares the Company's consolidated U.S. Income Tax return and related U.S. jurisdiction returns (e.g., for individual states). In preparing the tax return, the Tax department reviews the return for accuracy and completeness and ensures that the tax return information reconciles with the financial statements.

Qualified third-party Income Tax consulting services may be used for non-U.S. Income Tax preparation and filings. Notification of non-U.S. Income Tax status and filings must be forwarded to Corporate Tax, where filings are monitored and tracked.

E. Evaluation of Inquiries, Audits, and Tax Controversy

Corporate Tax must be notified of all inquiries, audits, and items of tax controversy. In the U.S., Corporate Tax serves as the central resource for all such inquiries. For non-U.S. subsidiaries,

	Policy and Procedures	
Procedure No. B27	Section: Accounting and Finance	Page 5 of 5
	Income Tax Preparation and Reporting	
Department Ownership	Issue/Effective Date:	Replaces previously issued

Corporate Tax must be immediately notified and shall provide or arrange for local support and resources as appropriate.

The Company requires that inquiries be written and list specific items to be studied. All inquiries must be addressed in a timely manner, with the inquiry and the results fully documented by the local controller and/or Corporate Tax department. Initial responses are usually brief and directly answer the questions asked without providing gratuitous information.

Corporate Tax must be notified if a follow-up inquiry and/or audit is required. It is Company policy that if an external auditing team is required to be on site, the external auditors be provided with adequate workspace, private telephones, and photocopiers. They are kept in fairly close proximity to the Tax department but not so they can overhear confidential discussions.

As necessary, Business Unit Vice Presidents and representatives from the Tax department shall participate in the audit and be included in the discussions of findings and recommended settlement solutions. In rare cases involving very technical issues of significant amounts, an outside consultant may be used.

Whenever possible, the Tax department strives to settle all audits at the lowest possible level (i.e., without legal escalation). An appellate conference or litigation shall be considered only in extremely unusual situations, and only if the Chief Financial Officer and the General Counsel agree to proceed. Typically, this requires preparation of a written protest and an oral presentation.

Controls/Areas of Responsibility

Corporate Tax maintains a list/log of all worldwide required Income Tax filings and status of outstanding issues/resolutions.

Corporate Tax recommends and implements feasible tax-planning strategies, consistent with the corporate direction and carefully considers all business concerns. Corporate Tax provides input for Company planning instruction, quarterly instructions to Finance Controllers, and Accounting and Finance policies and procedures. Additionally, as the business undergoes changes, the Tax department needs to be involved in the change process to ensure that tax is considered prior to finalizing the business decision.

To validate that the information is complete and accurate, internal controls, data processing and system checks, balances, and reconciliations are performed and documented.

Tax payments must be requested and documented through the Accounts Payable process and in accordance with the Accounts Payable policy and procedure.

Contact

Corporate Tax

Policy and Procedures		
Procedure No. B28	Section: Accounting and Finance	Page 1 of 5
	Insurance and Risk Management	
Policy Owner:	Issue/Effective Date:	Replaces previously issued

Prepared by: Date	Approved by: Date	Authorized by: Date

Scope

This Insurance and Risk Management policy and procedure applies to all Company divisions, departments, operations, programs, and support services at all locations worldwide. Every business unit and location shall participate in and comply with the Insurance and Risk Management Program. Definitions of key terms are located at the end of this document.

Policy

It is IDEAL LLP's (Company) policy to identify, measure, and eliminate or control the risks of loss to which the Corporation, and its people and assets may be exposed. Risks that cannot be controlled or eliminated become a subject for insurance protection.

It is management's responsibility to actively manage risk and to prepare the Company for responding to a fortuitous occurrence. Accordingly, an Insurance and Risk Management Program (Program) shall be prepared, put in place, and regularly maintained. Details of the Program are documented in the Company's Insurance and Risk Management Manual located on the Company's intranet or by request from the Insurance and Risk Management department.

The Program expresses the Company's commitment to community partnership through coordination in areas of mutual concern.

No Company business unit or legal entity is permitted to purchase the following type of insurance:

- General liability insurance
- Product liability insurance
- Property damage and business interruption insurance
- Inland transit and ocean cargo insurance
- Directors and Officers liability insurance
- Aviation or aircraft insurance

The Corporate Insurance department is the sole source for purchasing all property and casualty insurance worldwide.

Procedure No. B28	**Policy and Procedures** Section: Accounting and Finance **Insurance and Risk Management**	Page 2 of 5
Policy Owner:	Issue/Effective Date:	Replaces previously issued

Procedure

The purpose of the procedure is to establish a formal Insurance and Risk Management Program (Program) consisting of a set of written responsibilities, goals, and objectives aimed at achieving the following at any of the Corporation's worldwide locations:

- Identification and avoidance of the risks of physical injury or loss

- Reduction and control of the risks of physical injury or loss

- Protection of life during and after a loss

- Conservation of assets and resources

- Maintenance of business operations and earnings flow

- Placement of appropriate insurance coverage

- Management of insurance claims

The Corporate Insurance and Risk Management department administers the Corporate Insurance and Risk Management Program. From time to time, and at least annually, Corporate Insurance requests underwriting reports from divisional and financial management. Those reports request information to aid in the assessment and planning of the Company's worldwide insurance needs.

The Corporate **Insurance and Risk Management Manual**. The Manual summarizes each type of insurance protection and includes:

- Coverage descriptions—identify perils covered and excluded from the insurance contract.

- Deductible amounts, which may vary by country.

- Claim procedures:

  - All North American claims must immediately be reported to Corporate Insurance, which provides guidance and direction for proper claim handling.

  - Non–North American claims must be reported through the Business Area Controller or financial designate to the local country insurance broker.

  - Initial claim reporting must include the date, time, place, and a brief description of the event and further guidance shall be provided as to how to proceed through the process.

- Risk information reporting procedures—insurance underwriting data will be requested at least annually from the area controller or financial designate by Corporate Insurance.

- Loss control procedures—from time to time, outside insurance engineers will survey major locations to assess risks and recommend procedures and equipment required to help control risks.

	Policy and Procedures	
Procedure No. B28	Section: Accounting and Finance	Page 3 of 5
	Insurance and Risk Management	
Policy Owner:	Issue/Effective Date:	Replaces previously issued

Insurance Brokers

Determining and engaging with global or regional insurance brokers is the responsibility of the Insurance and Risk Manager and must be processed through Procurement.

Insurance and Risk Management fees must be processed through Accounts Payable and may be established as a Prepaid Assets/Expense.

Identifying/Submitting a claim

If and when a claim is required to be filed, register the issue with the local and/or Corporate Safety and Security. If an investigation is required, they will conduct or arrange for an investigation and assist with the required documentation.

The local business area must also contact the Corporate Insurance and Risk Manager, where appropriate insurance information may be gathered and submitted. All claims or potential claims are recorded in a log where they are monitored and tracked until they are resolved.

Documentation of the incident shall be gathered and maintained in accordance with Records Information Management and includes but is not limited to:

- Incident report and investigative report if required—initiated and approved by Corporate Safety and Security

- Statement of impact to the Company—reviewed and approved by the Business Unit and Finance management

- Claim submission—approved and submitted by the Insurance and Risk Manager (or designate)

- Correspondence with the Insurance and Risk Management service provider—through the Insurance and Risk Manager

- Resolution of the claim—through the Insurance and Risk Manager

Areas of Responsibility

Business Unit Executives shall consider Insurance and Risk Management a primary responsibility and shall ensure that the Corporate Insurance and Risk Management Program objectives are incorporated into the regular course of Company business. They are responsible for informing Corporate Insurance when conditions or events occur where additional (long- or short-term) coverage is required.

Supervision and management personnel shall ensure that employees under their direct supervision incorporate the Corporate Insurance and Risk Management Program procedures

Policy and Procedures		
Procedure No. B28	Section: Accounting and Finance	Page 4 of 5
	Insurance and Risk Management	
Policy Owner:	Issue/Effective Date:	Replaces previously issued

and objectives into their regular activities and are provided with appropriate Insurance and Risk Management training.

Employees will be required to comply with all Company rules, procedures, and directives governing the actions they are to take in preparation for and responding to an occurrence.

The Senior Manager of Corporate Insurance and Risk Management oversees and directs the Program to ensure objectives are met and in meeting the Company's commitment to proactively mitigate and manage the risks of loss to which it is exposed.

Controls/Areas of Responsibility

All insurance claims must be filed through Corporate Safety and Security and Corporate Insurance and Risk Management.

Information consolidated from the Global broker network provides data from which risk can be identified and measured. At least semiannually, identified risks and key process and spending metrics are sent to the Company's senior officials.

Contact

Corporate Insurance and Risk Management

<table>
<tr><td colspan="3" align="center">**Policy and Procedures**</td></tr>
<tr><td>Procedure No. B28</td><td align="center">Section: Accounting and Finance</td><td>Page 5 of 5</td></tr>
<tr><td colspan="3" align="center">**Insurance and Risk Management**</td></tr>
<tr><td>Policy Owner:</td><td align="center">Issue/Effective Date:</td><td>Replaces previously issued</td></tr>
</table>

Definitions

Risk: Pure or insurable risk is defined as the possibility of loss or no loss. This is differentiated from business or speculative risk, which includes the possibility of gain.

Pure risk falls into four categories:

- Risk of personal injury or loss of life
- Risk of direct physical damage to property
- Risk of indirect loss from damage to property (i.e., loss of income)
- Risk of legal liability loss

Coverage: The specific areas of loss for which the insurer will indemnify the Company.

Insurance: A written contract that enables the corporation to transfer all or a portion of the financial impact of a loss to another party (the insurer) for a negotiated consideration.

Insurance certificate: A legal document evidencing that certain types and amounts of insurance coverage are in force.

Insurance claim: A demand by the insured for recovery from the insurer in accordance with the terms and conditions of the insurance contract covering the occurrence.

Loss: Injury to persons, destruction of property, or depletion of assets or income.

Risk management: The process of systematically identifying, measuring, controlling, avoiding, or insuring the risks of loss to which the Company and its people and assets are exposed.

Risk measurement: The process of quantifying the physical and financial impact of a loss upon the Corporation.

Policy and Procedures		
Procedure No. B29	Section: Accounting and Finance	Page 1 of 6
	Intercompany Transactions	
Department Ownership	Issue/Effective Date:	Replaces any previously issued

Prepared by: Date	Approved by: Date	Authorized by: Date

Scope

The purpose of accounting for Intercompany transactions is to allocate assets, liabilities, revenues, and expenses to the appropriate legal entity in relation to the economic benefits and obligations associated with the operational activity incurred. This guidance applies to all Intercompany transactions that are expected to be settled (i.e., payments sent/received. This policy does not pertain to cross charges within a company (i.e., intracompany allocated).

The consolidated Financial Statements include the accounts of IDÆAL LLP and its majority-owned and controlled subsidiaries. All Intercompany transactions and balances must be eliminated during consolidation process.

Policy

It is IDÆAL LLP's (Company) policy to account for Intercompany transactions in a manner that results in the appropriate and timely recording of transactions as well as equal and offsetting entries to the Intercompany balance sheet or income statement accounts. Intercompany transactions must be reported as an Intercompany Accounts Receivable (A/R) or Intercompany Accounts Payable (A/P).

In no case shall transactions be accounted for as Intercompany on the balance sheet while they are pending approval from the counterparty.

Intercompany transactions and settlement must be in compliance with local laws and regulations. Exceptions to the following must be documented, citing the local law and regulation, and submitted to the Chief Accounting Officer (CAO) for review and approval.

Procedures

Intercompany transactions shall be classified as:

A. Revenue- and inventory-related transactions such as cross-border revenue, cost of revenue, product inventory, and warranty as coordinated through the Company's distribution center. Intercompany revenue-related transactions must be processed as invoices.

B. Cross-charges refer to allocations and other charges that affect the operating expense of one entity are incurred by and therefore more properly recorded to another entity. Intercompany cross-charges must be processed using the Intercompany transfer form (see Exhibit).

	Policy and Procedures	
Procedure No. B29	Section: Accounting and Finance	Page 2 of 6
	Intercompany Transactions	
Department Ownership	Issue/Effective Date:	Replaces any previously issued

C. Funds transfer includes requests for funds to or from Corporate Treasury and the local entity. Intercompany funds transfer must be processed using the Intercompany transfer form.

A. *Intercompany Revenue and Inventory-Related Transactions*

Intercompany revenue and inventory related transactions may be processed into the accounting systems up to five business days prior to the end of the accounting close unless otherwise approved by the Chief Accounting Officer (CAO). Those transactions that are not processed in time and relate to the current accounting period must remain on the initiator's books for processing the following month.

Intercompany revenue and inventory related transactions are processed the same as any other revenue or inventory transfer item except that all the Company's subsidiaries are assigned a Customer number which flags it as an Intercompany transaction. Sales order administration processes the sales order.

Based on a pre-approved formula Corporate Tax department provides the Intercompany transfer pricing formula.

B. *Intercompany Cross Charges*

An Intercompany Transfer Form shall be completed for all Intercompany cross-charge transactions. Cross-charges may include allocations or valid expenses that were incurred on behalf of another entity Cross-charges shall be processed quarterly, one month prior to the quarter end:

- Interest on promissory notes
- Cross-charges for salary and payroll-related expenses and interest on notes

It is the **responsibility of the manager initiating the invoice** to obtain all required information, including the general ledger department and account numbers and to complete the entire form. The controllers or financial designates of the initiating and receiving areas must approve the form **prior** to the transaction's being entered into the accounting system as an Intercompany A/R or Intercompany A/P.

Cross-charges shall:

- Have a minimum $5,000 USD, except for the following: cash receipts, interest on promissory notes, funding, and stock option purchase plan.
- Be recorded assuming the P&L exchange rate (see the Source and Use of Exchange Rate policy).

To eliminate cursory Cross-charging miscellaneous charges must be $5,000 per line item and not be accumulated to meet the minimum USD threshold. Charges less than the minimum should remain on the local Entity's books.

	Policy and Procedures	
Procedure No. B29	Section: Accounting and Finance	Page 3 of 6
	Intercompany Transactions	
Department Ownership	Issue/Effective Date:	Replaces any previously issued

Unless otherwise approved by the CAO, Intercompany Transactions shall be processed into the accounting system in the month they are incurred no later than five (5) workdays before the last work-day of the month. Intercompany balances should be processed in accordance with the accounting statement close schedule. At that time, any out-of-balance conditions (i.e., unreconciled and/or unre-solved transactions) should be reversed and remain on the initiator's books for processing the follow-ing month.

C. *Intercompany Loans or Funding*

- Are generally not permitted and must be approved by Corporate Tax, the Treasurer and CAO.

- Unless otherwise approved the Corporate controller transactions are to be processed into the accounting system in the month they are incurred no later than two workdays before the last workday of the month.

- Must be recorded assuming the actual spot rate used to secure the necessary funding.

Invoices and Intercompany Transfer Forms

The initiating manager is responsible for ensuring the receiving manager receives a copy of the Intercompany invoice and supporting documentation with instructions to forward it to their local controller or financial designate.

The offsetting entry for all Intercompany Transactions must be in the same currency as the initial entry. Each entity must enter their side of the Intercompany invoice in the same currency.

Due to foreign currency fluctuations, Intercompany entries booked as reversing journal entries (e.g., allocations are generally calculated on a year-to-date basis) must be treated the same way (i.e., reversing) within each entity.

Settlement

Unless otherwise approved by Corporate Treasury and Corporate Tax, Intercompany settlement is the month following the recording of the transaction. On a monthly basis, non-U.S. subsidiaries are required to pay down as much of their Intercompany balance as possible. During the annual planning cycle, the subsidiary or Business Entity and Corporate Treasury agree on the necessary closing cash balance which must be retained in order to adequately service the next period's oper-ating costs and expenses.

The subsidiary or entity is responsible for confirming the list of invoices to be paid down forward-ing the detail settlement information to the Intercompany accounting manager.

Since the amounts owed are in the same currency, as outstanding balances are settled, the coun-try which sends the payment may have a currency exchange gain or loss. The exchange gain or loss should be recognized on the Profit and Loss statement as part of other deductions.

Procedure No. B29	**Policy and Procedures**	Page 4 of 6
	Section: Accounting and Finance	
	Intercompany Transactions	
Department Ownership	Issue/Effective Date:	Replaces any previously issued

Treasury supplies the Intercompany Accounting designate with a schedule of incoming payments, and this schedule reflects the dates and amounts and indicates which banking institution the payment is coming into or from.

Once the cash is received, Treasury notifies the Intercompany Accounting designate, who then applies the cash to the appropriate entity and account.

At the end of the month, Corporate Accounting confirms that the Intercompany balances are in agreement. Appropriate personnel should investigate differences, and if adjustments are required, they should be made to the period in which they relate.

Tax Implications

In transferring goods and services that are used within for revenue generation, many countries require that these goods and services be transferred using a formula that includes the cost of the goods or services plus a pricing uplift. Corporate Tax must be contacted to assist with establishing the methodology that should be used to determine the amount of the transfer price related to Intercompany revenue and/or Intercompany cost of goods or services. The Intercompany charge shall be the gross of the cost plus applicable transfer pricing uplifts.

According to local income tax rules, certain types of transactions may require an addition of withholding tax as part of the settlement. In those jurisdictions where withholding taxes apply, this increases the amount that has to be paid (i.e., the agreed-to settlement amount is net of withholding tax).

Note that visa or customs forms, duties, and/or other taxes may apply when transferring goods and/or services across geographic borders.

Controls/Areas of Responsibility

The Intercompany Accounting designate is a member of Corporate Accounting, where the Intercompany A/R and A/P are monitored and reconciled. At the end of the period, the net of Intercompany A/R and A/P should be zero. Unmatched Intercompany transactions shall be reversed and must remain on the initiator's accounting records.

Intercompany transactions that arrive late (according to the accounting statement close schedule) are evaluated for materiality and must be approved by the CAO if they are to be processed for the period. Late transactions will be processed in the following month (i.e., the items remain on the initiating entity's books).

In accordance with the Account Reconciliation policy, all balance sheet accounts must be reconciled.

Policy and Procedures		
Procedure No. B29	Section: Accounting and Finance	Page 5 of 6
	Intercompany Transactions	
Department Ownership	Issue/Effective Date:	Replaces any previously issued

Both the initiating and receiving entities maintain Intercompany invoices and Intercompany Cross-Charges Transfer forms as part of the audit trail documents are to be retained in accordance with the Records Information Management policy and procedure.

Contacts

Intercompany Accounting Manager
Chief Accounting Officer
Corporate Tax

	Policy and Procedures	
Procedure No. B29	Section: Accounting and Finance	Page 6 of 6
	Intercompany Transactions	
Department Ownership	Issue/Effective Date:	Replaces previously issued

Exhibit

Intercompany Transfer Form

Initiator/sender of the charge:	**Receiver of the charge:**
Employee name: _____	Employee name: _____
Phone: _____	Phone: _____
Subsidiary/Business Area _____	Subsidiary/Business Area _____
Location: _____	Location: _____
Company Code and General Ledger Account:	Company Code & General Ledger Account:
Functional Manager Signature	Functional Manager Signature
Financial Authorization Signature	Financial Authorization Signature
For Wire Transfers Bank Name _____ Bank Number _____	For Wire Transfers Bank Name _____ Bank Number _____

Date	Description of the Charge	Local Currency	Exchange Rate	U.S. Dollars

Date represents the transaction date and refers to the accounting month to be processed. **Exchange rate** for processing cross-charges is the profit-and-loss (P&L) rate.

When complete, forward requests for wire transfers to Corporate Treasury and **all** requests are to be forwarded to **Corporate Accounting:** Attention **Intercompany.**

Policy and Procedures		
Procedure No. B30	Section: Accounting and Finance	Page 1 of 6
	Inventory	
Department Ownership	Issue/Effective Date:	Replaces previously issued

Prepared by: Date	Approved by: Date	Authorized by: Date

Scope

The term Inventory used within this policy refers to Company-owned Inventory such as materials, parts, accessories, components, finished goods, and used Inventory, whether stored within Company-controlled warehouses or manufacturing facilities or assigned to approved Suppliers.

Policy

It is IDÆAL LLP's (Company) policy to properly control Inventory and consistently apply a costing methodology so as to ensure accuracy of the records for materials, work in process, finished goods, used goods and parts. Inventory valuation shall be in compliance with U.S. Generally Accepted Accounting Principles (GAAP).

It is Company policy to monitor its Inventory using a perpetual Inventory method. The perpetual Inventory methodology employs rotating cycle counts, after which adjustments for discrepancies are made to the Inventory records.

It is Company policy to value Inventory using a standard cost methodology determined by the first-in, first-out (FIFO) cost basis.

The valuation method for each item of Inventory shall remain consistent from one accounting period to the next. Changes in value will be applied against Inventory reserve accounts such as shrinkage, excess and obsolete, and standard-to-actual reserve. Any changes in methodology must be reviewed and approved by the Chief Accounting Officer (CAO).

Procedure

This procedure includes the following topics:

A. Safeguarding the physical Inventory

B. Valuing the Inventory and using the reserve accounts

C. Relieving Inventory to Cost of Goods Sold

A. *Safeguarding the Physical Inventory*

The perpetual Inventory system is maintained within the Inventory database. As Inventory is received, it is recorded within the database. As the Inventory moves through the production cycle, it is monitored through the Inventory materials movement database. The database is designed to

Procedure No. B30	**Policy and Procedures** Section: Accounting and Finance **Inventory**	Page 2 of 6
Department Ownership	Issue/Effective Date:	Replaces previously issued

comply with asset tracking and product traceability procedures as defined within the ISO 9001 guidelines.

Inventory maintained at the supplier/original equipment manufacturer (OEM) location is validated and reconciled each month, with the Company sending out a statement to the Supplier. The supplier confirms the status of the inventory. Those items that cannot be confirmed must be immediately expensed through the reserve account.

If a Supplier is to ship a product directly to the Customer, the Supplier sends the Company a shipping notice, which triggers the receipt of goods into the Company's Inventory records and generates an invoice to the Customer.

Additional security and asset tracking is applied toward selected Inventory, which is considered to be of high value or a proprietary nature. To safeguard and protect this Inventory, it may be stored within locked cages or other limited access areas.

At least once a year, the complete Inventory count is verified by a rotating cycle count procedures.

B. *Valuing the Inventory*

Inventories must be valued at the cost associated with bringing the goods to the point of sale and making them available for sale.

Standard Cost estimates are created annually for each product during the planning cycle and reevaluated on a quarterly basis. The differences between the actual versus the standard costs are captured monthly and recorded in the standard-to-actual reserve.

Cost is defined as the historical cost or accounting book value for products or materials and has the following components:

1. Direct Labor which includes the total cost of employee compensation (salary and benefits), for work performed directly on the manufacturing of the product. Direct labor does not include the cost of supervision, administration, materials handling, shipping, or quality control.

    All employees performing direct labor are included in this definition.

2. Direct Materials refers to those materials that become an integral part of the finished product. For direct materials to be included as Inventory, the Company shall have clear title and be financially obligated to pay for the liability.

    Costs included as direct materials include:

    *   Vendor costs less any applicable purchase discounts

    *   Shipping and/or Transportation charges

<table>
<tr><td colspan="3" align="center">**Policy and Procedures**</td></tr>
<tr><td>Procedure No. B30</td><td align="center">Section: Accounting and Finance</td><td align="right">Page 3 of 6</td></tr>
<tr><td colspan="3" align="center">**Inventory**</td></tr>
<tr><td>Department Ownership</td><td align="center">Issue/Effective Date:</td><td align="right">Replaces previously issued</td></tr>
</table>

- Insurance for the Inventory while in transit and while in the warehouse and manufacturing location

- Handling costs associated with ordering, receiving, storing, and moving the Inventory

3. Overhead refers to those costs that cannot be directly assigned to a specific product/ configuration but nonetheless are directly associated with the production process.

   - Labor Overhead includes indirect labor, supervision, occupancy costs, utilities, repairs and maintenance, and depreciation.

   - Material Overhead includes procurement costs, material handling in receiving, quality control, operating supplies, and other supplies or materials that do not become part of the direct product.

Direct labor and overhead rates are applied to materials based on a designated activity type (i.e., classification of activity performed within the manufacturing process). Activity centers capture indirect overhead costs for a group of similar products.

Manufacturing Operations Finance is responsible for the coordination and analysis of the proposed worldwide standard cost changes as they arise. Individual departments are responsible for the cost components of the overall product standard cost.

Monthly accruals (for goods received where invoices have not yet been processed by Accounts Payable) shall be evaluated for inclusion in the cost of Inventory; see the Accrual policy and procedure. Prepaid Inventory (where advances have been made to acquire materials or Inventory) shall be treated in accordance with the Prepaid Assets/Expense policy and procedure.

Inventory Reserves

Adjustments to Inventory accounts shall be made to the appropriate Inventory reserve account. These accounts include shrinkage, excess and obsolete and standard to actual reserve. The reserves are determined based on historical performance and management discretion used to analyze the estimated and actual Inventory levels. The reserve balances are updated with any necessary accounting adjustments recorded on a monthly basis.

- The Inventory shrinkage or materials usage reserve refers to the anticipated differences that may occur between the Inventory quantity and valuation retained on the Inventory books compared to the physical Inventory count. This includes a reserve for defective Inventory, scrap, or waste during the production or storage process.

- The Excess and Obsolete reserve assesses the current period impact for excess and obsolete Inventory. Excess Inventory that is deemed to be no longer eligible for sale must be scrapped and written off to this reserve.

Policy and Procedures		
Procedure No. B30	Section: Accounting and Finance	Page 4 of 6
	Inventory	
Department Ownership	Issue/Effective Date:	Replaces previously issued

- The Standard-to-Actual reserve estimates the variance between the valuation impact of standard and actual costs as it relates to material, labor, and overhead.

Inventory Impairment Testing

Periodically, at least annually, as with other assets, the carrying value of Inventory shall be compared to the current market value. In determining current market values for each item of Inventory, the following must be considered:

- Prevailing bid price at Inventory date and at similar purchase volume of an average purchase of product or materials

- Current selling price of product or materials less an allowance for a normal profit margin

- Reproduction cost used to value goods in process and finished goods

- Expected future demand for the product or material

- Obsolescence of product technology

- Scrap or salvage value of material

Significant differences shall be recorded directly against the Inventory.

C. Relieving Finished Goods Inventory to Cost of Goods Sold

As goods are sold, they are moved from the Finished Goods Inventory accounts to the Cost of Goods Sold account based on the number of units sold at the standard costing rate.

Cost of Goods Sold Inventory includes:

- Items sent to Customers representing the fulfillment of shipments identified by valid sales contracts

- No-charge shipments authorized to be sent to customers for demonstration purposes, replacement purposes, or to address customer dissatisfaction issues

Items used for promotional or marketing purposes are directed to the marketing expense account.

Items sold through intercompany transactions are directed to the Intercompany Cost of Sales accounts.

Items sold to employees or used as contributions or donations are directed to the appropriate cost or expense line (e.g., employee sales—cost of goods sold or contributions).

	Policy and Procedures	
Procedure No. B30	Section: Accounting and Finance	Page 5 of 6
	Inventory	
Department Ownership	Issue/Effective Date:	Replaces previously issued

Returns

Product returns accepted by the Company must be recognized as a reduction to the Cost of Goods Sold and an increase to Finished Goods Inventory. Returned products must undergo quality inspection to determine if they are fit for resale; if so, they are valued at the then standard Cost of Goods Sold rates and classified as:

1. Equivalent to New (ETN)—the returned product is classified into Finished Goods Inventory at the then current standard cost rate

2. Sent for rework—the returned product is classified as work in progress or Construction in Process (CIP)

3. Scrapped and written off to the Excess and Obsolete reserve

Sales, Usage, and Variance Analysis Reports

To ensure accuracy of reporting, sales and usage reports are generated monthly with analysis of the number of units and the application of standard cost rates. Sales reports are cross-referenced to Inventory movement reports and reconciled to ensure that Inventory has been shipped and invoiced or properly coded.

Physical Inventory Count

The Company uses a perpetual Inventory system and relies on the accuracy of the information within the Inventory database. In addition, one third of the Inventory is physically counted every four months and reconciled to the Inventory system database. The Inventory chosen for this rotating count is chosen based on warehouse location.

High-value Inventory is retained in a secure location (e.g., locked cage) and physically counted and reconciled each quarter.

Company-owned Inventory sent out on consignment and located at noncompany locations is physically counted at least once a quarter.

Controls/Areas of Responsibility

Monthly unit sales and Inventory reports are monitored and reconciled to ensure accurate and timely recording of Inventory.

Valuation variances between the standard-to-actual carrying costs are tracked, analyzed, and reconciled monthly by Operations Finance.

The reserve accounts must be reconciled monthly in accordance with the Account Reconciliation policy to insure that accurate Inventory levels and valuations are reflected on Company financial statements.

Policy and Procedures		
Procedure No. B30	Section: Accounting and Finance	Page 6 of 6
	Inventory	
Department Ownership	Issue/Effective Date:	Replaces previously issued

Sales, usage, and variance analysis reports are circulated and reviewed by management each month. Reconciliation must be performed in accordance with the Account Reconciliation policy.

Changes to Inventory valuation or reserve account methodology must be approved by the Chief Accounting Officer.

Contacts

Manufacturing Operations Finance

Policy and Procedures		
Procedure No. B31	Section: Accounting and Finance	Page 1 of 3
Investment and Marketable Securities		
Department Ownership	Issue/Effective Date:	Replaces previously issued
Prepared by: Date	Approved by: Date	Authorized by: Date

Scope

This policy applies to all the Company's subsidiaries and locations worldwide.

Policy

It is IDÆAL LLP's (Company) policy to invest surplus cash to satisfy the following objectives:

- Preserve capital

- Ensure liquidity by defining maturities as required by cash flow projections

- Maximize yield within the constraint of maximum safety

- Optimize tax benefits

Country Controllers and non-U.S. geographic Treasury Managers must coordinate local Investments and Marketable Security positions and transactions with the Corporate Cash Manager.

All Investments shall be made by the Corporate Cash Manager or designate and based on approved guidelines as agreed to by the Corporate Treasurer. No other persons or business areas are authorized to make Investments except for interest-bearing deposits at the bank where the company has its accounts.

This policy prohibits taking speculative positions or the borrowing of funds for Investment purposes.

Procedure

When investing funds, priority shall be given to the following criteria, listed in order of importance:

- Security—refers to the relative risks involved with an Investment vehicle.

- Liquidity—refers to how quickly and easily the Investment can be bought, sold, or converted to cash in large quantities without adversely affecting the asset's price.

- Return—refers to the after-tax equivalent yield of an Investment.

Ongoing determination of risk factors is imperative to controlling Investment risk. This evaluation shall consider interest rate movements, currency movements, commodity movements, and country sovereignty (i.e., risk and ability to move cash across borders).

Policy and Procedures		
Procedure No. B31	Section: Accounting and Finance	Page 2 of 3
Investment and Marketable Securities		
Department Ownership	Issue/Effective Date:	Replaces previously issued

Safekeeping - All Investments shall be held with only approved brokers, dealers or banks as evaluated by Corporate Treasury. Investment instruments that are purchased by a subsidiary must be placed in similar safekeeping. If they are delivered to the subsidiary, the recipient at the subsidiary shall in no event be the same individual making the Investment.

Sovereign risk. This is the risk attached to a deposit, security, or loan held in a bank located outside of the U.S. This risk takes into consideration the political and economic stability of the country in which the Investment is domiciled. An international offshore banking facility limited to a booking center shall not be considered a sovereign risk issue. Also, the ability to move cash cross-border (availability of U.S. dollars) must be considered.

The funds invested by a non-U.S. subsidiary must be placed in a locally registered branch of the Company's approved banking facility. It must be noted that funds invested in a foreign branch of a locally approved bank are still subject to sovereign risk regardless of whether the bank remains a viable institution in good standing in the financial community.

Funds that are collected by foreign subsidiaries during the month shall be used to pay local obligations such as vendor payables, overdrafts, Intercompany debt, commissionaire payments, and notes. Remaining funds that are awaiting repatriation to the U.S. may be invested in highly liquid interest-bearing Investments having a maturity of 30 days or less. These Investments should be made and managed by someone designated by the Corporate Cash Manager, such as the subsidiary's Controller. The Investments must have the unqualified backing of the bank.

The types of Investments such as Marketable Securities shall be approved for Investment, within portfolio managed by Corporate Treasury. The portfolio shall include a mix of the following types of Investment vehicles:

- Securities and/or obligations issued by or guaranteed by the U.S. government and its federal agencies

- Repurchase agreements limited to U.S. government securities or agencies

- Other securities such as:

    - Commercial paper (CP)

    - Certificates of Deposit (CDs) or bank notes

    - Banker's Acceptances (BAs)

    - Auction rate securities

    - Corporate Bonds (including medium-term notes)

    - Taxable Municipal Bonds

    - Tax-Exempt Municipal Bonds

Policy and Procedures		
Procedure No. B31	Section: Accounting and Finance	Page 3 of 3
	Investment and Marketable Securities	
Department Ownership	Issue/Effective Date:	Replaces previously issued

- Floating-rate securities

- Money market funds

An instruction is issued to the bank or financial institution to enact the transaction and directs the bank or financial institution as to where the funds may be deposited. Each transfer and all trades are assigned a reference number and documented within the Wire Transfer Log. This log is reviewed by the Cash Manager daily to resolve any open issues and monitor transactions in progress.

A Monthly Investment Portfolio report is prepared by the Cash Manager submitted for review to the Treasurer and Chief Financial Officer (CFO). The report identifies the worldwide status of Investments and Marketable Securities and provides information as to the type of transaction, location, date it was acquired, original cost of the Investment and Marketable Securities, as well as the current fair market value, average maturity, and yield of the Investment.

The Monthly Investment Portfolio report, bank confirmations of wire transfers, and bank statements are used to assist with the account reconciliation.

Control/Areas of Responsibility

Administration of the Investment policy and execution of the Investment strategy shall be the responsibility of the Corporate Cash Manager.

The Investment policy is reviewed at least annually and approved by the Treasurer and the CFO.

The Corporate Treasurer must be notified immediately if any of the following events occur:

- The market value of any Investment instrument drops below 5 percent of the amortized value.

- The market value of the total portfolio drops below 5 percent of the total cost value.

- Any significant rating downgrade for any instrument or any institution.

Ongoing determination of risk factors is imperative to controlling Investment risk. This evaluation should consider interest rate movements, currency movements, commodity movements and sovereignty issues.

Contacts

Corporate Treasury

Policy and Procedures		
Procedure No. B32	Section: Accounting and Finance	Page 1 of 6
	Journal Entries: **Routine, Non-Routine, and Estimates**	
Department Ownership	Issue/Effective Date:	Replaces previously issued

Prepared by: Date	Approved by: Date	Authorized by: Date

Scope

The Company must maintain a strong accounting system capable of accurately recording the financial activity of the business. It is, therefore, imperative that financial reports reflect accurate account information as collected from Journal Entries and posted to the general ledger.

Consistent with the Public Company Accounting Oversight Board (PCAOB) guidelines, accounting transactions are classified as:

- Routine—defined as recurring financial activities reflected in the accounting records in the normal course of business (e.g., sales, purchases, cash receipts, cash disbursements, and payroll).

- Non-Routine—defined as activities that occur for the first time or only periodically (e.g., sale/ leaseback arrangements, mergers, acquisitions and divestitures, extraordinary items, litigation settlements) and require addressing specific financial reporting and operational control issues. A distinguishing feature of non-routine transactions is that data involved are generally not part of the routine flow of transactions.

- Estimation—defined as activities that involve management judgments or assumptions in formulating account balances in the absence of a precise means of measurement (e.g., determining the allowance for doubtful accounts, establishing reserves, changes to assumptions or methodology for depreciating or amortizing assets).

This policy and procedure applies to all currencies and accounting systems used by the Company.

Policy

It is IDÆAL LLP's (Company) policy that all Journal Entries (JEs):

- Represent valid approved and supported business transactions

- Be prepared and approved by only authorized employees

- Adhere to U.S. Generally Accepted Accounting Principles (GAAP) or, where there are deviations from U.S. GAAP, have been approved by the Chief Accounting Officer (CAO)

- Be recorded in a timely manner in accordance with the accounting close schedule

Policy and Procedures		
Procedure No. B32	Section: Accounting and Finance	Page 2 of 6
	Journal Entries: **Routine, Non-Routine, and Estimates**	
Department Ownership	Issue/Effective Date:	Replaces previously issued

JEs must be entered into the accounting system using the local currency of the country where the transaction originated. Intercompany journals and registers must be in the local currency.

Procedure

Whether routine, non-routine or estimations, manually prepared, or systems generated, JEs must comply with the following procedures.

Valid Transactions

In accordance with U.S. GAAP and as interpreted by the CAO, all JEs must represent valid business transactions.

The CAO or a designate must review and approve transactions or situations that do not comply with U.S. GAAP. A review of the accounting literature and approval of the accounting treatment shall be documented with a "Memo to File" and made available to the external and/or internal auditors.

Unless otherwise disqualified, business transactions shall be recognized on an accrual basis.

Manual JEs

When required for accurate transaction processing, a valid, supported JE shall be prepared processed as:

- Routine manual JEs recur each month; however, the dollar amount may vary. Examples include but are not limited to revenue, depreciation, amortization, interest expense, royalty, consolidation, and closing entries.

- Non-Routine manual JEs occur infrequently and require a high degree of subjectivity and judgment, with data or information provided from non-routine sources. Non-Routine transactions must be approved by the CAO; refer to the Non-Routine Transactions section (e.g., Sale/Leaseback arrangements).

- Estimation manual JEs are generally required for first-time estimations or when there is a change in the methodology. Subsequent entries may be systematized and considered routine (e.g., change to Allowance for Doubtful Accounts).

Systems-generated JEs

Whenever possible (i.e., where accounting systems permit) a system-generated JE shall be established for routine repetitive transactions. Controls must be present to ensure complete, accurate system processing of JE.

<table>
<tr><td colspan="3" align="center">**Policy and Procedures**</td></tr>
<tr><td>Procedure No. B32</td><td align="center">Section: Accounting and Finance</td><td align="right">Page 3 of 6</td></tr>
<tr><td colspan="3" align="center">**Journal Entries:**
Routine, Non-Routine, and Estimates</td></tr>
<tr><td>Department Ownership</td><td align="center">Issue/Effective Date:</td><td align="right">Replaces previously issued</td></tr>
</table>

Documentation and Authorization

Only individuals authorized by Corporate Accounting are to have access to use the accounting system. Corporate Accounting maintains authorization documentation which include the list and access rights of qualified users. At least annually, the list of authorized individuals shall be reviewed and validated (e.g., by person, department, or job role).

Systems-generated JEs

Access to and approval for system or database-generated JEs must be identified within the design and configuration of the system or database.

Standard, routine, and system-produced JEs must be validated at least quarterly that the scope and accounting treatment are correct. There must be detailed documentation to support an Accounting and Information Technology (IT) audit of the end-to-end process. System control checks and balances shall be embedded into the programs and reports, which validate that the information is complete and accurate.

Accounting Systems

JE shall be made to appropriate account codes as defined within Accounting policies, procedures, manuals, and official instructions.

Once the JE is entered into the accounting system, the system validates the account combination (e.g., account code, cost center/department).

The accounting system must include controls with checks and balances to ensure that:

- Only authorized employees may enter and approve JEs.

- Only valid, active accounts may be used.

- Debits and credits are in balance.

Documentation and Record Keeping

Manual JEs must include supporting documentation and an accurate description of the nature of the transaction with "prepared by" and "approved by" signatures and dates. Manual JEs must use the attached JE form or an approved (by Corporate Accounting) equivalent.

All JEs must have documentation and backup support that represents a valid, authorized business transaction. The quality and quantity of the documentation and backup support must be useful for those who prepare, approve, review, or audit the financial records.

Policy and Procedures		
Procedure No. B32	Section: Accounting and Finance	Page 4 of 6
	Journal Entries: **Routine, Non-Routine, and Estimates**	
Department Ownership	Issue/Effective Date:	Replaces previously issued

Supporting documentation for a complete audit trail must be retained for each JE. Examples of supporting documentation may include but are not limited to:

- Methodology and rationale to backup the calculation

- Reconciliation and reference to special or separate journals and/or ledgers

- Account analysis of transactional activity

- Source data that initiates the transaction (e.g., sales orders, customer invoice references, purchase orders, receipt of goods and/or services references, contracts, and agreements references

- Reference to supporting accounting literature

JE records and supporting documentation must be retained in accordance with the Company's Record Information Management policy and Retention Schedules.

Authorization for Transaction Types

Transaction Type	Recurring	Nonrecurring
Routine	JE processor's manager	Not applicable
Non-Routine	Not applicable	Refer to table below*
Estimation	Refer to table below*	Refer to table below*

*Approval for nonrecurring, non-routine and estimation transactions:

Country Business Unit Controllers	Up to $250k USD
Corporate Controller	Over $250k USD
Chief Accounting Officer	Over $1M USD

Accounting Close Schedule

All JE activity shall be posted to the ledgers in a timely manner in accordance with the monthly accounting close schedule.

Disclosure

Disclosure for non-routine and estimation transactions over $10,000 USD must be made to Corporate Accounting and the CAO as soon as the JE is anticipated or known.

	Policy and Procedures	
Procedure No. B32	Section: Accounting and Finance	Page 5 of 6
	Journal Entries: **Routine, Non-Routine, and Estimates**	
Department Ownership	Issue/Effective Date:	Replaces previously issued

Disclosure to Corporate Accounting and the CAO may be required for those non-routine and estimation transactions that cannot be quantified. When in doubt, refer to specific policies or contact the CAO.

Controls/Areas of Responsibility

The originator of the JE must maintain support for the JE and must produce it on demand for internal and/or external audit reviews.

It is the Counting or Business Unit Controller's responsibility to identify any transaction to the CAO, where the accounting treatment or interpretation of U.S. GAAP is not clearly understood.

Corporate Accounting is responsible for:

- Identifying employees authorized to enter JEs into the accounting system

- Approving (or delegating approval for) all JEs

- Ensuring that JEs reflect U.S. GAAP and Company policies

- Ensuring that the accounting treatment for non-GAAP transactions is properly reviewed and authorized

- Selecting and sampling JEs for periodic review of the justification and documentation

- Approving all maintenance and changes to financial information systems or other information systems that serve as source documentation to determine input for accounting transactions and/or JEs

Systems-generated controls must be established and monitored to ensure the timely, accurate, and complete processing of systems-generated JEs.

During the month-end accounting close cycle, the financial statements are reviewed to ensure that all the necessary and anticipated JEs are recorded.

Contact

Chief Accounting Officer

Procedure No. B32	**Policy and Procedures** Section: Accounting and Finance	Page 6 of 6
	Journal Entries: **Routine, Non-Routine, and Estimates**	
Department Ownership	Issue/Effective Date:	Replaces previously issued

Exhibit

Manual Journal Entry Form

Prepared by:		Date:
Reviewed by:		Date:
Approved by:		Date:
Entered by:		Date:

Period the JE must be processed For the Month:	Currency:
Business Unit:	Geography/Currency:

Describe the transaction—for the benefit of future readers, provide a lengthy, detailed description of why this entry needs to be recorded.

Account Number	Account Name	Debit (Dr) Currency	Credit (Cr) Currency
	Total	**Total Dr**	**Total Cr**

Once entered into the accounting system, retain supporting documentation with this form.

	Policy and Procedures	
Procedure No. B33	Section: Accounting and Finance	Page 1 of 7
	Capital, Operating Leases, and Real Estate Rental Property	
Department Ownership	Issue/Effective Date:	Replaces previous issue

Prepared by:	Approved by:	Authorized by:
Date	Date	Date

Scope

In addition to the guidance within this policy, refer to the Property, Plant and Equipment policy when considering Capital or Operating leases.

Policy

Assets must be acquired in accordance with the Procurement Policy and classified in accordance with the Property, Plant and Equipment Policy. Assets must be approved according to the Authorization and Delegation of Authority Policy.

It is IDÆAL LLP's (Company) policy to recognize leases in accordance with U.S. Generally Accepted Accounting Principles (GAAP).

In accordance with Statement of Financial Accounting Standard SFAS No. 13, "Accounting for Leases," leases must be capitalized as a long-lived asset if they meet any **one** of the following criteria:

1. Ownership of the asset is transferred.

2. Lease term is 75 percent or more of the economic life of the asset.

3. The present value of the lease payments is equal to at least 90 percent of the price to purchase the asset.

4. There is a bargain purchase price at the end of the lease.

If **none** of the above four conditions are met, the lease is considered an operating lease, with the lease payments expensed as they are incurred. Corporate Accounting shall review all lease agreements to determine the appropriate accounting treatment.

Regardless of whether the lease is considered a capital or operating lease, Corporate Treasury must review and approve all proposed leases and lease renewals with annual payments in excess of $12,000 (except for real estate rental agreements and automobile leases) **or** with an aggregate payment in excess of $120,000 USD.

Corporate Treasury must review the master lease agreements to determine the lease classification. A review by Corporate Treasury also ensures that the Company receives the most competitive financing rates available when leasing assets. See the Exhibit for an Accounting example for the treatment of a Capital Lease.

	Policy and Procedures	
Procedure No. B33	Section: Accounting and Finance	Page 2 of 7
	Capital, Operating Leases, and Real Estate Rental Property	
Department Ownership	Issue/Effective Date:	Replaces previous issue

Corporate Procurement or an approved delegated business area is responsible for negotiating contracts and monitoring the acquisition of Company-leased products.

Corporate Legal must review and approve all contracts and agreements.

Real Estate Rental Property

The Company recognizes rent expense on a straight-line basis, irrespective of variable payment amounts or escalating clauses, over the term of occupancy for lease or rental agreements, which include any of the following: free rent, landlord allowances, fixed escalation provisions (i.e., scheduled and specified rent increases or concessions from the lessor in the form of cash payments or assignments of current obligations).

This policy applies worldwide to any facility rented or leased longer than one year. For real estate policies with a term of less than one year, rent may be expensed as it is paid.

Procedure

In order to take advantage of the Company's purchasing power in a global marketplace, certain business areas are responsible for establishing, maintaining, and enforcing purchasing guidelines. Leased assets generally fall into one of these purchasing categories and as such **must** be approved by the global purchasing authority. For example:

- Corporate Facilities is responsible for acquiring Company automobiles and trucks as well as office equipment such as copiers, printers, audiovisual, fax, and so on.

- Corporate Real Estate is responsible for acquiring and contracting for building, building improvements, and leasehold improvements.

- Information Systems (IS) is responsible for acquiring computer hardware, software, and network systems

All business units considering acquiring assets with lease terms must have the agreement and the accounting treatment approved by representatives from Corporate Accounting, Fixed-Assets Accounting, Corporate Treasury, and representatives from Legal. These representatives are also referred to as the lease assessment team.

Lease Review Process

A "lease/buy" comparison shall be documented whenever a rental or leasing alternative is considered. The comparison must be prepared by the requesting business unit's Controller prior to review with the lease assessment team.

	Policy and Procedures	
Procedure No. B33	Section: Accounting and Finance	Page 3 of 7
	Capital, Operating Leases, and Real Estate Rental Property	
Department Ownership	Issue/Effective Date:	Replaces previous issue

The lease review shall consider significant financial and operational costs and expenses (e.g., implicit interest rates, down payments, end-of-term payments or guarantees, early termination, or other penalties). The lease review shall also consider legal, tax, and accounting issues (e.g., rights and obligations of ownership).

The department submitting the purchase request and/or purchase order must document and provide the following information:

- Business rationale for buy and/or lease decision
- Copy of lease proposal and related documentation showing:
    - Cost comparison of the equipment life (i.e., desired usage term within the Company)
    - Amount of the lease payments
    - Frequency and total number of lease payments
    - Lease agreement terms and conditions
- Confirmation that:
    - There is no bargain purchase option at the end of the lease
    - There are no residual guarantees at the end of the lease
    - Ownership of the equipment does not transfer to the Company during or at the end of the lease
    - The tax rate for non-U.S. deals is not affected; for example, the tax depreciation method (for non-U.S. deals) would apply for assets if purchased
- Third-party verification of the estimated:
    - Useful life of the equipment
    - Residual value of equipment at the end of the lease term

SFAS No. 13

If any one of the FAS No.13 (noted above in the policy section) conditions is met, the asset and related lease liability must be recorded as a capital lease. The net present value of the lease payments plus any additional financial obligation (such as a down payment, guaranteed renewal, or mandatory buyout option) is included when determining the asset value and obligation of the lease.

The asset shall be amortized over the life of the lease. The lease liability must be segregated as current (due within 12 months) and long-term debt.

<table>
<tr><td colspan="3" align="center">**Policy and Procedures**</td></tr>
<tr><td>Procedure No. B33</td><td align="center">Section: Accounting and Finance</td><td align="right">Page 4 of 7</td></tr>
<tr><td colspan="3" align="center">**Capital, Operating Leases,
and Real Estate Rental Property**</td></tr>
<tr><td>Department Ownership</td><td align="center">Issue/Effective Date:</td><td align="right">Replaces previous issue</td></tr>
</table>

Capital Leases

Upgrades, renovations, or repairs to a capital leased asset must be in accordance with the Long-Lived Asset Policy and are generally treated as being coterminus with the original leased obligation unless deemed otherwise and authorized by Corporate Accounting.

Termination and/or disposal of a capital leased asset must be in accordance with the Long-Lived Asset Policy. After the termination or disposal, additional costs and expenses plus any remaining net book value must be expensed. Any exception from this procedure must be approved by the Chief Accounting Officer (CAO).

Operating Leases

Operating lease refers to those leasing arrangements where any one of the four criteria above is not met. Operating leases shall be treated as expense with guaranteed Company obligations (e.g., penalties for early termination) set up as reserves or liabilities. Regional Controllers shall assess the Company liability, and Corporate Accounting must approve the accounting treatment and recognition. Generally, the operating lease expense is determined as an aggregate over the life of the lease with a straight-line methodology to determine the monthly expense.

Real Estate Rental Property

Corporate Accounting or the appropriate subsidiary or functional business area's Controller or financial designate shall compute the average rent expense to be recorded each month over the life of the lease. The difference between the straight-lined rent expense recorded and the actual rent payments is the Deferred Rent Liability.

For leases that contain provisions (refer to Definitions within the Exhibit, e.g., free rent period, variable rent escalation) scheduling additional, square footage to be occupied during the lease, separate computations shall be made on each parcel of space to determine average rent per parcel.

Accounting for Leases on Vacant Property

The accounting treatment for leases relating to vacant property is dependent on the events leading to the vacancy.

- If the vacancy is an isolated incident where local management has decided to consolidate offices to increase efficiency, then the costs associated with closing the office should be incurred and expensed as part of operations.

- If the office or facility being vacated was acquired as part of an acquisition and there is a plan in place to dispose the office on or shortly after the deal is consummated, then the estimated

	Policy and Procedures	
Procedure No. B33	Section: Accounting and Finance	Page 5 of 7
	Capital, Operating Leases, and Real Estate Rental Property	
Department Ownership	Issue/Effective Date:	Replaces previous issue

liability associated with this exit activity must be accrued for and included as part of the purchase balance sheet.

- If the vacancy is the result of a broader restructuring plan (as defined under FAS No. 146, "Accounting for Costs Associated with Exit or Disposal Activities"), then these costs, less an allowance for sublease income (regardless of whether there is a plan to sublease the property), can be accrued for as part of the restructuring (reserve) charge.

Controls/Areas of Responsibility

All rental and leasing agreements must be reviewed and approved by representatives from Corporate Legal and Corporate Accounting (or designates).

Corporate Accounting and Corporate Tax must approve the accounting and tax treatment for all rented and leased assets.

As with all assets and Company-committed obligations, local procedures shall be implemented to safeguard, monitor, and track rented and leased assets.

Corporate Facilities maintains real estate files for all locations (worldwide), which includes details for the agreements, start and end dates, and payment terms.

The business unit's area Controller or financial designate shall determine the average monthly lease payment.

In accordance with the Account Reconciliation policy, all Balance Sheet accounts must be reconciled each month.

Contacts

Corporate Accounting
Corporate Treasury

	Policy and Procedures	
Procedure No. B33	Section: Accounting and Finance	Page 6 of 7
	Capital, Operating Leases, and Real Estate Rental Property	
Department Ownership	Issue/Effective Date:	Replaces previous issue

Exhibit

Examples

Capital leases for **all** types of long-lived assets are to be coded to the capital lease account category in order to ensure the correct accounting treatment.

Fixed-Asset Lease Example: The Company has entered into a 60-month lease agreement for a Long-Lived Asset with an equivalent purchase price of $21,000. The anticipated residual value at the end of the 60 months is $0 and the implicit interest rate is 4 percent per year. Company payments are $375 per month.

- In this example, the Company should treat this asset as a capital lease because:

    - The Company will have possession of the asset for more than 75 percent of its economic life (the Company has the asset for 100% of its economic life).

    - The net present value of the payments equals $20,362, which is 97 percent of the purchase price of the asset. To be an operating lease, the net present value must be less than 90 percent of the purchase price.

Real Estate Rental Property Example: The Company has entered into a real estate lease for 60 months with the following payment terms:

Payment Terms:	Months 1 thru 6	Free
	Months 7 thru 24	$ 9,000 per month
	Months 25 thru 60	$12,000 per month

To compute the average monthly rent, sum the rental payments and divide by the number of months.

Months 1 thru 6	Free	=	$ 0
Months 7 thru 24	$ 9,000 per month	=	162,000
Months 25 Thru 60	**$12,000 Per Month**	=	**432,000**
Total Aggregate Payments		=	$ 594,000
Average Monthly rent (divide by 60 months)		=	$ 9,900 per month

In this example, a monthly debit of $9,900 shall be directed to rent expense with the credit going to Rent Payable.

	Policy and Procedures	
Procedure No. B33	Section: Accounting and Finance	Page 7 of 7
	Capital, Operating Leases, and Real Estate Rental Property	
Department Ownership	Issue/Effective Date:	Replaces previous issue

Definitions for Real Estate Rental Property

- **Average rent:** The sum of all cash payments made over the lease term, less any cash rebates, divided by the number of months in the lease term. See Exhibits for examples of this computation.

- **Cash rebate:** A cash payment from the landlord at the outset of the lease, which may be used for leasehold improvements or as an inducement to sign the lease.

- **Deferred rent:** Rental payments that are temporarily reduced or eliminated for some portion of the lease.

- **Deferred rent liability:** A liability equal to the amount of accrued free rent or accrued fixed rent escalation on the balance sheet at any time. This liability arises when either a cash rebate is received and/or when the actual cash payment to lessor for rents is less than the average rent expense over the life of the lease. See Exhibit for examples of this computation.

- **Fixed rent escalation:** A clause contained in the lease agreement, which stipulates that future rents will increase by a specified amount. Types of fixed escalation clauses include fixed-dollar or percentage increases and increases that contain a minimum fixed escalation factor e.g., where a rental escalation clause states ". . . rent will be increased annually by 3 percent," such language is considered a fixed escalation factor.

- **"Free" rent period:** A portion of the lease term during which no rent is charged, normally at inception. Deferred rent and cash rebates are to be treated as free rent for the purposes of this policy.

- **Landlord allowances:** The equivalent sum provided by the landlord to the tenant for lease-hold improvements.

- **Variable rent escalation:** A clause contained in the lease agreement, which stipulates that future rents will increase, based on some variable factor such as the Consumer Price Index. **Lease agreements with these types of increases are exempt from the provisions of this policy since the change in any specific index cannot be estimated.**

	Policy and Procedures	
Procedure No. B34	Section: Accounting and Finance	Page 1 of 6
	Letter of Representation, **Quarterly Financial Sub Certification Process**	
Department Ownership	Issue/Effective Date:	Replaces previously issued

Prepared by: Approved by: Authorized by:
Date   Date   Date

Scope

In accordance with Securities and Exchange Commission (SEC) regulations and the Sarbanes-Oxley Act, the Chief Executive Officer (CEO), Chief Financial Officer (CFO), and other principal company officers are required to sign or certify Management Letters of Representation.

According to the regulations, it is management's responsibility to:

- Establish and maintain adequate internal control over financial reporting for the company.

- Assess the effectiveness of the company's internal control over financial reporting.

- Provide a statement identifying the framework used by management to evaluate the effectiveness of the company's internal control over financial reporting.

- Issue the certifications to the Company's registered public accounting firm that audited the Company's financial statements.

Disclosure controls and procedures include, without limitation, controls and procedures designed to ensure that the information required to be disclosed for external financial reporting purposes is accumulated and communicated to the company's management, as appropriate, to allow timely decisions regarding required disclosure.

Since the CEO, CFO, and others do not have intimate knowledge of all business processes, information presented in the financial statements and related SEC filings, selected employees who have knowledge of financial and business issues across the company are asked to sign (subcertify) that the information provided from their areas of responsibility is complete, accurate, and conforms to the company's policies, procedures, and internal controls.

Policy

It is IDEAL, LLP's (Company) policy that selected business process and area owners, as well as their financial and legal counterparts, are responsible for providing a subcertification to the CFO and CEO on a quarterly basis. The Quarterly Financial SubCertification Letter (Letter) asks individuals to certify that the information provided from their areas of responsibility is complete, accurate, and conforms to the Company's Code of Ethical Conduct, policies, procedures, and internal controls.

	Policy and Procedures	
Procedure No. B34	Section: Accounting and Finance	Page 2 of 6
	Letter of Representation, **Quarterly Financial Sub Certification Process**	
Department Ownership	Issue/Effective Date:	Replaces previously issued

It is the Company's policy that a Financial Review Committee (FRC) made up of representatives from Finance external reporting, Internal Controls, Legal external reporting, and Compliance oversee this policy and approve the details of this program including but not limited to the distribution list, the preparation of the Letter, and tracking the disclosure and resolution of issues identified within management's submission of the Letter.

Procedure

The Internal Controls department (IC) is responsible for updating the materials and executing the program. Each quarter, the IC updates the process owner matrix, which produces the distribution list of those who are required to subcertify the various sections of the Letter.

The process owner matrix defines the Company's processes and names a business owner and the corresponding financial and legal designates. All are required to sign the Letter. Additionally, management may decide to include others who they feel may have access to knowledge or transactions that may materially affect the financial statements and/or SEC submission.

The Letter is reviewed and updated according to changes in regulations or management emphasis. The FRC provides feedback, reviews, and approves the distribution list and Letter. The Letter is made up of three sections:

1. Representation of Financial Data and Business Practices

2. Financial Statement 302 Disclosure and Subcertification

3. Internal Controls 404 Subcertification

The distribution list identifies those individuals and the section of the Letter they must subcertify.

The Quarterly Financial Sub Certification package includes the matrix, Letter, and draft version of the 10Q or 10K. The request for Subcertification and the package is sent by the CFO.

The recipients of the Letter shall conduct due diligence reviews to a degree that will satisfy the claims to be made within the Letter (e.g., accurate and complete). Exceptions or deviations (also called issues or findings) from the representations must be identified within the space provided within the Letter.

Once received, the issues or findings are evaluated and assessed to determine issues/findings that are (1) immaterial and considered a local issue to remediate, (2) cross-referenced to other issues or findings previously identified and currently under remediation, and (3) new to the issue and findings list. Once categorized, the issues/findings are logged into a database (Sub Certification issues log) for monitoring and tracking the issue through the remediation process.

Policy and Procedures		
Procedure No. B34	Section: Accounting and Finance	Page 3 of 6
Letter of Representation, **Quarterly Financial Sub Certification Process**		
Department Ownership	Issue/Effective Date:	Replaces previously issued

All issues and findings are evaluated and assessed as to whether they require changes to and/or disclosure to the current quarter's financial statement reporting. All issues and findings must be evaluated and resolved prior to submission to the SEC.

Findings and issues are reviewed with the FRC; the Disclosure Operating Committee. The Risk Oversight, and Compliance Committee prior to review with the CEO and CFO.

Controls/Areas of Responsibility

- Compliance with this policy is the responsibility of each functional area's executive manager and controller. Nonconformance areas must be investigated, monitored, and resolved.

- IC function ensures that there is 100 percent compliance (i.e., responses received) and that significant processes and business areas are represented.

- External Financial Reporting and Legal will review the outstanding items to determine the completeness and accuracy of the financial statement presentation and SEC filings. Nonconformance areas will be investigated, monitored, and resolved.

- The FRC meets monthly to ensure that remediation is occurring and to monitor and track findings and issues identified as a result of comments and to prepare for the next quarter's issuance of the Letter and related package.

Contact

Internal Control

	Policy and Procedures	
Procedure No. B34	Section: Accounting and Finance	Page 4 of 6
	Letter of Representation, **Quarterly Financial Sub Certification Process**	
Department Ownership	Issue/Effective Date:	Replaces previously issued

Exhibit

Sample Letter of Representation
(insert content for areas highlighted in yellow)

I confirm to the best of my knowledge and in the acting capacity of my responsibilities the following representations regarding the financial information provided to the Company as of <u><date for the submission of this Letter></u> and for the quarter ending <date>.

My representations to the Company are based on the execution of standard disclosure controls and procedures, review for adequacy of internal controls over financial reporting and appropriate documentation supporting significant or unusual items and accounting adjustments, inquiry of key operating and financial personnel, and other evaluation procedures I consider necessary to collect and disclose, in a timely manner, information required to be recorded or disclosed in our financial information.

To the best of my knowledge and belief, I <name and title> representing <area of responsibility> confirm the following:

A. *Representation of Financial Data and Business Practices*

1. In accordance with the Company's Code of Ethical Conduct and in my role, the financial data provided to the internal Finance department and our external auditors is inclusive of all relevant information, is true and accurate, and is prepared in conformity with U.S. Generally Accepted Accounting Principles (GAAP) and Company policies and procedures. The data fairly presents in all material respects the financial position, results of operations, and cash flows of my area of responsibility.

2. I am not aware of any accounts, transactions, or agreements not authorized or properly recorded in the financial records underlying the financial information provided or not in accordance with policies in all material respects. There are no false statements of fact or omissions that would make the information underlying the financial information provided as misleading in any material fact for the periods covered by this Letter.

3. I have no knowledge of any violations of laws or regulations with regard to Company business practices. Additionally, I have no knowledge of any transactions or proposed transactions involving a foreign official as defined in the U.S. Foreign Corrupt Practices Act (FCPA) of 1977 as well as the anti-bribery policy for the purpose of corruptly obtaining or retaining business or gaining improper advantage in accordance with the anti-bribery provisions of the FCPA.

4. I am not aware of (a) any fraud[1] involving management or employees who have significant roles in the system of internal control over financial reporting or any fraud involving others that could have a material effect on

---

[1] I understand that the term *fraud* includes misstatements arising from fraudulent financial reporting and misstatements arising from misappropriation of assets. Misstatements arising from fraudulent financial reporting are intentional misstatements or omissions of amounts or disclosures in financial statements to deceive financial statement users. Misstatements arising from misappropriation of assets involve the theft of an entity's assets where the effect of the theft causes the entity's financial statement not to be fairly presented.

<table>
<tr><td colspan="3" align="center">Policy and Procedures</td></tr>
<tr><td>Procedure No. B34</td><td align="center">Section: Accounting and Finance</td><td align="right">Page 5 of 6</td></tr>
<tr><td colspan="3" align="center">Letter of Representation,
Quarterly Financial Sub Certification Process</td></tr>
<tr><td>Department Ownership</td><td align="center">Issue/Effective Date:</td><td align="right">Replaces previously issued</td></tr>
</table>

the financial information provided, (b) any violations of laws or regulations whose effects have not been considered for disclosure in the financial information provided or as a basis of recording a loss contingency, (c) any communications from regulatory agencies concerning noncompliance with or deficiencies in financial information provided, or (d) any failure to comply with contractual agreements where such failure would have a material effect on the financial information provided that has not been discussed or for which a provision has not been recorded.

5. I understand that, although I am not expected to have knowledge in relation to areas for which I am not responsible, this certification relates to any knowledge that I in fact have about the Company.

6. I am aware of no material transactions that have not been properly recorded in the accounting records. Furthermore, no material events have occurred subsequent to the period covered in this representation Letter that have not been appropriately disclosed but prior to the release of the 10Q. It is my responsibility to report the event(s) to the controller's office. With respect to the period between the date of this Letter and the date the Form 10Q is filed, communication of any material changes since the date of this representation letter should be provided to the controller's office immediately.

7. I sign this certification without qualification, except as may be indicated below: _____

_____

_____

B. For Financial Statement Subcertifiers (302 Disclosure Subcertification)

8. I have reviewed the relevant sections of the draft Quarterly Report on Form 10Q for the quarter ended (also browse the "Quarterly Report") that is to be filed with the SEC based on my area of responsibility and any other materials I believe to be relevant in providing this certification. In connection with preparation and/or review of the Quarterly Report, I have provided or caused to be provided for consideration for inclusion in the Quarterly Report all information that I believe may be material for purposes of disclosure in the Quarterly Report. To the best of my knowledge, the quarterly report does not contain any material misrepresentations or omit a material fact necessary to make the statements in the Quarterly Report not misleading.

9. I understand that the Chief Executive Officer, Chief Financial Officer, and other Company officers will rely on this certification to support their evaluation concerning the effectiveness of the Company's disclosure controls and procedures.

10. I sign this certification without qualification, except as may be indicated below: _____

_____

_____

	Policy and Procedures	
Procedure No. B34	Section: Accounting and Finance	Page 6 of 6
	Letter of Representation, Quarterly Financial Sub Certification Process	
Department Ownership	Issue/Effective Date:	Replaces previously issued

C. 404 Subcertification

11. I am responsible for establishing and maintaining adequate internal control over financial reporting in my area of responsibility (as defined above) to provide reasonable assurance regarding the reliability of financial reporting and the preparation of financial statements for external purposes in accordance with Generally Accepted Accounting Principles. The assertions made in this subcertification are to report changes internal control over financial reporting which have occurred during the Quarter ended.

12. I have received satisfactory answers to any questions I have raised (or have knowledge that were raised) that could have a potential financial statement impact or that could require disclosure in the financial statements except as noted below:

_____

_____

_____

13. I sign this subcertification without qualification, except as indicated below: _____

_____

_____

I <Name and Title> have reviewed the following sections <identify A, B, C sections that refer to you with a checkmark> with due diligence as these sections relate to <Area of Responsibility> and unless otherwise noted in the specified item numbers; I confirm that to the best of my knowledge, I am in compliance.

Signature:

_____   _____

Print   Signature

_____   _____

Title   Date of Representation (handwrite date)

Once completed retain a copy for your records and forward to the Internal Control function.

	Policy and Procedures	
Procedure No. B35	Section: Accounting and Finance	Page 1 of 4
	Payroll and Salary Expense	
Department Ownership	Issue/Effective Date:	Replaces previously issued

Prepared by: Approved by: Authorized by:
Date   Date   Date

Scope

This policy applies to all worldwide business units and locations. This policy applies to hourly and salary employees for standard wages, commissions, bonuses, and compensated absences.

Policy

It is IDÆAL LLP's (Company) policy to pay employees accurately, on a timely basis, and in compliance with all applicable laws and regulations of the jurisdictions where the company conducts business.

The Company pays employees according to their offer letter/wage contracts and calculates and records payroll (including payroll deductions) accurately and completely in the period the payroll/salary expense is incurred.

It is the Company's policy to accrue a liability when specific conditions are met for employees to receive compensation for future absences. Refer to the Compensated Absences policy and procedure.

Procedure

Wages and salaries are determined based on competitive comparisons, industry standards and local economic indicators. Payroll and salary baselines are generally established for the beginning of each fiscal year; however, changes may be initiated and approved during the year.

Salary expenses are planned as part of the annual planning process in accordance with the Financial Planning and Analysis guidance and include:

- Regular and overtime wages

- Commissions bonuses and awards

- Employer's portion of all taxes and benefits

- Other compensation as defined by income tax regulations, (e.g., tuition reimbursement)

Each employee provides information and direction for their discretionary withholding items. This information is retained and controlled within designated Human Resources (HR)/Payroll systems. HR must approve all changes to an individual's pay rate information and maintains control over employee master data.

<table>
<tr><td colspan="3" align="center">Policy and Procedures</td></tr>
<tr><td>Procedure No. B35</td><td align="center">Section: Accounting and Finance</td><td align="right">Page 2 of 4</td></tr>
<tr><td colspan="3" align="center">Payroll and Salary Expense</td></tr>
<tr><td>Department Ownership</td><td align="center">Issue/Effective Date:</td><td align="right">Replaces previously issued</td></tr>
</table>

Hourly paid employees are eligible to receive compensation for overtime worked in accordance with the HR policy and the planning guidance. The baseline hours worked varies by country (i.e., local regulations). Unless dictated by local laws and regulations, hourly employees are paid every two weeks.

Salaried employees are paid twice a month on or about the 15th and the last day of the month (unless dictated by local regulations) and receive their annual salary ratably over the year, based on 24 payroll checks per year.

Supplemental earnings such as commissions, bonuses, and awards are determined in accordance with Company policy and are subject to local and withholding tax. Supplemental earnings must be approved by HR and in accordance with the authorization/approval policy.

Salary expense as reported within the Company's reporting records is comprised of gross amounts paid to employees as well as the employer's portion for all taxes and benefits.

The Company's payroll cycle shall be consistent with its business needs and operations. Salary and Payroll expense accruals must be matched with the period the expense is incurred. If the last payroll run does not coincide with the last day of the month, a month-end accrual must be calculated, posted, and then reversed in the following accounting period.

For all employees, payroll is generated based on the information submitted through manual time sheets and time reporting systems. The supervisor or manager approves the time. The Payroll department processes the data or approves it for submission to an approved outside payroll service provider e.g., within the U.S. <insert vendor name> is used.

Whether internally or externally prepared, the related administration and recording of the transaction (i.e., establishing the expense and liability) for the applicable taxes and other withholding items must be performed.

- Tuition reimbursement. – Employees are provided the opportunity to participate in continuing education that maintains or improves the skills required in the course of their employment. The Payroll department processes tuition reimbursements as referenced in the tuition reimbursement policy, after receiving the approved and confirming documentation from HR. Tuition reimbursement is subject to withholding taxes.

- Lost checks. – Employees should report lost or otherwise missing checks to the Payroll department immediately so that a stop payment order and replacement check may be issued.

- Unclaimed checks. – As part of the monthly reconciliation process, a list of all unclaimed checks is forwarded to the employee's manager for follow-up. After 90 days a copy is sent to the accountant in charge of Abandoned Property; refer to the Escheat, Abandoned Property, and Unclaimed Checks policy and procedure.

The manager completes a Change in Human Resource (HR) Status form (see Exhibit) for changes to employee status, including hiring, promotions, change to departments or job position, pay

<table>
<tr><td colspan="3" align="center">**Policy and Procedures**</td></tr>
<tr><td>Procedure No. B35</td><td align="center">Section: Accounting and Finance</td><td align="right">Page 3 of 4</td></tr>
<tr><td colspan="3" align="center">**Payroll and Salary Expense**</td></tr>
<tr><td>Department Ownership</td><td align="center">Issue/Effective Date:</td><td align="right">Replaces previously issued</td></tr>
</table>

status, termination, or other change in employment. Employees completes the HR Status form for changes regarding changes to withholding taxes A change in status must be approved by an HR employee relationship manager, who then forwards it to the Payroll department.

Deferred Compensation Arrangements

If future compensation is contractually agreed, then the rules for accruing the liability must be followed. Refer to the Accrual policy and procedure. If the deferred compensation is likely to occur and is estimable, then it must be accrued for in the period the expense is incurred. Company is liable for the obligation, as the compensation is deemed earned. If the deferred compensation extends beyond one year, the amount to be accrued must be the present value of the estimated payments. If elements of current and future employment are present (i.e., deferred compensation is based on the employee's term of employment), only the portion attributable to the current service should be accrued.

If the aggregate of deferred compensation contracts with individual employees are equivalent to a pension plan, the contracts shall be accounted for in accordance with Accounting for Pension Plans.

Refer to the Accounting for Restructure and Reorganization policy and procedure if the deferred compensation is part of a company restructuring or reorganization program.

Controls/Areas of Responsibility

Employees are responsible for reviewing and verifying their pay remittance information and updating their personal information as necessary.

The Human Resources department is responsible for all employee-specific personal, salary, wage, and withholding information for retention within the employee's file.

The employee's Supervisor or Department manager must use the standard Change of Status form provided by HR for requesting changes to the employee's master data and/or payroll information.

The Payroll department reconciles changes in employee status to the master control report and the payroll register weekly. Differences are investigated and resolved.

A financial analyst for each business area/location is responsible for understanding the administrative responsibilities and accounting implications related to the processing of payroll and recording the salary expense.

Contact

Payroll

Policy and Procedures		
Procedure No. B35	Section: Accounting and Finance	Page 4 of 4
	Payroll and Salary Expense	
Department Ownership	Issue/Effective Date:	Replaces previously issued

Exhibit

Change in Status

Employee Name	Employee ID Number
Department	Date

Mark the changes that apply.

	Wage		Department
	Job Title		Transfer
	Change in Pay Rate		Change in Job Level/Promotion
	Family Information (e.g., Name, Address, Phone, Car)		Other: Explain

Identify or describe the current and new information.

Current Information/Description	New Information/Description

Employee Signature	Date
Manager Name (print)/Signature	Date

Once complete, forward to HR for processing.

HR Representative	Date
HR Opinion	

Employee completes the form and forwards to manager for approval, then the form is routed to HR where a copy is retained within the employee's file and copy is then forwarded to the Payroll Department.

Employee completes the form and forwards it to his/her manager for approval, and then the form is routed to HR where it is reviewed and approved. Once approved by HR, the employee's manager and the employee are notified and a copy is forwarded to Payroll with the original form retained with the employee's file in HR.

Internal Use Only

Policy and Procedures		
Procedure No. B36	Section: Accounting and Finance	Page 1 of 4
	Petty Cash	
Department Ownership	Issue/Effective Date:	Replaces previously issued

Prepared by: Approved by: Authorized by:
Date   Date   Date

Scope

Petty Cash funds allow cash to be made available to departments to facilitate cash payment for minor expenses while maintaining proper control. A Petty Cash fund must be used only for the purpose for which it is established.

The policy applies to all worldwide business units, functional Business areas, or departments that wish to establish and maintain a Petty Cash fund.

Policy

With the establishment of corporate credit cards and procurement cards, the Company discourages the establishment of Petty Cash funds. It is IDÆAL LLP's (Company) policy that, where appropriate, a Company location may request establishing an imprest Petty Cash fund (i.e., vouchers with receipts plus available cash must equal the fund amount) to be utilized for minor business expenses.

The Petty Cash fund **must** be maintained as cash on hand and **not** through the establishment of a local bank account. However, where available, it is preferable to use a corporate credit card, procurement card, or Check Request Form (reference Accounts Payable – Third Party Trade policy and procedure) where the expense recording flows directly through the appropriate accounts.

Corporate Treasury shall maintain an inventory list of all locations with Petty Cash funds and must approve the names of those assigned Petty Cash responsibilities. Replenishments to the fund follow the Accounts Payable-Third Party Trade policy and procedure.

Procedures

Establishing/Increasing the Fund

Requests to establish or increase the balance to a Petty Cash fund must be approved by Corporate Treasury and the Business Unit's or Area's Manager and Controller and processed through Accounts Payable. A Check Request Form including the following information must be completed and forwarded to Accounts Payable:

- Business Unit or functional Business Area Name/Department number

- Explanation as to why a Petty Cash fund is required and the anticipated types of reimbursements e.g., taxi, postage expense

	Policy and Procedures	
Procedure No. B36	Section: Accounting and Finance	Page 2 of 4
	Petty Cash	
Department Ownership	Issue/Effective Date:	Replaces previously issued

- Petty Cashier's name and contact information

- Where (i.e., the actual physical location) and how (e.g., locked box) the fund will be secured

- Gross amount requested for the fund

- Business Unit's or Area's Manager and Controller signatures and date

Unless otherwise approved by the Corporate Treasury, the fund must not be established for more than $200 USD and shall be designated to cover authorized out-of-pocket expenses and advances for **minor** business expenses. The local Controller must designate a Petty Cash Fund Cashier who is responsible for the control and disbursement of the fund. A control log must be established and must be maintained as a "checkbook," noting deposits and withdrawals (see Exhibit).

Advances/Reimbursements

Petty cash shall be used only when absolutely necessary, when immediate cash payment is required, and must not be used to circumvent proper purchasing or payment procedures.

Reimbursements must not be made for personal items, memberships, subscriptions, dues, furniture or equipment, payments for personal services, or travel advances. The fund shall not be used to cash personal checks or as advance loans.

The employee must submit a signed request for a petty cash reimbursement using an approved voucher (see Exhibit) and attach the original receipt or invoice, which contains the date, amount, and nature of the transaction. An employee must not approve his or her own petty cash transaction.

The Petty Cash Fund Cashier (Cashier) must review the request to ensure that the item is an allowable petty cash expense, enter the information into a log, retain the supporting voucher and documentation, and disburse the funds.

For advances or draws, the employee must attach the receipt for the items purchased and return any change to the Cashier within the next business day. A petty cash voucher must then be completed with the receipt attached.

Safeguarding the Asset

Petty cash funds and supporting documentation (vouchers, receipts) must be kept in a safe location (e.g., locked in a safe, vault, or desk drawer) and must not be commingled with any other funds. All suspected thefts must be treated confidentially (as there may be an ongoing investigation) and reported to the location manager and Corporate Security.

The local Controller, Internal Controls, and/or Internal Audit may audit Petty Cash funds at random times.

<table>
<tr><td colspan="3" align="center">**Policy and Procedures**</td></tr>
<tr><td>Procedure No. B36</td><td align="center">Section: Accounting and Finance</td><td align="right">Page 3 of 4</td></tr>
<tr><td colspan="3" align="center">**Petty Cash**</td></tr>
<tr><td>Department Ownership</td><td align="center">Issue/Effective Date:</td><td align="right">Replaces previously issued</td></tr>
</table>

At least monthly, the Cashier must reconcile the vouchers, receipts, and remaining funds to the log. At least quarterly, the local Controller shall review the petty cash log and validate the reconciliation.

Replenishment

The Petty Cash fund shall be replenished as frequently as required and must be replenished at each quarter-end. The reconciliation form must be completed and forwarded to Accounts Payable for processing together with the vouchers and receipts. Accounts Payable reserves the right to deny reimbursement for inappropriate expenditures.

A check is made out to the Cashier in an amount required to replenish the Petty Cash fund to its allowable level. The Cashier cashes the check and deposits the cash into the Petty Cash lockbox.

Closing the Fund

When the Business Unit's or Area's Manager and Controller deem that the fund is no longer required, instead of requesting replenishment, they must return all vouchers and remaining cash to Accounts Payable and notify Corporate Treasury that the Petty Cash fund has been closed.

Vouchers and cash shall be mailed by overnight shipment to Accounts Payable, where Accounts Payable will arrange to have the cash deposited into the Company bank account.

When there is a change in Cashiers, the Petty Cash fund must be reconciled and closed, with the new Cashier establishing a new fund in the new name.

Controls/Areas of Responsibility

Accounts Payable maintains the accounting journal entries and list of active Cashiers. Corporate Accounting reconciles the Petty Cash account monthly.

The Petty Cash Fund Cashier is responsible for the security of the fund and managing the fund, the activity log, supporting documentation, and reconciliation.

Accounts Payable must issue replenishment funds only with complete voucher documentation and fund reconciliation.

When reviewing or auditing a location, Internal Controls or Internal Audit should audit the Petty Cash fund and report the results to the Business Unit or Area Manager and Corporate Treasury.

Contact

Corporate Treasury

Policy and Procedures

Procedure No. B36	Section: Accounting and Finance	Page 4 of 4
	Petty Cash	
Department Ownership	Issue/Effective Date:	Replaces previously issued

Exhibit

Sample Petty Cash Log

1. The following sample setup must be used to keep track of transactions:

Location _____

Date	Description	Amount of Voucher (+ or −)	Running Balance
	Beginning Balance		

Prepared by:

Petty Cashier Name/Signature/Date _____

Reviewed by:

Controller/Signature/Date _____

2. The following sample voucher must be used when disbursing cash to employees:

Sample Reimbursement Voucher

Employee Name/Date _____

Department Name/Number _____

Charge General Ledger Code _____

Explanation of Expense (List separately and attach receipts)

Date	Description	Amount
	Total	$ xxx

Employee Signature _____

Petty Cashier Signature _____ **Date** _____

Policy and Procedures		
Procedure No. B37	Section: Accounting and Finance	Page 1 of 3
Physical Counts and Evaluation **for Inventory, Property, Plant and Equipment**		
Department Ownership	Issue/Effective Date:	Replaces any previously issued

Prepared by:	Approved by:	Authorized by:
Date	Date	Date

Scope

This policy and procedure applies to all worldwide entities and relates to inventory held for resale and fixed assets (i.e., property, plant and equipment; long-lived assets).

Policy

It is IDEAL LLP's (Company) policy to perform periodic counts and validate the accounting book value of inventory held for resale and property, plant and equipment (PP&E) assets according to the approved schedule.

It is Company policy that inventory held for resale be recorded within the financial records and valued in accordance with the inventory policy and procedure. It is Company policy that all Company-owned inventory (wherever it resides) must be reconciled to the Inventory and financial records.

It is the Company's policy that PP&E assets be recorded within the financial records and valued in accordance with the PP&E policy and procedure. It is Company policy that all Company-owned PP&E assets (wherever they reside) must be reconciled to the financial records.

Procedures

Inventory held for resale

Company-owned inventory relates to products held for resale and stored at warehouses or storage locations.

Inventory held for resale is generally produced and packaged by third-party vendors. To avoid warehousing excess inventory, the Company maintains a just-in-time inventory methodology. As inventory is received into the warehouse locations, it is charged to Cost of Goods Sold. Inventory is recorded at the actual cost of acquisition.

However, where appropriate, the Company warehouses inventory held for resale. Inventory movement is tracked using an inventory control management system. The inventory logistics manager arranges for physical inventory counts to be conducted so as to ensure that:

- All high-value inventories (i.e., top 10 percent of the inventory values) is physically counted and reconciled every quarter.

- Inventory at distribution sites is physically counted and reconciled at least once a year.

- Locations where a significant variance has occurred must use problem-solving techniques to identify and remediate the process that caused the discrepancy.

Policy and Procedures		
Procedure No. B37	Section: Accounting and Finance	Page 2 of 3
	Physical Counts and Evaluation **for Inventory, Property, Plant and Equipment**	
Department Ownership	Issue/Effective Date:	Replaces any previously issued

At least annually, using a fair market value methodology, the inventory is evaluated to determine if it is valued appropriately. If the value of the inventory on the Company's financial records exceeds the fair market value, the inventory values must be adjusted, with a loss recorded within the financial statements.

The business unit's controller must assess the inventory counts based on the forecasted product sales with excess and/or obsolete inventory disposed of and written off to the excess and obsolete reserve account.

PP&E (i.e., fixed assets) may be located within the Company's offices, warehouses, and distribution centers as well as remote (e.g., home) office locations.

After an initial baseline confirmation of the quantity and value of PP&E, selected samples representing at least one half of the asset base must be confirmed each year, so that at least every two years, the total PP&E population has been verified.

The functional area responsible for the asset as identified within the PP&E policy and procedure is responsible for monitoring and tracking asset movement.

Baseline Confirmation

Internal Audit establishes an approved physical inventory count plan which must be prepared for each PP&E asset classification. Asset type, location, and Company asset tag with identifying asset number must be logged into a database. The value of the asset is assigned based on the original documentation as to when the asset was acquired.

The asset record is validated within the asset database. Historic depreciation rates shall be used to reconcile the asset to its net book value.

Go-Forward Confirmation

After the baseline confirmation and on a go-forward basis, input to the PP&E asset database and asset tagging shall be confirmed at the point where the asset is received into a Company location (i.e., receiving dock, warehouse, and office).

As part of the annual planning cycle, each functional area prepares an asset verification plan including a methodology and schedule for tagging and conducting the physical count and investigating variances. Finance Planning and Analysis must approve and monitor the progress and results.

The Asset Verification plan shall indicate when and how at least one half of each asset category will be physically counted and reconciled to the asset database each year.

Because of the sensitive nature of the type of inventory and/or equipment, the physical count for inventory and PP&E held by Research, Development, and Engineering is the responsibility of Research, Development, and Engineering. However reconciliation rules apply.

The PP&E database retains a list of each asset through its asset life cycle that is, from the time the asset is installed and eligible for depreciation until the asset has been removed from Company use.

Policy and Procedures		
Procedure No. B37	Section: Accounting and Finance	Page 3 of 3
Physical Counts and Evaluation **for Inventory, Property, Plant and Equipment**		
Department Ownership	Issue/Effective Date:	Replaces any previously issued

For accounting purposes, each asset retains the date acquired, additions and/or adjustments to the asset's costs, accumulated depreciation, and remaining net book value. The asset should remains on the books until it has been sold, destroyed, or otherwise removed from active life.

Acquisitions

Inventory and PP&E acquired as part of a merger or acquisition must be 100 percent counted with values assigned within three months of the acquisition's becoming final. Assets must be tagged in accordance with the above procedure.

Physical County Discrepancies

Discrepancies include an over or under of the inventory count and/or the quality or usefulness of the assets and inventory. Discrepancies between the inventory records and the physical count must be recorded as in the period they become known.

Controls/Areas of Responsibility

Accounting procedures must be in accordance with U.S. Generally Accepted Accounting Principles (GAAP) and in compliance with the PP&E policy and procedure.

Employees who are responsible for the plan and implementation of the physical asset count should not be the same employees responsible for input, change to, or reconciliation of the asset database system.

Representatives from Internal Audit or Corporate accounting shall oversee the physical count process and ensure that the plan for the physical count is executed in a timely, accurate manner and the results are reconciled with the general ledger.

The plan and execution of the physical counts are the responsibility of the financial designate for that functional area e.g., real estate, facilities, furniture, and fixtures are coordinated by Facilities Finance; Information Technology (IT) equipment is coordinated by IT Finance.

The physical count for product inventory held for resale is the responsibility of the Indirect Sales Channel business unit and their financial designate.

On a go-forward basis, all PP&E assets capitalized must be tagged with an approved Company asset tag and must be counted at least every two years.

The functional business area where the asset is located is responsible for safeguarding the asset through the asset life cycle (e.g., from acquisition, repair and renovation, and disposition).

PP&E asset accounting is responsible for the accounting representation of the asset, including maintaining integrity in the asset's value, including the asset's accounting net book value.

Contacts

Corporate Accounting

	Policy and Procedures	
Procedure No. B38	Section: Accounting and Finance	Page 1 of 3
	Prepaid Assets/Expenses	
Department Ownership	Issue/Effective Date:	Replaces previous issue

Prepared by:	Approved by:	Authorized by:
Date	Date	Date

Scope

Because the Company uses an accrual method of accounting and in order to match expenses to the period in which they are incurred, assets or expenses that are paid in advance of their use may be classified as prepaid assets/expenses. Rent, insurance, interest, and advertising are examples of expenses that may be considered prepaid.

Policy

It is IDÆAL LLP's (Company) policy to recognize prepaid assets and expenses as prepayments made to secure the use of assets or the receipt of goods or services at a future date.

Prepaid Assets and expenses are generally recognized as current on the Balance Sheet and amortized to an expense account on a straight-line basis over the period in which the benefits are received. Proper documentation must be maintained for each item, with the account balance reconciled monthly.

In addition, the Company has established the following standards when recording Prepaid Assets and Expenses:

- Only valid asset and expense items shall be included as prepaid assets and expenses.

- Individual asset and expense items shall have a cost greater than $1,000 USD.

- Individual asset and expense items with costs less than $1,000 USD must be expensed as incurred.

- Corporate Accounting shall approve and maintain a list of those countries where the "above $1,000 rule" is not appropriate due to local laws, practices, or tax considerations.

The acquisition and payment of the prepaid asset or expense must be in compliance with the Procurement policy and procedure and the Accounts Payable policy and procedure.

Procedure

On occasion, because of industry norms and/or agreement terms and conditions, a prepayment of an asset of expense may be required.

Policy and Procedures		
Procedure No. B38	Section: Accounting and Finance	Page 2 of 3
	Prepaid Assets/Expenses	
Department Ownership	Issue/Effective Date:	Replaces previous issue

Each business area's Controller or financial designee is responsible for the identification and subsequent tracking of its respective prepaid asset/expenses. Once a prepaid asset or expense has been identified, the financial designate shall determine the portion of the amount paid that is prepaid. The balance in the prepaid asset or expense account is amortized to an expense account on a straight line basis over the period in which the benefits (services) are received.

> For example, if the Company pays its six-month insurance premium in advance, the amount recorded as prepaid after the first month would be five sixths of the premium.

> Unless otherwise approved amounts are charged to the Profit-and-Loss (P&L) accounts on a straight-line basis over the appropriate period.

> Another example, if the Company prepays for equipment that has not yet gone into service, and the equipment is NOT part of a work in progress project, then the equipment may be deemed a Prepaid Asset until it has gone into service at which time it will be capitalized as a Property, Plant and Equipment Asset.

The requesting and authorizing department must highlight and note the amount to be classified as prepaid asset/expense with the start and end dates for the prepaid period. Requests for a check or wire payment shall be submitted to Accounts Payable (A/P) for processing. Prepaid asset/expense amounts shall be properly recorded in a subledger at the time the expense is paid.

The Business Unit Controller or financial designee shall monitor the various types of prepaid asset/expenses and maintain a separate schedule of prepaid items to be reconciled with the general ledger each month.

Supporting documentation for the journal entry must be maintained, with a copy forwarded to A/P and should include (but is not limited to) the following:

- Description of the asset, service, or benefit

- Vendor and contact information

- Reference to approved purchase order

- Prepayment benefit period, with start and end dates of the prepayment

- Amount of the prepayment and the total amount to be paid

- Amortization method—straight line over the period unless otherwise approved by Corporate Accounting

- Formula controls to ensure that the prepaid account does not move into a negative position

- Any other pertinent information

Policy and Procedures		
Procedure No. B38	Section: Accounting and Finance	Page 3 of 3
	Prepaid Assets/Expenses	
Department Ownership	Issue/Effective Date:	Replaces previous issue

For financial integrity and accuracy, documentation and records retention standards apply to all prepaid journal entries. Documentation includes approved and appropriate backup to support the prepaid amount, (e.g., when the amount is obtained from another area of the business, support must be provided). Refer to the Records Information Management schedules to determine the record retention period.

Journal entries for prepaid assets/expenses shall be completed in accordance with the Company's Journal Entries and Non-Routine Transaction policy and monthly accounting close cycle.

In accordance with the Account Reconciliation policy and procedure, the Prepaid Asset and Expense balance must be reconciled each month.

Calculation and Amortization

The prepaid amount is determined based on the amount prepaid (including partial prepayments or deposits). Unless otherwise approved by the Chief Accounting Officer, the prepaid amount should be amortized over the expense period in equal (straight-line) amounts.

For rent and real estate prepayments, refer to the Capital, Operating Leases and Real Estate Rental Property policy and procedure.

Control/Areas of Responsibility

The requesting area and its regional controller are responsible for the accurate and timely recording of eligible prepaid assets/expenses.

Authorization and approvals for spending must be in accordance with approved spending limits. The purchase order must clearly indicate if the terms include prepayment or down payment arrangements.

Each business area's controller or financial designate shall reconcile and validate the monthly activity and closing balance of this account.

Accounting for prepaid assets/expenses shall be conducted in the most efficient and accurate way possible. Standard and/or recurring journal entries must be established whenever possible, in order to minimize the time spent processing routine entries.

Contact

Corporate Accounting
Accounts Payable

Policy and Procedures		
Procedure No. B39	Section: Accounting and Finance	Page 1 of 6
	Revenue Recognition	
Department Ownership	Issue/Effective Date:	Replaces previously issued

Prepared by: Date	Approved by: Date	Authorized by: Date

Scope

This policy sets forth the guidelines by which the Company recognizes revenue.

The Company generates revenue from the sale and licensing of products for use by Customers, and providing professional services, such as consulting and education. Sales are executed through the following channels: direct sales (i.e., through the Company's salespeople, telesales) and indirect sales (i.e., through Company-approved dealers and resellers).

The Company establishes a Customer Master sales agreement, then accepts Customer purchase orders as sales orders.

Policy

It is IDÆAL LLP's (Company) policy to recognize revenue according to U.S. Generally Accepted Accounting Principles (GAAP). It is the Company's policy that revenue will begin to be recognized in the financial statements when **all** of the following criteria for revenue recognition have been met:

1. Persuasive evidence of an arrangement exists (e.g., a contract duly signed by both the customer and the Company).

2. Delivery has occurred or services have been fully rendered, and risk of loss has been passed to the customer.

3. The sales price is fixed or determinable (e.g., no right to cancel or receive refunds for price or other concessions outside the Company's standard sales terms).

4. Collectibility of the sale is probable.

If any of the above criteria have not been met, revenue must be deferred until such time as the above criteria are all met.

Procedure

This procedure addresses the following topics:

*   Contracts and agreements

*   Each of the four revenue recognition criteria

*   Orders involving multiple elements

	Policy and Procedures	
Procedure No. B39	Section: Accounting and Finance	Page 2 of 6
	Revenue Recognition	
Department Ownership	Issue/Effective Date:	Replaces previously issued

Contracts and Agreements

In order for an agreement to be considered final, the following minimum evidence is required:

- A valid and approved Company sales contract, or once a customer master agreement is in place, the Company accepts the customer's purchase order for additional products and/or services
- Signed and dated by the Company and a recognized customer representative (i.e., who has authority to enter into a sales agreement)
- Contain specific information and detail as to the:
    - Products and/or services the Company shall provide to the customer, including delivery dates
    - Payment terms the customer shall provide to the Company, including a payment schedule

Additional information contained within the contract that may affect recognition of revenue includes but is not limited to:

- Specified future product deliverables
- Acceptance clauses
- Refunds and/or rebates on current or future products

There must be **no** side letters or agreements. Any non-Company standard terms and conditions must be approved by Corporate Legal and Corporate Finance.

Pricing models and payment terms and conditions may affect the ability to recognize revenue. Therefore, the Company treats the pricing and discounting of products and services separately from the terms the customer negotiates to pay for the product. Depending on specific sales terms and conditions, the Company may not be able to recognize revenue in the period the sale is enacted.

If in doubt, contact the Chief Accounting Officer for clarification as to when revenue is eligible for recognition.

Products Sold through the Direct or Indirect Business Channel

The Company sells products to customers and distributors. Sales are recognized when the customer assumes the rights and privileges of ownership and the above four criteria above are met. Sales are generally considered final, with customers having a limited "right of return or exchange."

Policy and Procedures		
Procedure No. B39	Section: Accounting and Finance	Page 3 of 6
	Revenue Recognition	
Department Ownership	Issue/Effective Date:	Replaces previously issued

Generally, sales to distributors include an extended accounts receivable payment term (see the Collectability section); to allow for the sale to pass through to end-user customers.

Reseller arrangements generally use the Company's products within their own product or as a supplement to selling their own products. Therefore, depending on the type of Reseller Agreement, the sale may be reflected as a product sale or, more often, a license or right to use the product. Reseller Agreements are generally negotiated as royalty agreements.

Professional Services Sold through the Direct or Indirect Business Channel

Revenue from professional service arrangements (i.e., consulting and/or education) is generally recognized as the services are performed and in accordance with the terms of the sales contract. The standard accounting methods of revenue recognition on professional service contracts are:

- Time- and material-based engagements where revenue is recognized as time is incurred.

- Fixed-price engagements where revenue is recognized on a percentage-of-completion or completed-contract method.

Travel expenses associated with the delivery of professional services and billed to the client shall be reported as other revenue.

Revenue associated with professional services delivered by subcontractors are generally reported net revenue of what the Company billed the customer and the cost of the subcontractor.

As each contract/agreement is reviewed and approved by the Company, a contract review checklist documents the various clauses to determine if and when revenue may be recognized according to the four criteria.

According to generally accepted accounting principles the following four criteria are required to be met before revenue can be recognized:

1. Persuasive evidence that an arrangement exists

2. Delivery has occurred

3. The sales price is fixed or determinable

4. Collectability is reasonably assured

1. Persuasive evidence of an arrangement. Revenue shall be recognized only upon receipt of a contract signed by both the customer and the Company. *Note:* The contract may be labeled Contract, Document of Understanding, or Statement of Work.

The customer/client must **sign** the contract and the company must accept the contract no later than the last calendar day of the month if the revenue is to be considered in that month's revenue.

Policy and Procedures		
Procedure No. B39	Section: Accounting and Finance	Page 4 of 6
	Revenue Recognition	
Department Ownership	Issue/Effective Date:	Replaces previously issued

The contract must actually be received and countersigned by a Company authorized signatory prior to midnight on the last day of the calendar month.

Contracts must indicate a contract start date (i.e., commencement date), which must be effective at or prior to the month-end for which the contract is booked.

Side letters or other written or verbal terms are not permitted as amendments or additions to the approved contract.

2.   Delivery has occurred. For revenue to be recognized within a given month, the products and/or software must actually ship (or be delivered electronically) as identified within the contract to the customer site or customer-specified location no later than the last day of the month. Refer to Shipping Terms below.

Acceptance Clause

Generally, any acceptance clause requires that the revenue be deferred until the acceptance clause has been deemed complete and the customer has "accepted" the product, software, or service. Therefore, any type of customer acceptance clause must be reviewed and approved by the Corporate Controller.

"Acceptance" language identifies that the sale is conditional on the customer's acceptance of the product and/or service and generally is applicable only when the installation/implementation project is complete.

The Company does not include "acceptance language" within standard contract terms and conditions, except for government contracts. If "acceptance" language is included as part of the customer's sales order or contract standard terms and conditions, it must be explicitly waived in the body of the contract. If it is not waived, revenue cannot be recognized until the Company receives written confirmation that acceptance has occurred. If uncertainty exists about customer acceptance, the delivery criteria have **not** been met.

Future Deliverables

No reference to future concessions or contingencies (including additional product features and functionality to be developed or delivered) should be written into the contract. This is considered a future deliverable and eliminates the ability to recognize the agreement and/or establish a service project until all future concessions or contingencies have been delivered or until the customer's ability to exercise the option has expired.

Software licenses generally include the ability to upgrade to a new version of a product. Upgrades are not considered a new product and therefore should not be considered a future deliverable.

Policy and Procedures		
Procedure No. B39	Section: Accounting and Finance	Page 5 of 6
	Revenue Recognition	
Department Ownership	Issue/Effective Date:	Replaces previously issued

For arrangements that include beta products (i.e., those products not made generally available to the public), revenue must be deferred until the product becomes generally available.

Shipping Terms

The Company's standard shipping terms are FOB Shipping Point (i.e., the product title and risk passes to the customer when the product leaves the Company's distribution center). If the terms are changed to FOB Destination, delivery is deemed to be complete when the product is received by the client and the Company receives "proof" that delivery has occurred.

3.   Sales price is fixed or determinable when the customer's payment obligation is unconditional. This means that there must be **no contingency** language, for example, subject to legal approval or approval of the board of directors, options to cancel or extend the use of a product, provisions for refunds.

Fiscal funding clauses refer to returning the product or canceling the contract if/when funding is no longer available. Fiscal funding clauses are accepted only for government contracts.

Orders Involving Multiple Elements

Orders involving multiple elements include orders for Company products and/or professional services and where the price to the customer is quoted as a bottom-line amount (i.e., price of the individual multiple elements are not identified).

As long as the multiple elements are signed at the same time, are fully committed (e.g., no opportunity for product substitution or discounts on future products), and satisfy U.S. GAAP criteria, the revenue may be recognized up front; otherwise, the revenue must be ratably recognized over the longest committed term of the multiple elements.

The value assigned to each element of a multiple element contract is based on Vendor-Specific Objective Evidence (VSOE). Unless otherwise known (i.e., documented from previous sales), the overall contract discount percent is applied to each element's list price.

4.   Collectibility of the sale is probable. The Company's standard payment terms are net 30 days; extensions require Regional Controller approval. Refer to the Accounts Receivable: Third-Party Trade and Customers—Credit, Collection, and Cash Applications policy and procedure.

Collectibility must be reasonably assured; therefore, sales to delinquent or slow-paying customers may require revenue recognition to be deferred until such time as it is reasonably assured of being collected. The Corporate controller must approve revenue recognition for customers who are delinquent or slow paying.

Special situations and/or clauses which are not addressed in this policy and procedure requirement assessment and approval by the Corporate Controller and/or the Chief Accounting Officer.

	Policy and Procedures	
Procedure No. B39	Section: Accounting and Finance	Page 6 of 6
	Revenue Recognition	
Department Ownership	Issue/Effective Date:	Replaces previously issued

Controls/Areas of Responsibility

In accordance with the Account Reconciliation policy, all balance sheet accounts must be reconciled monthly. Full reconciliations must be performed in the middle month of the quarter, with roll-forward reconciliations including opening balances required for the other months.

A revenue recognition checklist that corresponds to the Company's standard terms and conditions and the revenue recognition criteria must be completed and attached to the Company's contract documentation for **all** sales orders before revenue is recognized.

For professional service contracts, a percent of completion worksheet must support the revenue to be recognized and attached to the contract documentation.

Documentation must be retained in accordance with the records information management schedule. Documentation is required to support the complete audit trail from contract and order to collection. Sales Finance must ensure that documentation related to the above procedures are retained for reconciliation, control, and audit purposes. Documentation includes and is not limited to:

- A signed contract, agreement, and schedules
- Shipping schedule and proof of delivery (if applicable)
- Pricing and discount analysis
- Billing and payment schedules
- Customer/client creditworthiness documents

Contacts

Corporate Controller

Chief Accounting Officer

Policy and Procedures		
Procedure No. B40	Section: Accounting and Finance	Page 1 of 3
	Source and Use of Exchange Rates	
Department Ownership	Issue/Effective Date:	Replaces previously issued
Prepared by: Date	Approved by: Date	Authorized by: Date

Scope/Background

The following establishes the responsibility and procedure for defining and using various exchange rates when reporting non-U.S. currency transactions. Also included are the guidelines for complying with Financial Accounting Standard (FAS) No. 52, "Accounting for Foreign Currency Translation."

This policy and procedure applies to all worldwide business units and locations.

Policy

IDÆAL LLP (Company) has designated Corporate Treasury as the sole resource for providing currency exchange rates for use in financial transactions and reporting, and Corporate Accounting has the responsibility to input the exchange rates into the accounting system. Company subsidiaries use the exchange rates provided to translate local currency transactions into U.S. dollars (USD).

It is the Company's policy to recognize exchange gains and losses in accordance with U.S. Generally Accepted Accounting Principles (GAAP) and in the period they occur.

Procedures

The following definitions refer to this topic and may be used within the document:

- **Exchange rates** are defined as a rate where one unit of currency can be exchanged or converted into another currency. Exchange rates are an expression of the amount of one unit of currency it would take to equal one unit of another currency.

- **Foreign (includes Non-U.S.) currency** is the functional currency of the legal subsidiary being referred.

- **Foreign currency transactions** arise when a parent or subsidiary:

    1. Buys or sells goods or services whose prices are denominated in a foreign currency other than its designated reporting currency,

    2. Borrows or lends funds, and the amounts payable or receivable are denominated in a foreign currency,

    3. Is a party to a foreign currency spot rate or forward option contract, or

    4. For other reasons acquires or disposes of assets or incurs or settles liabilities denominated in a foreign currency.

Policy and Procedures		
Procedure No. B40	Section: Accounting and Finance	Page 2 of 3
	Source and Use of Exchange Rates	
Department Ownership	Issue/Effective Date:	Replaces previously issued

- **Foreign currency translation** refers to the process used to express functional currency i.e., non-U.S. financial statements into the reporting currency i.e., U.S. dollars (USD).

- **Functional currency** is defined by FAS 52 as the currency of the primary economic environment in which that subsidiary operates i.e., the currency of the environment in which the subsidiary primarily generates and expends cash.

- **Revaluation** is part of the consolidation process where any transaction denominated in other than the reported currency is remeasured into the parent company's reporting currency.

Exchange rates are used in converting transactions for representation within the Company's financial statements. The Company calculates and uses the following exchange rates:

1. **Income Statement or Profit-and-Loss Statement (P&L) rate** refers to a 30-day average of daily spot rates used to translate the foreign currency P&L for the period into U.S. dollars. This rate is gathered as daily spot rates quoted in the *Wall Street Journal* using a simple average and is averaged for the month. The current period's Income Statement is translated at the previous month's average P&L exchange rate.

2. **Product and professional service pricing rate** refers to a three-month average of P&L rates. In order to minimize insignificant fluctuations this rate may be updated quarterly when there is a plus or minus five percent movement from the previously issued pricing rate.

3. **Statement of Financial Position, Balance Sheet (B/S) rate** is determined using the last day of the month's spot rate and is used when translating the foreign currency B/S into USD. The spot rate is taken from the last day of the month's P&L input.

4. **Spot rate** certain individual transactions (e.g., intercompany loans, funding, and intercompany payments) are transacted at the actual bank rate used to acquire the specific funds. Corporate Treasury provides this rate confirmation as required on a transaction-by-transaction basis.

5. **Plan or budget rates** are the forward-looking exchange rates used when translating the Income Statement and Balance Sheet for plan and forecast purposes. Plan or budget exchange rates are communicated with plan guidance. The plan rate is based on the product and service pricing rate and includes management discretion. Once established, the plan or budget exchange rates are not changed during the planning year. Plan variances due to exchange differences shall be calculated and documented.

Once the exchange rates have been compiled from the independent published sources, the rates are input to the accounting system and made available to the company's worldwide financial community.

Corporate Accounting reviews the rates and prepares an upload file to the consolidation database. Corporate Accounting verifies that the upload is complete and accurate.

<table>
<tr><td colspan="3" align="center">**Policy and Procedures**</td></tr>
<tr><td>Procedure No. B40</td><td align="center">Section: Accounting and Finance</td><td align="right">Page 3 of 3</td></tr>
<tr><td colspan="3" align="center">**Source and Use of Exchange Rates**</td></tr>
<tr><td>Department Ownership</td><td align="center">Issue/Effective Date:</td><td align="right">Replaces previously issued</td></tr>
</table>

Subsidiaries and non-U.S. countries submit their monthly results in local currency to Corporate Accounting. As part of the consolidation process, Corporate Accounting converts individual country results from local currency to USD; subsidiary and country controllers are responsible for verifying that the exchange used for their transactions is reasonable and accurate.

FAS 52 Exchange Gains/Losses

In accordance with FAS 52, "Accounting for Foreign Currency Translations," exchange gains/losses occur when the subsidiaries' accounting records that are denominated in other than the reporting currency and are translated into the reporting currency as part of the month-end consolidation process.

The Income Statement is translated at the P&L rate. Assets and liabilities are translated at the B/S rate, with the equity components translated at historic (i.e., carryforward) rates.

As part of the consolidation process, U.S. exchange gains and losses are determined and recorded by Corporate Accounting as an other income/expense on the P&L.

The final translation (of the B/S) adjustment is accumulated as a separate component within equity and reported in the Cumulative Translation Account (CTA).

Controls/Areas of Responsibility

- Corporate Treasury is responsible for issuing exchange rates as per the methodology above and secured from an independent, published source.

- Corporate Accounting is responsible for:

  - Reviewing the rates and posting (uploading) the rates into the consolidation database

  - Validating the rates to ensure that the posting of the rates was done accurately

- The local subsidiary and country controllers are responsible for checking the specific exchange rates used by their subsidiary. If errors are noted, Corporate Accounting shall be notified to investigate and correct as necessary.

- Treasury and Corporate Accounting must approve exceptions to these rates.

Contacts

Corporate Treasury
Corporate Accounting

	Policy and Procedures	
Procedure No. B41a	Section: Accounting and Finance	Page 1 of 4
	Travel, Entertainment, and Expense	
Department Ownership	Issue/Effective Date:	Replaces previously issued

Prepared by:
Date

Approved by:
Date

Authorized by:
Date

Scope

Since the maximum travel cost savings result from trip avoidance, it is the responsibility of all employees to conscientiously avoid unnecessary business travel by first exhausting the alternatives. Virtual communication (e.g., teleconferencing, webex) should be considered as a substitute for travel.

The Company strives to:

- Provide all travelers with a clear and consistent understanding of the Company's business Travel, Entertainment, and Expense (T&E) policies and associated procedures.

- Provide business travelers with a reasonable level of service, safety, and comfort at the lowest possible cost.

- Maximize the Company's ability to negotiate discounted rates with preferred suppliers, thereby reducing travel expenses.

Policy

It is IDÆAL LLP's (Company) policy to reimburse employees for valid expenses that are required and necessary for business operations, approved by management, and in compliance with regional guidelines and as described within the Travel, Entertainment, and Expense Manual (separate document). In addition to this policy and procedure, local country laws and regulations apply.

Regional and/or Business Unit guidelines may be more restrictive than the U.S. guidelines but not less.

- U.S. employees and those who travel within the United States must refer to the Travel, Entertainment, and Expense Manual.

- Europe, Asia, South America, and other regional employees may contact the regional general manager for specific guidelines.

It is Company policy to restrict the number of employees traveling together on the same airline. Restrictions on airline travel include:

- No more than four Senior Vice Presidents (SVP) or higher-ranking officials may travel on the same aircraft.

	Policy and Procedures	
Procedure No. B41a	Section: Accounting and Finance	Page 2 of 4
	Travel, Entertainment, and Expense	
Department Ownership	Issue/Effective Date:	Replaces previously issued

- Any waiver to this policy for large events such as the annual sales conference may be granted only by the Chief Executive Officer (CEO) or SVP Sales and the Chief Financial Officer (CFO).

- Employees shall use regularly scheduled airline service. Use of chartered aircraft (including helicopters) and other non-regularly scheduled air transportation service must be avoided. In instances where use of chartered aircraft is requested, a minimum of one week's advance written approval is required from the Company's global Insurance/Risk Manager and CEO. In addition, any such preapproved charter **must** be arranged **only** through the Company's senior Corporate travel specialist. **Use of Company aircraft is *strictly controlled* and *must* be approved by the CEO.**

- An employee may not fly in an aircraft owned or operated by him/her or by any member of his/her household while traveling on Company business.

- Employees may not pilot, operate, or act as a crewmember of, any aircraft while on Company business.

On occasion and only to support client (i.e., end-user customer) need, T&E expenses may be applicable to nonemployees. Non-Company employees are subject to the parameters and limits as described within the T&E policy and procedure manual. In addition to line management, non-Company employee T&E claims must also be approved by the general manager of the business unit. Regional controllers must confirm the accounting treatment for such non-Company employee T&E.

Procedures

Annual T&E Plan

By using the annual planning guidance issued by Financial Planning and Analysis, each department or cost center must plan an annual T&E budget. The annual budget should be determined using historical T&E activity, future anticipated activity, and management discretion. Actual to plan T&E spending must be monitored and managed, with significant over-/underspending and/or expense timing differences explained to Financial Planning and Analysis and reflected within the quarterly forecasts.

Corporate Credit Card Program

Where applicable, eligible employees shall use the Procurement Card (P-Card) or Corporate Credit Card rather than file claims through the T&E process. For additional information on the P-Card refer to the Procurement policy and procedure, and for the Corporate Credit Card refer to the T&E Manual.

	Policy and Procedures	
Procedure No. B41a	Section: Accounting and Finance	Page 3 of 4
	Travel, Entertainment, and Expense	
Department Ownership	Issue/Effective Date:	Replaces previously issued

Approval

Employees planning a business trip or other expense must secure proper approval from their line management. To claim T&E reimbursement, the line manager or a delegate shall review and approve all claims.

Once it is determined that a trip is necessary, it is Company policy to provide equitable standards, control costs, and ensure consistent and fair treatment of all individuals who travel on Company business. An individual should neither gain nor lose personally because he or she has incurred reasonable business expenses.

The T&E Manual references this policy and procedure and contains details as to the items and amounts that may and may not be included for travel and expense reimbursements. The Company assumes no obligation to reimburse employees for expenses that are not in compliance with this policy. Employees who willfully disregard this policy may be subject to disciplinary action up to and including termination of employment.

Eligible Expenses

Only authorized reasonable and necessary business expenses will be considered for reimbursement. Employees issued a corporate credit card must use it for all business travel expenses for which the corporate card is accepted, and must use the receipts as backup for their expense reimbursement.

Reimbursement

All travel-related expenses incurred by individual employees must be reported either with the manual form (Exhibit) or through a Company-approved designated payment system.

Expenses paid in foreign currencies shall be converted per the actual or an average exchange rate received at time of conversion for the trip, and such documentation must be submitted with the expense report. Credit card expenditures shall be converted at the exchange rate charged by the credit card company, and a copy of the invoice or credit card statement must be provided to support the conversion rate used.

Employees should complete a T&E report within 30 days for expenses incurred on company business. Expense reports submitted after 30 days must also be approved by the business unit's business and finance manager. Expense reports older than 90 days may not be honored.

Accrual

When the employee has incurred T&E expenses and the expense reimbursement has not been processed by the end of the accounting period, the employee must notify their supporting accounting manager that the expense has been incurred and must be accrued in accordance with the Company's Accrual policy.

Policy and Procedures		
Procedure No. B41a	Section: Accounting and Finance	Page 4 of 4
	Travel, Entertainment, and Expense	
Department Ownership	Issue/Effective Date:	Replaces previously issued

Employee Termination

All T&E claims must be submitted and be processed prior to the employee leaving the company. On their last day of employment, employees leaving the Company must relinquish their corporate card, at which time the card will be destroyed and the account canceled. Remaining charges not claimed and accepted as T&E are the employee's responsibility to resolve.

Controls/Areas of Responsibility

Reimbursement is issued only to valid and active Company employees.

Corporate Procurement is responsible for updating this policy and negotiating all travel-related contracts and for the relationship between the Company and the travel vendor. It assists Accounts Payable with interpreting the travel and expense manual and resolving questions or disputes.

Accounts Payable is responsible for processing reimbursements, auditing travel expense reports, and serving as liaison between the Company's employees and payment system provider.

Vice presidents/directors/managers are responsible for approving international and domestic travel before it occurs, overseeing the management of their division's travel expense, and ensuring that each employee is thoroughly familiar with this policy and complies with it. Managers are responsible for reviewing and approving expense reports, identifying fraudulent activity, and initiating the necessary actions for investigation and disciplinary action.

Contacts

T & E Manager
Accounts Payable

IDÆAL LLP

Travel, Entertainment, and Expense Manual

CONTENTS

TRAVEL, ENTERTAINMENT, AND EXPENSE
POLICY AND PROCEDURE MANUAL

OVERVIEW

Since the maximum travel cost savings result from trip avoidance, it is the responsibility of all employees to conscientiously avoid unnecessary business travel by first exhausting the alternatives. Teleconferencing is the primary alternative to travel that must be considered, in the following order of preference:

- Audio or teleconferencing

- Web conferencing

- Videoconferencing

However, once it is determined that a trip is necessary, IDÆAL LLP (Company) seeks to provide equitable standards, control costs, and ensure consistent and fair treatment of all individuals who travel on Company business. An individual should neither gain nor lose personally because he or she has incurred reasonable business expenses.

This Manual is an addendum to the Company's Travel, Entertainment, and Expense (T&E) policy and procedure. This Manual provides additional detail of the Company's T&E policy and procedure to employees who incur reimbursable business travel, entertainment, and expenses on the Company's behalf.

Dollars quoted are in U.S. dollars and should be converted at an approved country exchange rate (e.g., plan and budget exchange rate).

Objectives

The objective of this Manual is to:

- Provide travelers with a clear and consistent understanding of the Company's business T&E procedures and acceptable reimbursement.

- Provide business travelers with a reasonable level of service, safety, and comfort at the lowest possible cost.

- Maximize the Company's ability to negotiate discounted rates with preferred suppliers, thereby reducing travel expenses.

Regional and/or business unit guidelines may be more restrictive than this Manual but not less.

Scope

The T&E Manual applies to all Company employees, including all Senior Executives. Senior Executives must use prudent judgment and may make alternative arrangements as long as the arrangements and reimbursements are approved by the Chief Financial Officer (CFO) or General Counsel.

The policy, procedure, and Manual shall be communicated to all employees, consultants, and company vendors who travel on Company business. Unless otherwise approved by the unit's business and financial manager reimbursement for non-Company employees will be the same as for employees.

The following does not apply to those requesting reimbursement for relocation, moving and living, tuition, and international assignments.

The following may vary for those who work remotely and/or are field personnel whose job requires that they work at non-Company or customer locations for extended periods.

Assistance

You may direct questions, concerns, or suggestions regarding this manual to:

- Corporate Procurement, Director of Travel <phone, e-mail>

- Accounts Payable (A/P), Manager for Travel Administration, <phone, e-mail>

- Safety and Security, <travel emergency hotline, phone, e-mail>

Responsibility and Enforcement

Corporate Procurement is primarily responsible for managing the Company's corporate travel program, updating this policy, and negotiating all travel supplier contracts. It also assists Accounts Payable (A/P) with policy interpretation and the resolving of questions and disputes.

Negotiations with vendors, including but not limited to airlines, hotels, and car rental agencies, are the responsibility of the Procurement department.

Regional i.e., North America (NA), Europe Middle East and Africa (EMEA), Asia Pacific and Japan (APJ) Latin America (LA) Procurement representatives are responsible for managing the Company's travel program locally. Regional Procurement representatives assist A/P with interpretation and the resolving of questions and disputes.

A/P is responsible for reimbursement compliance, providing interpretation, resolving questions and disputes, auditing, and processing T&E reimbursement requests. A/P serves as the liaison between Company employees, and Company-approved vendors who provide service e.g., travel agency, credit card company, reimbursement service provider.

Vice Presidents/Directors/Managers are responsible for approving international and domestic travel before it occurs, overseeing the management of their organization's travel expense, ensuring that each employee is thoroughly familiar with this manual and for reviewing and approving expense reimbursement requests (also known as expense reports). Managers are responsible for identifying fraudulent activity and initiating the necessary actions for investigation and disciplinary action.

Employees are responsible for complying with the policy, procedure, this Manual and process for reimbursement. Employees must use common sense and good judgment in spending the Company's money while conducting authorized Company business. Employees shall be reimbursed for all reasonable and necessary expenses.

Analysis and reports will be produced and circulated identifying travelers who fail to book their travel through a Company-approved travel agency, fails to book the appropriate airfare, hotel, or rental car rate and/or otherwise do not comply with the policies or procedures identified within this Manual.

The Company assumes no obligation to reimburse employees for expenses that are not in compliance with this manual. Employees who willfully disregard the guidelines may be subject to disciplinary action up to and including termination of employment.

Corporate Credit Card

Those who travel on Company business at least three times per year are recommended to apply for the Corporate credit card (Card). Others may apply for the Card, which requires management approval. There is no application cost or annual fee to the employee. It is primarily a corporate-sponsored personal liability program.

Note: **No personal expenses are to be charged to the Card. Failure to use the Card in accordance with this procedure may result in disallowance of the incurred expenses.**

Employees may participate in the Card Membership Rewards Program, but the membership dues are a nonreimbursable expense.

If there are Company locations that do not have the Company Credit Card Program implemented, employees will be reimbursed using their own credit cards. All other T&E and reimbursement guidelines apply.

Reservations

The Company has contracted with <ABC> Travel Agency (Agency) to be its primary provider of travel reservation services worldwide. This is to assure that all employees benefit from a consistently high level of authorized service at negotiated rates, Therefore, worldwide employees are required to use the Agency for booking reservations, including air travel, lodging, car rental, and rail reservations (limousine reservations may be made directly with the limousine companies), including en route changes. Travel arrangements booked through another travel agency, public Internet sites, or by any other means may not be reimbursed.

Travelers must book their travel as far in advance as possible (i.e., preferably at least 14 days in advance) to secure lower airfares and hotel rates. Airlines and hotels utilize sophisticated yield management software and third-party services, so prices may increase as the travel date approaches.

Traveler Profiles

For the purpose of providing optimum reservation services, the Company and the Agency maintain online traveler profiles that contain relevant personal information, including traveler type, addresses, phone numbers, credit card numbers, frequent flyer numbers, airline seating preferences, special needs, and other preferences. It is the traveler's responsibility to update his or her profile when there is a change in personal data. Personal preferences that you indicate must fall within the provisions of this travel manual. Traveler profiles are subject to the Company's privacy rules, and shall be kept confidential.

Leisure/Vacation Travel Arrangements

The Company's partnership with the Agency and other vendors has been established to service the Company's corporate business travel needs only. Agencies may require a separate traveler profile for leisure, vacation, and personal travel arrangements.

Spouse/Companion Travel

The Company will not reimburse travel expenses incurred by a spouse or other individual accompanying an employee on business unless there is a bona fide business purpose for taking the spouse or other individual.

Expense Allocation

Expenses must be claimed after a trip and accounted for in the traveler's own cost center. In exceptional circumstances, if a subsidiary agrees to pick up an expense for a traveler, it must be accounted for in that subsidiary's books and not cross-charged as an Intercompany Transaction.

SAFETY AND SECURITY

As a global company, when conducting business in countries where cultural and environmental conditions differ, familiarize yourselves not only with customs, climate, and currency of countries to be visited, but also risks associated with travel.

Any trip to be taken through or near countries where war is in progress or anticipated must be reported to the Company's Insurance and Risk Manager and the employee must provide a list of the countries to be visited and visitation dates (this is for insurance purposes only).

From time to time, the Company may issue travel advisories. Employees must follow travel advisories or other communications issued by the Global Safety department.

Employees should keep a copy of personal information, passport, and visa documentation in a suitcase and leave a copy with your manager or designate. This will assist in expediting the issuance of a temporary passport/visa while abroad should your passport get lost/stolen while traveling.

Safety hints:

- Be vigilant against pickpockets and petty thieves; do not leave your passport in your luggage or in your hotel room.
- Use hotel safes and other protective arrangements.
- Check security requirements prior to departure so that you are not delayed.

Health

Please investigate if there are any documented health concerns for the country or region to which you are traveling.

The Company's basic insurance program covers employees traveling abroad who may require medical attention. In the event that medical attention is required, arrange for the necessary medical care, then contact the benefits hotline for assistance in getting the claim reimbursed.

AIR TRAVEL

Authorized airline class of service is based on the employee's level and the duration of the flight.

Traveler Category	Flight Duration	Policy Fare
All employees	Less than 6 hours	Coach (economy)
	6 hours or more	Business class

Notes:

1. All international (i.e., between countries) trips must be preapproved by your manager.

2. Requests for upgrades to a higher class of service for medical reasons must be supported by a note from the employee's doctor and approved in writing by a senior vice president (SVP). Copies of the approval must be forwarded to the director of Travel Administration before the trip is booked.

3. Any exceptions to the above class-of-service policy must be preapproved, in writing, by a senior president or Executive Leader. Each individual exception must be approved—no blanket exceptions may be granted (except in the case of a documented chronic medical condition).

Restrictions on Airline Travel

Where feasible and unless otherwise approved:

- No more than four Sr. VP or higher ranking officers may travel on the same flight.

- No more than four key employees from the same department may travel on the same flight.

- No more than 12 employees may travel on the same flight.

- Employees are to use regularly scheduled airline service. Use of chartered aircraft (including helicopters) is strictly **prohibited.** In rare instances, chartered aircraft may be used only with the advance approval of the Company's Insurance and Risk Manager and the Company's CEO. In addition, any such preapproved charter **must** be arranged **only** through Corporate Travel.

- An employee may not fly in an aircraft owned or operated by him/her or by any member of his/her household while traveling on Company business.

- Employees may not pilot, operate, or act as a crewmember of any aircraft while on Company business.

Airfare

The Company has contracts with several major airlines under which it receives substantial discounts. Travel counselors are conversant with the contracts, and the discounts are loaded into the reservation system. Accordingly, employees must accept the lower applicable airfare as offered by the self-booking tool or travel counselors, subject to the following parameters:

- The Company's preferred airlines must be used.

- Penalty and nonrefundable fares must be used and **booked as soon as your travel plans are firm** if the fare offered is the most cost effective. Timing is vital, as substantial savings are available on tickets purchased at least seven 7 to 14 days in advance. The cost of changing a restricted ticket is often significantly less than the difference in cost between it and an unrestricted ticket, and a nonrefundable ticket can be used by the same individual for future travel in the event the original trip has to be canceled—but only if it is changed before the original travel date.

- To secure a lower airfare cost, use of alternative airports may be considered.

The Company strongly encourages the consideration of cost saving options, but leaves it to the individual traveler's discretion, based on the particular needs of the trip, whether or not to accept them.

Failure to utilize the lower fare and/or to fly on a preferred airline as defined above may result in nonreimbursement of incremental airline ticket costs above the fare that was declined.

Saturday Night Stayover

To provide overall savings to the Company, employees may, at their discretion, opt for a discounted airfare that requires a Saturday night stayover. The Company will reimburse the normal expenses of lodging, local transportation, breakfast, lunch, and dinner (but **not** entertainment), **provided these additional expenditures are significantly less than the airfare savings.**

Airline Frequent Flyer Programs/Upgrades

In recognition of the extra effort put forth by employees when traveling away from home, the Company allows individuals to retain frequent flyer benefits for use at their discretion. Participation in such programs must not influence flight selection that would result in incremental cost to the Company beyond the lower applicable fare as defined above.

Employees may opt to use frequent flyer mileage, points, or awards to upgrade from an authorized class of service to a higher class of service when traveling for the Company, provided this is consistent with obtaining the lower applicable fare. However, if there is a monetary cost in upgrading, or if a higher, more readily upgradeable, fare would be required, such costs are not reimbursable.

Any membership dues in frequent flyer programs are a personal expense.

Airline Club Memberships

The Company will reimburse **one** airline club membership for each SVP and above. In addition, SVPs, at their discretion, may extend one club membership to travelers under their line of command who travels frequently (i.e., 25,000 air miles annually) on Company business. Such memberships must be purchased directly from the airlines.

Electronic Tickets (E-Tickets)

E-tickets for air travel have largely replaced the use of paper tickets and should be used wherever possible. You may receive an e-mailed invoice/itinerary. This invoice/itinerary must be attached to your expense report.

Advance Ticket Purchase

Since the Company encourages the purchasing of tickets as far in advance of a trip as possible, it also allows reimbursement for the same before the trip is taken to allow for timely payment of the employee's corporate credit card account. However, if the trip is not taken, refer to Unused/Voided Airline Tickets.

Unused/Voided Airline Tickets

Unused airline tickets or flight coupons often have a cash value and must never be discarded or destroyed. You must notify the agency immediately about unused paper and e-tickets, and promptly forward paper tickets to enable the agency to expedite a credit to the Company's account, or to apply the ticket toward a future trip. If a change in your itinerary occurs that requires a reissuance of your ticket, **always** request that your unused portion be credited against your new ticket's cost. Note: **Do not automatically** buy a new ticket, because this can substantially increase the Company's cost.

Lost or Stolen Airline Tickets

Upon discovery of a lost or stolen ticket, immediately report the loss to the travel agency, where a replacement ticket will be arranged.

Airline tickets are the responsibility of the traveler, and it is the traveler who will be held responsible for the value of lost tickets. The Company will not absorb the cost of a lost ticket or fees charged by the airlines for processing the lost ticket application. Note: use of E-tickets should avoid this issue.

GROUND TRANSPORTATION

Employees traveling on Company business must use the most economical and practical mode of transportation, giving due consideration to factors such as scheduling, distance, and safety, in addition to cost. Ground transportation should be shared whenever possible.

Personal Cars

Use of personal vehicles is the preferred mode of transportation for local trips not exceeding 300 miles round trip.

In the United States (US), the employee's manager is required to preapprove such use. Employees are entitled to reimbursement for mileage at the current Internal Revenue Service (IRS) rate or the Runzheimer plan rate in the US. For non-US mileage, refer to geographic industry and income tax allowances.

Parking

Personal cars parked at airports by employees are to be in the most economical parking area, usually long-term parking.

To and From Airports and Terminals

Travelers should use an economical mode of transportation to and from airports, rail terminals, and bus terminals, such as the following:

- Buses and subways (before taxis)
- Hotel and airport shuttle services
- Personal automobile
- Rides provided by local personnel, when visiting another Company office

Rental Cars

Travelers may rent a car at their destination when other forms of transportation are impractical, more expensive, or not available; or when entertaining customers. When traveling in groups, employees should make every effort to share cars.

- Reservations. All car rental reservations must be made through the Agency. This is to ensure that the Company's preferred vendors are used, with the negotiated rates and insurance coverage.

- When the Agency cannot arrange for rental car reservations, the employee or Agency should obtain the best deal. In this circumstance employees should take Loss Damage Waiver insurance (LDW), collision damage waiver insurance, and theft damage waivers from the car rental supplier.

- All car rentals must be charged to the employee's Corporate credit card.

- Rental car categories. Rentals must be no larger than intermediate (midsize) cars, except that a full-size, four-door car may be rented when:

  - Three or more individuals are traveling together.

  - Entertaining a customer.

  - No compact or intermediate group car is available.

  - A no-cost upgrade can be secured (always ask for this!).

  - Transporting corporate materials such as booth displays.

  - The employee has a preapproved medical reason or physical disability.

- Insurance. Except as indicated above, LDW, liability, and all other insurance should be declined.

- Inspection. Physically inspect the vehicle, and be sure to have any damage noted on the rental contract **before** leaving the agency.

- Refueling. Employees are to return the car with a full tank of gas to avoid excessive refueling charges at the rental company—unless doing so would cause you to miss your flight.

- Accidents. Should the rental car be involved in an accident, you must immediately report it to the following and complete any required forms:

  - The rental car company

  - Local authorities, as required by law

  - Company's Director, Travel Administration

  - Company's Insurance and Risk Manager

Taxis or Car Service

The use of taxis is generally limited to those situations in which other means of transportation are not feasible or are more costly. An example would be an airport run for which no shuttle service is available and the cost of driving and parking one's personal vehicle would be more than the cost of the taxi or car service.

All taxi fares must be paid directly by the employee and reclaimed from the Company on an expense report. Billing to the Company from the taxi provider is not acceptable.

HOTEL RESERVATIONS AND LODGING

Reservations

Hotel reservations must be made through the Company-approved agency; failure to do so may result in nonreimbursement of any incremental cost to the Company over the rate that would have been available. Exception: Hotels that are part of a meeting/conference/trade show package may be used, by notifying the Agency to ensure that the Company is receiving appropriate corporate rates.

There are several reasons for this requirement:

- The Company has negotiated the contract and discounted rates at specific properties.

- The Agency has access to discounted rates at thousands of additional hotel properties worldwide. When traveling overseas, the Company's regional procurement office can assist with appropriate properties.

- Should the employee need to be contacted in an emergency, Corporate Travel and/or the Agency will have the necessary information available in their records.

Hotel Frequent Guest Programs

As with airline frequent flyer awards, employees may retain awards derived from hotel frequent guest programs for business or personal use, but participation in these programs must not influence hotel selection if it would result in incremental cost to the Company above what is available through the Company's contracts or through the Agency. Any such incremental cost would not be reimbursable.

Room Guarantee/Cancellation

Unless otherwise instructed, all rooms will be guaranteed for late arrival with the traveler's Corporate credit card. Should it become necessary to cancel the reservation, the traveler must inform the Agency and/or call the hotel directly, if after business hours—be sure to obtain a cancellation number and person's name. **If the traveler fails to cancel when there was sufficient time to have done so, and cannot provide a legitimate excuse, any resulting "no-show" charge will not be reimbursed.**

MEALS AND ENTERTAINMENT

General

As with other business travel expenses, reimbursable expenses for meals and entertainment must be supported by adequate records that clearly establish that they were (1) ordinary and necessary (i.e., not lavish, or extravagant), (2) reasonable in amount, and (3) incurred for a valid business purpose. The following criteria must be reported:

- Name(s), company affiliation(s), and business relationship(s) of all persons in attendance

- Business purpose of the meeting and nature of items discussed

- Original, itemized receipts

Tipping for Meals

Tips included on meal receipts will be reimbursed up to 15 percent of the meal cost, before tax.

Personal Business Meal Expenses while Out of Town

Personal meals are defined as reasonable meal expenses incurred by the traveler when dining alone on an out-of-town business trip. Out of town is defined as away from normal place of employment for more than 5 hours and more than 30 miles away from that place of employment. Such meals will be reimbursed at actual cost, when supported by receipts, up to a total daily not-to-exceed amount of $50, with a single meal limit of $35, for both domestic and international travelers. These amounts are inclusive of tax and tip.

Management/Team Meetings

Management/team meeting meals with colleagues must have a demonstrable business purpose, which must be explained on the expense report. Unless otherwise approved by the business unit SVP, reimbursement will be at actual cost, up to a maximum of $35 per person per meal. Examples of this category of expense are:

- Group meeting expenses approved by an appropriate level of management per the department manager's practices.
- Hospitality for business guests or employees from out-of-town facilities.
- The most senior-level employee is required to pay for the business meal of employee-to-employee meals. No participant at the meal may be the approver of the meal expense.
- The following details must be given on the expense report in respect of employee meals/meetings:
  - Names of employees in attendance and their Company subsidiary
  - Business purpose

Professional Membership Dues, Conferences, and Meetings

In order to encourage employee participation in professional memberships and attendance at meetings and seminars, related fees, continuing professional education credits, conferences, and meetings may be reimbursed. Professional memberships must be approved by the Chief Financial Officer, Chief Information Officer, General Counsel, and/or Executive Vice President, Human Resources and must be registered with Corporate Procurement. Annual membership dues, conferences, meetings, and events are reimbursable with approval from the employee's manager and:

- Up to $1,000 annually for membership dues prorated for the employee's first and final year of employment.
- Up to 75 percent of registration fees for seminars, conferences and similar educational programs and approved in advance; 100 percent of T&E as defined within the manual related to attending the seminar, conference, or similar educational program

Business Entertainment and Entertainment Meal Expenses

Business entertainment meals which are taken with clients, prospective clients, partners, or vendors during which a specific business discussion takes place. Entertainment event expenses include events such as nightclubs, theater, and sporting events attended with a person who has an actual or potential business relationship with the Company in which a business discussion takes place immediately before, during, or immediately after the event. Unless otherwise approved by an SVP, the maximum reimbursable amounts are:

• Entertainment meals: $100 per person

• Entertainment events: $100 per person

Note: For client-related meals and entertainment, the amounts are additive (i.e., you may expense the actual cost of each up to $200).

Large (over $1,000) divisionally sponsored meetings, sales meetings, off-site meetings, and the like may be processed using a purchase order as defined by Corporate Procurement.

Overtime Meals

Overtime i.e., when working after normal business hours or on weekends or holidays meals may be reimbursed when they are consumed on Company's or the client's premises and will be reimbursed when they are at actual cost up to a maximum of $10 per employee per meal.

End-of-Project Celebrations

Such occasional, special events shall be reimbursed at actual cost up to a maximum of $35 per employee. The project and business reference must be documented within the expense report.

Holiday Parties

Every effort should be made to have no more than one holiday party event per business group per location (i.e., employees should not be attending more than holiday party). The maximum total cost that may be incurred by a given cost center annually is $50 per employee times the number of employees in that cost center. No holiday gifts may be expensed.

TELECOMMUNICATIONS

Hotel Telecommunications Usage

All necessary business-related telephone calls, faxes, and computer usage are reimbursable. To avoid costly surcharges added by hotels to telephone bills, travelers should:

• Use a phone card or calling card whenever possible.

• Use hotel lobby phones.

• Use 800 numbers, free phone, or lower rate numbers for business calls whenever possible.

Cellular/Mobile Phones and Devices

Where a business need has been identified, cellular/mobile phones are provided to employees for business use and must not be abused for personal use. When using cellular/mobile phones, employees shall consider whether their use is the more economical communication means available at that time. The employee is responsible for the safekeeping of the phone and/or the device. The employee will be charged for any replacement or costs which occur due to the employee's negligence e.g. loss or theft.

Telephone Calls for Business Purposes Made on Employee's Private Telephone

To be reimbursed for business calls made on an employee's private phone i.e., land line or cellular/mobile phone, employees must attach their original, itemized phone bill to their expense report, clearly identifying calls related to business. The Company will not reimburse any element of line rental or standing charges. Applicable sales taxes should be added to the call costs.

Broadband and Other Internet Connections

Reimbursement of broadband or other Internet access for the employee's personal address may be made subject to the following:

- Fully supported valid business justification.

- Prior approval of cost center manager, finance, and information technology services.

- Local tax rules and regulations apply.

The bill must be in the employee's name and reimbursed through a T&E request form.

APPROVALS AND EXPENSE REPORTING

General Information

The Corporate Credit Card shall be used for Company business, travel, entertainment, and expenses. Only authorized reasonable and necessary business expenses will be reimbursed to employees. Refer to Appendix for NonReimbursable Expenses for items generally not reimbursed; exceptional circumstances must be documented and approved by an SVP.

Such expenses must be paid directly by the employee. Employees issued a Corporate Credit Card must use it for all business expenses for which the Corporate Credit Card is accepted, and must use the receipts as backup for their expense reimbursement.

Cash Advance

Where the Corporate Credit Card is not available and if required, a cash advance may be arranged. Advances shall cover only anticipated out-of-pocket cash expenses.

The Corporate guidelines for travel advances are $250 per day for in-country travel and $350 per day outside of the base country travel.

Cash advances must have approval from an SVP and require at least 10 days advance notice.

- Funds will be processed via the expense report system and paid by direct deposit into a nominated bank account.

- No more than one advance will be issued to an employee at any given time.

- In circumstances where an advance has been paid to the employee, an expense report must be submitted within 10 days of the business travel to settle the advance.

- In the event that a terminating employee has an unsettled advance, this amount will be deducted from the employee's final salary.

Currency Exchange Rates

Expenses in foreign currencies shall be converted at a rate representative of the average exchange rate in effect during the trip. When possible, currency conversion should be accomplished at a bank or similar financial institution where rates will be the most advantageous. The exchange rate used must be documented, and in practice this can be:

- The actual rate incurred supported by receipts to prove the rate used, e.g., credit card statement, foreign exchange receipt

- The rate in force at the date of travel

Expenses Report Procedure

Employees must complete an expense report to: claim expenses incurred on company business; this must includes a description of the purpose of the travel or expense so that we can determine that the expense is for business purposes; or reconcile any cash advances and/or Company-paid tickets or expenses incurred on company business.

Employees **must retain original receipts** and attach them to their expense report with positive indication that they were paid for and to serve as documentation for the IRS or local income tax agency that these were actual business expenditures. **The following receipts are required** if not available, attach a memorandum of explanation with the department manager's approval:

- A copy of travel invoice/itinerary as issued by the agency.

- The hotel bill showing payment and the credit card receipt.

- Car rentals: auto rental bill showing payment and credit card receipt.

- Receipt for restaurant meals and other business-related items that exceed $25.

- Telephone bills for calls made on personal credit cards.

- International travel to third world countries where receipts are difficult to obtain (e.g., taxis). The employee must itemize trips with destination and amount if receipts were unobtainable.

- Invalid receipts—the following receipts are unacceptable:

  - Receipts altered in any way

  - Photocopies of original

  - Handwritten "tear stubs" (i.e., portion of the invoice, bill or receipt)

When an employee is claiming for meals/meetings involving only others including employees, customers, business partners, and vendors, the following details must be provided on the expense report:

- Names of employees in attendance and their Company subsidiary

- Business purpose

When employees entertain other persons for business purposes, the expense report or an attached memorandum must detail the following:

- Type of entertainment

- Location

- Guests names and business affiliation

- Business purpose of the entertainment

- Amount and date

Review and Approval of Expense Reports

Employees considering travel, entertainment, and/or expenses must obtain their Manager's (or higher-level following the chain of command line management) authorization.

- **No employee may approve his/her own cash advance or expense report. Approval must be at least the next level of supervision or management.**

Responsibilities:

- Managers must monitor and ensure that the business expenses incurred by their employees are properly authorized and the travel expense report is properly completed and approved.

- Each employee is responsible for assuring that each expense report has appropriate approval(s).

- Each employee is responsible for the safekeeping of funds and tickets advanced to him/her and must account for them within 10 days after completing the business for which they were drawn.

The expense reports have sections in which to reconcile amounts of outstanding advances that an employee has received against any expenses he/she has incurred for company business.

- Due Employee—the Company will pay an outstanding balance due to the employee upon presentation of the expense report.

- Returned Balance Due Company—within 10 business days after the completion of a business trip, the employee must submit to A/P an expense report with a check attached in settlement of any unused travel advance. *Note:* Do not send cash through the mail. Make checks payable to the Company.

APPENDIX

NONREIMBURSABLE EXPENSES

In addition to the nonreimbursable items set forth in the travel policy, the following items are not reimbursable. Of necessity, this list cannot be exhaustive or substitute for good judgment and common sense.

Adult entertainment expenses	Laundry expenses when the trip is not in excess of three business days' duration
Alcoholic beverages unless part of approved entertainment expenses	Lavish or extravagant costs
Barbers and hairdressers	Loss or theft of cash advances
Briefcases	Loss/theft of personal funds/property
Car washes	Lost airline tickets and processing fees
Car accessories including maps	Lost baggage
Charitable and political contributions	Luggage
Child care	Magazines, books, newspapers (personal reading matter without a specific business need)
Clothing and other personal items	Massage/sauna/health club/spa usage
Commuting costs to/from employee's home office	Membership dues for airline clubs (except as noted)
Credit card/charge card annual fees	Movies (in-flight and in-hotel) and video games
Excess baggage charges, unless required by the Company	"No-show" charges for hotels
Excessive personal telephone calls	Office equipment
Excessive rental car refueling charges (i.e., when done by the rental car company)	Personal postcards and postage
Expenses older than 90 days	Pet care
Finance charges or delinquency fees from the credit card company or any source	Rental car cellular telephone charges
Flowers or gifts	Shoeshines
Golf fees, or other sporting event fees (when not part of customer entertainment)	Snacks or meals outside of breakfast, lunch and dinner
House-sitting	Souvenirs/personal gifts/cards/flowers
Illegal activities or items	Tobacco products
In-flight telephone charges unless for emergency or critical business need	Toiletries
Insurance, noncompulsory or optional (e.g., travel, baggage, personal or rental car), except as provided in the travel policy	Traffic or parking violation fines and court costs
	Unexplained expenses

BONUS POLICIES AND PROCEDURES

	Policy and Procedures	
Procedure No. C01	Section: Corporate	Page 1 of 8
	External Communications and Public Relations	
Department Ownership	Issue/Effective Date:	Replaces previously issued

Prepared by: Approved by: Authorized by:
Date   Date   Date

Scope

This document applies to all worldwide business units, subsidiaries and company employees.

The Corporate Pubic Relations (PR) department, or appointed designees, manage external communications strategies, press releases, correspondence, inquiries, and relationships with the media communities. External communications includes and is not limited to disclosure of customer contracts, partnerships, products and technology announcements, business operation information, and the release of quarterly and financial results.

This document excludes marketing communications and business partner related marketing initiatives.

Policy

It is IDÆAL LLP's (Company) policy to have a single, unified voice in communicating Corporate-level news and business objectives with the media.

The PR strategy is to create appropriate positive media attention in major business publications, business news, and within the trade and vertical press.

Procedure

The following describes procedures and/or roles for:

A. Press and analyst inquiries

B. News preparation

C. Financial and investor inquiries

D. Business partners / Third Party releases

E. Employees

A. *Press and Analyst Inquiries*

Persons identifying themselves as members of the media or industry analyst community, such as journalists, reporters, columnists, editors, or others related to the field, must be forwarded to the designated spokesperson within each country, usually to a PR designee within the Corporate Communications department.

Policy and Procedures		
Procedure No. C01	Section: Corporate	Page 2 of 8
External Communications and Public Relations		
Department Ownership	Issue/Effective Date:	Replaces previously issued

Press and analyst representatives encountered at public venues, such as trade shows, events, conferences, seminars, and the like, must be directed to a PR spokesperson or designee.

If there is no PR designee in country, then all inquires shall be forwarded to the regional or divisional representative of the Global Communications Programs team or if in direct contact the Corporate PR team.

All Corporate-level inquiries for North America (NA) must be directed to Corporate Communications/Public Relations. All Corporate-level inquiries in another country must be directed to the country manager.

In responding to press inquiries, the PR designee shall:

- Assess and evaluate the request (local vs. Corporate issue).

- Assess and evaluate the impact of responding or not responding.

- Determine if the necessary information is available to respond.

- Prepare a response.

- Secure the necessary authorizations and approvals.

All PR materials must contain appropriate contact information, including the Company's PR designee.

B. *News Preparation*

News preparation and releases are formal documents subject to review by the Company's legal counsel and senior management. Responsibility for the public distributions of news regarding new agreements, technological breakthroughs, new product announcements, and/or any other business-related activities **must be coordinated by the Corporate PR department.** PR requires at least 10 days advance notice for all third-party and Company press releases. Breaking news, litigation, or crisis communications require immediate response and must be fast-tracked to External Communications and PR.

Local, in-country PR designees shall be responsible for:

- Assessing the impact and preparing local responses as it relates to local business specific issues

- Managing all media inquiries and follow-up inquiries

- Obtaining customer and/or in-country approvals prior to release

The Global Communications Program team shall be responsible for:

- Preparing and gaining Corporate approval for general press releases

Policy and Procedures		
Procedure No. C01	Section: Corporate	Page 3 of 8
External Communications and Public Relations		
Department Ownership	Issue/Effective Date:	Replaces previously issued

- Communicating and distributing those press releases to country PR designees

- Issuing the press release through appropriate channels

Local country releases must not be scheduled prior to the corporate release.

C. *Financial and Investor Inquiries*

All financial and investor inquires **must** be directed to the Corporate Investor Relations department. Investor Relations is responsible for preparing responses to inquiries, releasing selected mandatory financial information and announcing other finance and investor related topics including and not limited to:

- Significant financial movement

- Significant business contracts

- Strategic alliances/partnerships, or technological advances/announcements

D. *Business Partner/Third-Party Release*

All news and press releases from Business Partners and/or third parties must have prior approval from Corporate PR and Corporate Legal.

E. *Employees (Non-PR Designates)*

Employees may **not** share Company information and perform the following activities without the written consent and prior approval of Corporate PR:

- Authorize press releases, press conferences, or distribution of company news over any news-wire, news service, Web site, or distribution service.

- Take photographs and/or video recordings on premises at any Company location.

- Take part in or respond to press inquiries or interviews, either on or off company premises.

- Forward e-mails, documentation, internal correspondence, or other Company confidential materials to anyone, including but not limited to members of the press. All employees, partners, and alliances are subject to nondisclosure agreements regarding confidential and proprietary materials.

- Engage in Internet chat rooms or online investor communities or post messages to Internet bulletin boards to discuss, comment on, or debate any business activity related to the Company.

Policy and Procedures		
Procedure No. C01	Section: Corporate	Page 4 of 8
External Communications and Public Relations		
Department Ownership	Issue/Effective Date:	Replaces previously issued

- Engage in any discussion with industry analysts or financial journalists.

- Comment on or provide information to online investor communities regarding the Company's business activities (Reference Material Nonpublic Information and Insider Trading Policy).

- Engage in public forum addresses that discuss, comment on, or debate any business activities or operations related to the Company. Speaking opportunities must be limited to the employee's regular course of business as approved by the Company.

Employees may not comment on, speculate on, or attempt to explain any situation on behalf of the Company. If an employee mistakenly or unknowingly acts as a Company spokesperson, he/she must immediately contact a member of the Company PR team in their respective region and provide details on exactly what was discussed and the name of the reporter/organization to which they spoke. Further discussion with the media must be avoided unless the Company's PR department specifically asks the employee to participate in an interview.

Translation

It is the in-country PR designee's responsibility to prepare or arrange for translation into English for Corporate Legal review or from English into the local language for local releases.

Approval and Authorization

The PR designees must obtain approval from in-country management, Corporate business unit management and Corporate Legal prior to any/all news or press releases.

Any news releases involving customer contracts or partnerships must have the approval of the customer, customer account, or channel representative.

External Support

The use of PR external support and agencies must be approved by Corporate PR and must follow the purchase requisition/purchase order procedures. PR expenses must be approved by the business unit's controller or financial designate.

Controls/Areas of Responsibility

Corporate PR maintains a contact list of approved venues and contacts and compares and updates this list to actual activities and events.

In order to ensure that processes are followed and that press inquiries and press release requests are appropriately evaluated, Corporate Communications has established a request form that shall be used when requesting support for external communications. Refer to the Exhibit for additional guidance.

Policy and Procedures		
Procedure No. C01	Section: Corporate	Page 5 of 8
External Communications and Public Relations		
Department Ownership	Issue/Effective Date:	Replaces previously issued

- A press release request form is filled out by the owner of the news.

- PR evaluates the request and determines whether it is newsworthy for distribution in a press release, a joint release, a third-party release, or not at all.

- PR moves the project forward accordingly and assign an appropriate owner within the External Communications group.

- PR writes the press release and/or work with the business unit or regional area to write the press release.

- An approval sheet will be attached to the release as it flows through the approval process within Company. Approval is required from the Business Unit and/or Regional General Manager as well as Finance or Legal, as appropriate. External Communications monitors this approval process.

- All press releases need the approval of Corporate Communications, a member of the Executive Senior staff, and Company's Legal Counsel.

Contact

Public Relations/External Communications

<table>
<tr><td colspan="3" align="center">**Policy and Procedures**</td></tr>
<tr><td>Procedure No. C01</td><td align="center">Section: Corporate</td><td align="right">Page 6 of 8</td></tr>
<tr><td colspan="3" align="center">**External Communications and Public Relations**</td></tr>
<tr><td>Department Ownership</td><td align="center">Issue/Effective Date:</td><td align="right">Replaces previously issued</td></tr>
</table>

Exhibit

External Communications and Public Relations

The following Exhibit is to be used when preparing an external communication request by third-party business partners and Public Relations (PR) designees.

Identify the Value

Press releases can be a valuable way to get a company's message across. However, editors receive literally hundreds of releases each day, so it's a good idea to make sure the release passes the "so what, who cares" test.

In your request, identify the following:

- What is the news?

- What is compelling about the news?

- What exactly do you wish the news release to accomplish?

- What about the news is time sensitive and important to a reporter?

Approval Process

The third-party, business partners, or PR designees' request **must** follow the Company's approval process if it directly or indirectly mentions the Company or contains a quote from a Company employee. To ensure a prompt and effective turnaround to the request, Corporate PR **needs 5 to 10 working days to handle most requests,** longer if various product groups or technical experts are required for the review.

Third parties/business partners shall:

- Contact their Company business partner manager and notify them of the intention, including as much background and information, as appropriate.

- Forward a request form and copy of the proposed release, including the issue date to Corporate PR.

- Include the name, e-mail address, and phone number for the third-party business partner's PR person, who will serve as the intermediary between the third-party business partner and the Company.

- List the names and contact of others within the Company who have been working on the solution, application, or contract.

Once this is submitted, Company PR shall:

- Review the accuracy.

Policy and Procedures		
Procedure No. C01	Section: Corporate	Page 7 of 8
External Communications and Public Relations		
Department Ownership	Issue/Effective Date:	Replaces previously issued

- Create and/or secure an approved quote. The decision to include a quote, the content of the quote, and who will be quoted will be of the sole discretion of the Company PR team.

- Check with appropriate Company groups to red-flag and resolve open issues and create any talking points if required for the internal spokespeople.

- Return the approved release and quote or document and explain remaining open issues and alternatives.

Quotes from Company Spokesperson

Generally, quotes from a Company spokesperson shall be short and focus on the business/customer benefits of the product/service/application. Corporate PR identifies an appropriate spokesperson.

Use the following considerations, when determining situations when and where quotes may be used:

- Company will not provide quotes that judge the value of one product relative to other competitive offerings (i.e., Company cannot say we offer the "best" or "most").

- Quotes shall address the support, capabilities, and benefits provided by working with the Company.

- The Company prefers quotes that discuss how the combination between a third-party business partner's service and the Company's expertise will benefit the customer.

- Text must **not** reflect a joint announcement. The third-party business partner, not the Company, is taking the action.

- The words *partnering, partners,* and *partnership* may **not** be used when referring to the business partner's relationship with the Company. Alternative language such as "work together to deliver" may be used. The phrase *strategic relationship* may **not** be used (implies a specific, legally described relationship).

- All press releases need to carry a trademark definition at the end of the release. A blanket disclaimer, such as "All product and company names herein may be trademarks of their respective owners", is recommended.

- Company PR contact information must **not** be included unless specified by Corporate PR.

- The Company boilerplate must not be included unless specified by Corporate PR and must be verified that it is the most current version.

Red-Flag Words

The following are terms that must not be in the press release and may be changed or deleted by the Company Legal department. Avoid using these words unless they can be substantiated Company's Legal department will ask for independent verification e.g., analyst report, market data.

- *Partners, partnership, partnering.*

- *New, first, leader*

Policy and Procedures		
Procedure No. C01	Section: Corporate	Page 8 of 8
External Communications and Public Relations		
Department Ownership	Issue/Effective Date:	Replaces previously issued

- *Buy, purchase, own, owner*
- *No. 1, standard, industry standard*
- *Strategic*
- *Alliances*
- *Strategic alliance*
- *Company commitment, committing*
- *Joint*
- *Global*
- *The leading provider of . . . (rather, it should be a leading provider of . . .)*

Appropriate Verbiage for a Business Partner Press Release

- *Relationship*
- *Deal*
- *Agreement*
- *Marketing agreement*
- *Work with*
- *Co-marketing*
- *Lead generation*
- *Work together*
- *Leverage*

Editing Style Guide

Abbreviations: Do **not** abbreviate the names for Company products or technology.

Acronyms: Place in parentheses after the term has been spelled out. Acronyms may be used for computer industry terms to ensure familiarity and clarity even if not referred to again in the same document.

Policy and Procedures		
Procedure No. C02	Section: Corporate	Page 1 of 4
Material Nonpublic Information and Insider Trading		
Department Ownership	Issue/Effective Date:	Replaces previously issued

Prepared by:	Approved by:	Authorized by:
Date	Date	Date

Scope

This policy applies to employees, officers, and directors of IDÆAL LLP (Company) with respect to transactions in the Company's securities.

Federal securities laws prohibit trading in the securities of a company on the basis of "inside" information. Anyone violating these laws is subject to personal liability and could face criminal penalties.

This policy is not intended to replace the responsibility to understand and comply with the legal prohibition on insider trading.

Policy

It is IDÆAL LLP's (Company) policy that annually all employees review and attest that they are in compliance with the policies and procedures governing material, nonpublic information and the prevention of insider trading.

Nonemployees working on behalf of the Company are included within the policy and procedure. Executives or managers working with these nonemployees must ensure that a nondisclosure agreement has been signed and that they are aware of this policy and procedure.

It is the policy of the Company to oppose the misuse of material nonpublic information in securities trading and the unauthorized disclosure of any nonpublic information acquired in the workplace.

- No insider may buy or sell Company securities at any time when they have material nonpublic information relating to the Company.

- No insider may buy or sell securities of another company at any time when they have material nonpublic information about that company, including, without limitation, any company that is followed in the ordinary course of our business, and any of our customers, vendors, or suppliers when that information is obtained in the course of services performed on behalf of the Company.

- No insider may disclose ("tip") material nonpublic information to any other person, including family, and no insider may make recommendations or express opinions on the basis of material nonpublic information with regard to trading in securities.

- No insider who receives or has access to Company material nonpublic information may comment on stock price movement or rumors of other Company developments that are of possible

Policy and Procedures		
Procedure No. C02	Section: Legal	Page 2 of 4
Material Nonpublic Information and Insider Trading		
Department Ownership	Issue/Effective Date:	Replaces previously issued

significance to the investing public unless it is part of defined role and responsibility (such as Investor Relations) or as specifically authorized in writing by the Chief Executive Officer (CEO) or Chief Financial Officer (CFO) in each instance.

- If you comment on stock price movement or rumors or disclose material nonpublic information to a third party, you should promptly contact the Company's Compliance Officer, Investor Relations department, and General Counsel.

If you are a member of the Board of Directors, an Executive Officer, a Senior Vice President, or a Vice President, you automatically are subject to the mandatory trading window described below. Additionally, Company employees, by virtue of their position with the Company, are subject to the mandatory trading window. If you are unsure as to whether your position with the Company subjects you to the mandatory trading window, you are advised to contact the Company's General Counsel.

Procedure

Nonpublic information relating to the Company is the property of the Company, and the unauthorized disclosure of such information is forbidden. The following procedures are designed to maintain confidentiality with respect to the Company's business operations and activities.

Limitations on Access to Company Information

Directors, officers, and Company employees shall take all steps and precautions necessary to restrict access to and secure material nonpublic information by, among other things:

- Maintaining the confidentiality of transactions.

- Complying with the terms of nondisclosure agreements between the individual and the Company.

- Conducting their business and social activities so as not to risk inadvertent disclosure of confidential information. Unauthorized persons must not conduct reviews of confidential documents in public places in a manner so as to prevent access.

- Restricting access to documents and files including computer files containing material nonpublic information to individuals on a need-to-know basis including maintaining control over the distribution of documents and drafts of documents.

- Promptly removing and cleaning up all confidential documents and other materials from conference rooms following the conclusion of any meetings.

- Disposing of all confidential documents and other papers after there is no longer any business or other legally required need, through shredders when appropriate.

Policy and Procedures		
Procedure No. C02	Section: Legal	Page 3 of 4
Material Nonpublic Information and Insider Trading		
Department Ownership	Issue/Effective Date:	Replaces previously issued

- Restricting access to areas likely to contain confidential documents or material nonpublic information.

- Avoiding the discussion of material nonpublic information in places where others could overhear information such as in elevators, restrooms, hallways, restaurants, airplanes, or taxicabs.

Personnel involved with material nonpublic information, to the extent feasible, must conduct their business and activities in areas separate from other Company activities.

Either positive or negative information may be considered material and nonpublic. Material information does not have to be related to the Company's business. For example, the contents of a forthcoming newspaper column that is expected to affect the market price of a security can be material. **If asked about any of the above matters by someone who is not an insider, the Company's strict policy is that for so long as such information is "nonpublic," you must respond that the Company's policy is not to comment on such matters.**

Definitions

Insider refers to

1. Members of our Board of Directors, our corporate officers, and our employees;

2. Our consultants and other persons associated with us and our subsidiaries, including distributors, sales agents, and joint venture partners, who receive or have access to our material nonpublic information; and

3. Household and immediate family members of those listed in (1) and (2).

Any person who possesses material nonpublic information regarding the Company is an insider for so long as the information is not publicly known. Any employee or consultant to the Company can be an insider from time to time and would at those times be subject to this Policy.

Material Nonpublic Information

Information should be regarded as material if there is a reasonable likelihood that it would be considered important to an investor in making an investment decision regarding the purchase or sale of the Company's securities.

There are various categories of information that are particularly sensitive and, as a general rule, must always be considered material. Examples of such information and is not limited include:

- Financial results and Projections of future earnings or losses or liquidity issues

- News of a pending or proposed acquisition, merger, or joint venture

- Gain or loss of a substantial customer or supplier

- Information regarding a new product

- New equity or debt offerings

Public Information

Information is "nonpublic" if it is not available to the general public. In order for information to be considered public, it must be widely disseminated in a manner making it generally available to investors through such media as Dow Jones, Reuters Economic Services, the *Wall Street Journal,* Associated Press, or United Press International or through a public filing with the Securities and Exchange Commission (SEC) and have been in the public domain for a period of at least two trading days.

Blackout periods—The Company has four blackout periods, which begin at each quarter-end e.g., March 31, June 30, September 30, and December 31 of each year, and end when two full trading days have passed on the New York Stock Exchange (NYSE) **after** an announcement of Company results for the preceding fiscal period.

A good general rule of thumb: **When in doubt, do not trade.**

Securities include common stock, preferred stock, and options to purchase common stock, warrants, convertible debentures, and derivative securities.

Controls/Areas of Responsibility

Employees are responsible for understanding and complying with this policy and procedure.

Managers who manage nonemployees must ensure that the nonemployee has signed a nondisclosure agreement and that they have read and understood this policy and procedure.

Corporate Legal is responsible for providing communication as to when blackout dates begin and end.

Corporate Legal is responsible for providing and arranging for education and training on material nonpublic information and insider trading to all employees.

Contacts

General Counsel

	Policy and Procedures	
Procedure No. C03	Section: Accounting and Finance	Page 1 of 5
	Procurement	
Department Ownership	Issue/Effective Date:	Replaces previously issued

Prepared by:	Approved by:	Authorized by:
Date	Date	Date

Scope

This policy and procedure applies to all procurement areas and individuals who are required to purchase goods and services on behalf of the Company.

The general areas of purchases are identified as:

1. Raw materials

2. Capital expenditures

3. Noncapital expenditures or noninventory expenses.

Policy

It is IDÆAL LLP's (Company) policy that procurement activities, whether within the Corporate Procurement department or delegated to functional business areas, must follow the process identified within the Procurement Manual.

In order to take advantage of the Company's functional subject matter experts and purchasing power in the global marketplace, it is the Company's policy that certain business areas are responsible for establishing, maintaining, and enforcing purchasing guidelines. Although the following functions retain worldwide responsibilities when determining when and how to use eligible providers, negotiating, contracting, and other related procurement activities remains with the Procurement department or designates.

- Corporate Information Technology (IT) is responsible for approving all IT network, hardware, software, and IT peripheral office equipment (e.g., faxes) and services.

- Corporate Legal is responsible for approving eligible outside legal service providers and their use.

- Corporate Real Estate and Facilities is responsible for investments in Land, Land improvements, Real Estate, and Building Leases and Leasehold Improvements.

- Corporate Tax is responsible for approving eligible outside tax service providers and their use.

- Corporate Treasury is responsible for approving eligible services and service providers related to insurance, vehicle, and fleet management.

- Freight and transportation service providers are assessed by Corporate Logistics.

	Policy and Procedures	
Procedure No. C03	Section: Accounting and Finance	Page 2 of 5
	Procurement	
Department Ownership	Issue/Effective Date:	Replaces previously issued

- Human Resources is responsible for the approving eligible providers of benefits for employees.

- Internal Audit is responsible for approving when and how to use eligible outside audit service providers.

The purpose of assigning worldwide purchasing responsibilities is to ensure a consistent approach for selecting vendors who will provide the best terms, conditions, and product to meet Company standards and requirements.

Corporate Treasury shall assess financing decisions including capital and/or operating leases.

Contracts to secure goods and/or services on behalf of the Company must use Company-approved contracts and standard terms and conditions and/or have contracts and agreements reviewed and approved by Legal.

Where local regulations permit, the Company's standard purchase terms and conditions include vendor payment terms as 60 days. Payment terms less than 60 days must be approved by the VP, Global Procurement. Generally, leases, utilities, rents, and tax are excluded from the 60-day standard: payment terms.

Procedure

Procurement activities may occur via:

- Purchase requisition initiated by the business area and forwarded to the Corporate Procurement department where a vendor is selected and a purchase order is issued

- A Procurement Card (P-Card) is provided to employees for the purpose of acquiring specific sundry items such as office supplies

- A Travel, Entertainment, and Expense (T&E) form is used to reimburse employees for travel, entertainment, and business expenses

Regardless of the type of procurement vehicle and commensurate with the level of spending, the following process shall followed and documented

Corporate Procurement or the delegated functional areas shall follow the detailed purchasing activities as defined within the Procurement Manual

Once the need has been identified and validated, the local business area initiates the process by developing the scope of work or the requested service. Together with line management and finance support, the scope of acquisition is evaluated and approved

Policy and Procedures		
Procedure No. C03	Section: Accounting and Finance	Page 3 of 5
	Procurement	
Department Ownership	Issue/Effective Date:	Replaces previously issued

The initiating area develops the scope and generates a purchase requisition (PR). As part of the request, the following must be considered as part of the total cost to the Company:

- Costs to acquire

- Down payments, setup fees, relocation, and removal or disposition of assets

- Ongoing or recurring charges that may result e.g., subscriptions, upgrades, maintenance

- Peripheral considerations that must accompany the request e.g., workstations, equipment for consultants, training, furniture

- Costs associated with the termination of the contract or disposal of the goods

The Corporate Procurement department serves and supports the initiating area by further developing the scope of the acquisition, placing and evaluating competitive bids, supporting the decision-making process, and tracking and monitoring vendor performance. Whether performed by Corporate Procurement or by the initiating area, these activities must be performed and documented for each procurement decision.

Depending on the level of spending and the type of commodity the Company is acquiring, it may be necessary to request competitive or comparative bids in the form of Request for Proposal (RFP) or Request for Information (RFI) from selected bidders. RFP, RFI packages may be requested from representatives of the Procurement Department.

It is recommended that the final criteria for evaluating and selecting a vendor be determined prior to sending out the RFP/RFI. In evaluating vendors, the Company shall consider varying factors, including prior vendor history of financial stability; quality of the product, goods, and/or service; and other quantitative or qualitative factors.

Assessing the impact across functions and gaining business and financial management approval supports the decision-making process. Commensurate with the scope of the activity, a project Task Committee may be required.

Financial authorization and approval must accompany each Purchase requistor (PR) as indicated in the table below. The following table identifies the chain of command approval required before spending shall occur. Use the plan or budget exchange rate to convert amounts of approval limits from U.S. dollars to local currency.

Additional documentation and support is required as the financial commitment increases. For fixed assets (also known as property, plant and equipment or long-lived assets), acquisitions over $10,000 USD, require a capital acquisition request form. Once completed and approved, this form must be forwarded to the Fixed Asset department for approval prior to sending it to Procurement. See the Property, Plant and Equipment policy and procedure.

Policy and Procedures		
Procedure No. C03	Section: Accounting and Finance	Page 4 of 5
Procurement		
Department Ownership	Issue/Effective Date:	Replaces previously issued

Approvals from business Management	Approvals from Finance	Maximum US $ Authorization
Manager or Senior Manager	Finance Manager	Up to $10K
Vice President	Director of Finance	Up to $100K
Senior Vice President or General Manager	Vice President of Finance	Up to $250K
Senior Vice President or General Manager	Corporate Controller	Up to $1M
Chief Executive Officer	Chief Financial Officer	Over $ 1M

Once approved by line management, Finance, and Legal (if required), a purchase order (PO) is created and sent to the vendor with a copy of the Company's purchase order terms and conditions.

A Company representative must always negotiate the best price, terms, and conditions for the Company. Depending on whether Corporate Procurement or the initiating department is coordinating or managing the procurement process, negotiating with the vendor shall be conducted to ensure that the Company receives the best possible price terms and conditions. When dealing with vendors, refer to the Company's Code of Ethical Conduct.

Corporate Legal must review Company and Vendor Contracts Unless the vendor is using the Company's standard purchasing contracts with standard terms and conditions, Corporate Legal or representatives (Legal) must review and approve the contract. Recurring contracts that have already been approved by Legal and where the terms and conditions have not changed do not require additional Legal approval.

All amendments to existing contracts, where scope of work and additional funding is modified, shall also be routed through Corporate Legal for review and approval, except for Company-generated contract amendments that solely add funding to the original scope of work and/or extends either the period of performance or contract termination date.

The initiating department shall monitor additions and/or changes to the scope of the procurement activity. The cumulative effect of change orders must be compared to planned and approved spending. As spending levels increase, additional line and financial management authorization may be required.

The initiating or receiving area must verify that the goods are received in accordance with the specified terms and conditions. Damaged goods and incomplete shipments must be noted and communicated to the vendor and to finance. As appropriate, adjustments must be requested from the vendor.

	Policy and Procedures	
Procedure No. C03	Section: Accounting and Finance	Page 5 of 5
	Procurement	
Department Ownership	Issue/Effective Date:	Replaces previously issued

Post–vendor award activities shall be performed by the initiating department and should include reconciling invoices to goods received and/or services rendered. The initiating department and/or Corporate Procurement may conduct audits of the procurement process, quality audits of the vendor. Corporate Procurement must be notified of any vendor audits and the findings.

Validated and approved vendor invoices must be directed to Accounts Payable for prompt payment.

A systematic review of open POs within the accounting system shall be performed to ensure closure for those POs no longer required.

Records Management

Purchase information, including but not limited to PRs, capital appropriation requests, RFP/RFI, supplier responses (accepted and rejected), POs, purchase acknowledgments, and supplier/vendor correspondence, shall be in accordance with the records information management policy. See the Records Information Management policy and related schedules to identify documents that must be retained.

Controls/Areas of Responsibility

Only selected employees may establish or change the vendor master data record. Purchasing and Accounts Payable (A/P) are responsible for the accuracy of the vendor master data. Additions, deletions, and changes to this database must be approved, logged, and monitored.

Delegation for procurement activities is governed and maintained by the Corporate Procurement department.

There must be appropriate separation of duties among those initiating the purchase request, placing the PO, approving the receipt of goods and services, and authorizing the vendor's invoice for payment.

The business area secures all necessary approvals and authorizations.

A capital/investment committee made up of the business unit, corporate planning and Corporate Treasury evaluates and approves the request for project and capital spending.

A/P verifies that the appropriate authorization accompanies the settlement of each invoice.

Corporate Legal evaluates and approves vendor agreements.

Contacts

Corporate Procurement

Policy and Procedures		
Procedure No. C04	Section: Corporate	Page 1 of 16
	Records Information Management	
Policy Owner:	Issue/Effective Date:	Replaces previously issued

Prepared by:
Date

Approved by:
Date

Authorized by:
Date

Scope

Records and information are created, during the normal course of business, to document transactions and support effective decision making. In an era of ever-increasing litigation and regulatory control, records and information must be formally managed and maintained, as specified by applicable laws, regulatory agencies, and/or operational and contractual requirements.

The purpose of records information management is to:

- **Comply with applicable laws** ensuring that all records are retained:

  - As long as they have operational use

  - In accordance with local laws and regulations

  - For the period as stated in applicable jurisdictions

- **Comply with contractual and internal operational requirements** ensuring that records that affect the obligations and operations of the company are being retained and to support external and internal audit access requirements

- **Provide an efficient records information management** process and monitor the procedures through the records life cycle

- **Manage a Records Management Program** that enables employees to manage, retain, and destroy documents in a consistent manner

Record(s) as referred to within this policy include:

- Record(s) such as books, papers, maps, photographs, machine-readable materials, or other documentary materials, regardless of physical form or characteristics. Records include content, context, and structure. Records are received or generated in connection with the transaction of business and preserved as evidence of the organization, functions, policies, decisions, procedures, operations, or other activities.

- Electronic records include numeric, graphic, and textual information that may be recorded in any machine-readable media form.

- Nonrecords and nonelectronic records are documents or other materials made, acquired, and/ or preserved for reference, exhibition, or convenience and are not required to be maintained.

- Vital records, core business records are those records containing information essential to the continuation or survival of an organization in the event of a major business interruption or

Policy and Procedures		
Procedure No. C04	Section: Corporate	Page 2 of 16
	Records Information Management	
Policy Owner:	Issue/Effective Date:	Replaces previously issued

disaster. They contain information necessary to recreate an organization's legal and financial status, resume operations and preserve the rights and obligations of stockholders, customers, partners, employees, and other constituent groups.

Records Information Management topics:

	Page
Overview	2
Records Information Management	3
Electronic Records	4
Retention and Archiving	7
Records Hold	8
Approval for Destruction of Records	9
Record Compliance Audit	9
Records Management Responsibilities	9
Procedures	13
Controls/Areas of Responsibility	16

This policy applies to IDÆAL LLP (Company) and its subsidiaries' employees, nonemployee directors and officers, consultants, and financial and legal advisors who create, receive, maintain, or control records as part of their work on behalf of the Company. Employees who oversee the work effort of nonemployees must ensure that nonemployees understand and abide by this policy, procedure, and related retention schedules.

POLICY

Overview

It is the Company's policy to have a worldwide Records Information Management (RIM) Program that provides for the identification, management, protection, systematic review, retention, and destruction of company records and information in accordance with government regulations and legal, fiscal, and corporate operational and historical requirements.

In addition, RIM classifies records according to defined categories and indicates the length of time that they must be retained by law or for specific company purposes, and when they may be reviewed for archival retention or destruction (see the Record Retention Schedule).

Revisions, modifications, or deviations to/from this policy or the retention schedule, with respect to any particular record or group of records, is permitted **only** upon the approval of the Records Information Manager.

Ownership of Records

The Company holds ownership and title to all records created, received, acquired, or maintained in the normal course of business by any employee or organizational component. These records are the property of the Company; they shall not be used for personal or private purposes, and shall be destroyed only in accordance with approved official records retention schedules and procedures.

All records created, utilized, or stored on the Company's premises, or under Company control i.e., off-site storage facilities shall be retained and eventually destroyed according to this policy.

Records Information Management

It is important to keep full and accurate records of the Company's activities and transactions. Therefore, it is Company policy to manage Corporate records effectively and efficiently in order to facilitate accomplishment of business objectives and administrative needs; preserve official records in accordance with applicable statutory and regulatory requirements; and promote access to information by employees, partners, suppliers, customers, agents, and independent contractors, as required.

Business units and functional departments accomplish this through adequate and proper documentation. The management of records shall be considered in all policy decisions, procedures, and essential transactions in a manner that promotes accountability, establishes a historical record, protects the Company's legal and financial rights, and promotes the privacy of employees. This is accomplished through:

1. Establishing a framework and plan for managing and overseeing a comprehensive RIM Program.

2. Providing a framework that guides the electronic records policy to promote effective management, communication, sharing, and transfer of information, regardless of the medium or format in which it exists.

3. Informing the Company's directors, officers, employees, agents, consultants, and independent contractors of their responsibilities to manage records and ensure that the records management staff receive adequate training to carry out their responsibilities.

4. Managing records throughout their information life cycle, including the following components:

   - Records creation/collection—an official record shall be created to appropriately document all corporate functions, policies, decisions, procedures and essential transactions.

	Policy and Procedures	
Procedure No. C04	Section: Corporate	Page 4 of 16
	Records Information Management	
Policy Owner:	Issue/Effective Date:	Replaces previously issued

Departments shall develop record-keeping requirements for all official records for which they are responsible.

- Records maintenance and use—record filing, indexing, and storage systems shall be designed and documented to the extent appropriate and necessary, to maximize the usefulness of records and allow retrieval throughout their life cycle.

- Records disposition—records retention schedules shall be submitted to and approved by the RIM Committee. No records may be destroyed without approval (see Destruction Process below). Once dispositions are approved, they must be carried out in a timely manner and in accordance with Company guidelines.

5. Creating an inventory of official records as requested by the RIM Committee. Records that are not needed on site for current business needs should be archived by the Records Information Management department.

6. Creating and monitoring safeguards commensurate with the risks and magnitude of harm that would result from the loss, misuse, unauthorized access to, or modification of information. Appropriate safeguards shall be adopted to ensure security.

7. Developing standardized filing systems/structures as appropriate to provide an effective mechanism that facilitates ease of use, access, and disposition. Records shall be organized and indexed in such a manner as to be easily accessible to employees and to allow for integration across departments and information systems.

8. Establishing and monitoring a business continuity plan to protect vital records. The policy shall define responsibilities for identifying and appropriately safeguarding records defined as crucial to the continuing operation of essential functions during an emergency and those essential to protecting the rights and interests of the Company and the individuals directly affected by its activities.

9. Eliminating personal information when it appears in a business document and retaining and treating the business content as an official record.

Electronic Records

The Company's electronic records are official records and include electronic records generated or received by directors, officers, employees, agents, consultants, and independent contractors in the course of work-related duties.

Electronic records shall include information and files created by individual employees using desktop applications such as e-mail, word processing, graphics, and spreadsheet software. Records created in desktop computing environments shall be saved and maintained in accordance with their record retention schedules based on the classification of the content.

Care must be taken to ensure that in no case shall duplicate or convenience copies be retained longer than the original document.

Retention and storage for electronic records shall be treated the same as hardcopy records; that is, their maintenance shall be in accordance with the Company's RIM policies and their disposal shall be in accordance with the approved records retention schedules. Retention periods shall be based on the content of the electronic record and not the type of electronic medium where the content is stored. Electronic records are subject to legal processes, such as discovery and in response to subpoenas.

Records that are created electronically, including email shall be made, sorted, and made available electronically. Electronic versions of records shall not categorically be regarded as valueless extra copies of paper versions. Electronic records are **not** identical to their paper counterparts and they are deemed to be unique and distinct from printed versions of the same record. Records stored electronically may have search, manipulation, and indexing capabilities that are not common to their paper counterparts.

Tools of the workplace such as e-mail and Personal Digital Assistants (PDAs) are subject to legal subpoena and discovery actions and, as such, come under the RIM guidelines. E-mail retention should be incorporated into the Information Systems architecture, where the associate must redirect it to be archived to an archival folder. **Unless otherwise classified, e-mail shall be retained for no more than 365 days.**

Information systems that retain information used in the conduct of business, administrative, or support activities shall be deemed electronic records systems. Systems that capture data (i.e., databases) in real time but do not retain data shall not be deemed electronic records systems.

Databases used in the conduct of the business shall be deemed as electronic records systems. Database records include the data organized for input into the database, the data stored according to the logical structure of the database, and data output as reports or views. Database records shall also include the specifications for the input screens, the logical schema, and the definitions for output.

Web pages that document the mission and current organizational structure, as well as certain key business functions, policies, procedures, and essential business transactions, are deemed official records.

Previous versions of a web page that do not qualify as records are deemed nonrecords and may be overwritten or deleted from the system within 30 days of the final posting of the updated version of the web page.

The unauthorized removal, concealment, falsification, mutilation and/or unauthorized disposition of official electronic records are strictly prohibited. Violators may be subject to penalties, such as fines and dismissal.

Policy and Procedures		
Procedure No. C04	Section: Corporate	Page 6 of 16
	Records Information Management	
Policy Owner:	Issue/Effective Date:	Replaces previously issued

Rules governing updates, alterations, and deletion of data in databases shall be consistent with the approved records retention schedules that apply to the data. RIM for electronic records includes:

1. Implementing standard record coding schemas to identify records and folders within a database.

2. Maintaining electronic records in accordance with the approved schedules and incorporating disposition instructions into the design of the automated system.

3. Maintaining adequate technical documentation to enable the records to be retrieved, read and understood. When a system is modified, documentation must be retained describing the previous state and schema of the system and data.

4. Maintaining electronic records in an accessible format throughout their life cycles. When records are dependent on specific hardware or software:

    *   The hardware and software shall be maintained as long as the records are maintained.

    *   Compatibility shall be ensured when changing hardware or software.

    *   Records may be converted to another media to enable them to be retrieved, read, and understood.

5. Controlling records throughout the total life cycle and including the following components:

    *   On-line retention period. An on-line retention period shall reflect the length of time that data will remain on primary storage devices; for example, on magnetic disks.

    *   Near-line retention period. A near-line retention period shall reflect the length of time data shall remain on site but off-line, maintained in secondary storage devices; for example, on optical media.

    *   Off-line retention period. An off-line retention period shall reflect the length of time that data shall remain off-line and generally off site; for example, on magnetic tapes.

    *   Total electronic retention period. The total electronic retention period shall reflect the length of time that data shall remain in computer-processable form, after which data shall be purged entirely from any and all storage devices supporting the system.

6. Safeguarding by implementing and maintaining an effective Records Security Program that:

    *   Ensures that required personnel receive training and understand the processes and procedures for managing both electronic and nonelectronic records, including safeguards for sensitive electronic records

    *   Ensures that only authorized personnel have access to records

    *   Provides for backup and recovery of electronic records to protect against loss

Destruction of Electronic Records

1. For purposes of RIM, there are five types of electronic records:

    a. Electronic documents

    b. Web pages

    c. E-mail messages and attachments

    d. Electronic business system outputs

    e. Digital scanning outputs

2. Acceptable methods of destruction for electronic records include reformatting, rewriting (expunging), or degaussing. The use of electronic programs that expunge or provide electronic "shredding" of data shall be used to ensure the complete destruction of electronic records, where possible. Alternatively, the physical destruction of the storage medium shall be performed.

3. Using the "delete" function to remove files from hard drives is **not** sufficient to destroy any electronic record. Hard drives should be reformatted and scrubbed when personal computers are returned at end of lease, for disposal or for reassignment to another associate.

Retention and Archiving

1. The retention and destruction of records shall be based upon legal, administrative, operational, financial, and research needs, through the development and maintenance of appropriate records retention schedules, procedures, and systems.

2. The RIM department shall maintain common and uniform records retention schedules and list all records series created or received by one or more departments and the retention periods for each series. The records retention schedules shall contain such other information regarding the disposition of records as required (e.g., local and central archiving durations, authority required prior to disposal).

3. Each records retention schedule shall be reviewed on a regular basis (at least every two years) and amended as needed, to ensure that it is in compliance with disposition instructions issued by the statutory and regulatory bodies and that it comes to reflect the record-keeping procedures and needs of the Company.

4. The Corporate Legal and Audit or Tax departments must approve all records retention schedules or amended schedules before their adoption.

5. All department heads, managers, employees, agents, and contractors shall adhere the retention schedules for the records in their possession.

<table>
<tr><td></td><td colspan="2" align="center">**Policy and Procedures**</td></tr>
<tr><td>Procedure No. C04</td><td align="center">Section: Corporate</td><td align="right">Page 8 of 16</td></tr>
<tr><td></td><td colspan="2" align="center">**Records Information Management**</td></tr>
<tr><td>Policy Owner:</td><td align="center">Issue/Effective Date:</td><td align="right">Replaces previously issued</td></tr>
</table>

6. A record whose retention period has expired in accordance with its records retention schedule shall be destroyed unless there is an open records hold or suspension request pending on the record.

7. In the event that a department has insufficient facilities to store records locally, the local Records Coordinator shall coordinate with the RIM department for the early archiving of records. This early transfer to the records center shall not impact the total retention period. For example, if the total retention for a record series is 48 months (24 months within the department and 24 months within the records center) and the records are transferred from the department to the records center after 12 months, then the records must be maintained in the records center for a total of 36 months.

8. In the event that a department is not sure of which retention schedule applies to a specific record series, a departmental records coordinator shall request assistance and clarification from the RIM department. The RIM department shall determine and advise the departmental records coordinator of the appropriate retention schedule. In the event that retention of a specific record series is not covered in the published retention schedules, RIM shall initiate actions to add the record series and its approved retention to the published retention schedule.

Records Hold

1. No Company record or nonrecord materials, whether stored at the records center, off-site warehouses, or active in business units and departments, that are involved in or expected to be involved in public records requests, grievances, audits, investigations, litigation, or other legal processes shall be transferred, destroyed, or overwritten until they have been released for transfer, destruction, or reuse by the Corporate Legal and Audit or Tax departments. This includes **relevant** nonrecord materials such as working papers, drafts, and data stored on system backup media.

2. When records are involved in or expected to be involved in public records requests, grievances, audits, investigations, litigation, or other legal processes, the General Counsel (or delegate) shall promptly circulate a written preservation notification to the appropriate custodian of records and the affected Company personnel directing a suspension of document destruction procedures with respect to documents relating to such matters. A copy of all record holds shall be forwarded to the RIM department.

3. No director, officer, employee, agent, consultant, or independent contractor shall destroy any document relevant to the subject matter of an investigation or litigation without specific written authorization from the Corporate Legal and Audit or Tax departments, depending on which department initiated the records hold.

4. Any questions regarding the retention of documents, whether the particular matter falls within a corporate governance, regulatory, or legal concern or whether specific documents are or may be relevant to a particular audit, investigation, or litigation, shall be directed to the Corporate Legal, Audit, or Tax departments, depending on which department initiated the records hold.

5. Upon completion of the public records requests, grievances, audits, investigations, litigation, and the like, the General Counsel (or delegate) shall promptly circulate a release of the written preservation notification to the appropriate custodian of records, the affected Company personnel and the RIM department.

Approval for Destruction of Records

1. All official records and nonrecords must be destroyed in accordance with the policies and procedures described in the procedure of this manual.

2. Records, regardless of format, shall never be destroyed prior to the end of its assigned records retention schedule life. Even records whose retention periods have expired shall **not** be destroyed when:

   a. The record is needed for an audit or investigation,

   b. Litigation is pending or is in progress, or

   c. "Record hold" is otherwise in effect.

3. It shall be the responsibility of each individual to determine if a record hold is in effect prior to destroying records. If there is doubt, contact Corporate Legal.

4. No documentation or approval is required to destroy nonrecords and other documents that fall within the category of normal administrative practice unless such nonrecords is otherwise subject to a "legal hold."

Records Management Compliance Audit

1. Business units and departments, or their designated records coordinators shall undertake periodic monitoring, auditing, and other activities to ensure staff compliance with RIM policies, programs, and procedures.

2. Adherence to RIM policies shall also be monitored through the regularly planned audits by the Internal Audit department. The audit will seek to highlight procedural nonconformance and, where necessary, recommend changes to procedures or controls.

Records Management Responsibilities

The director of RIM manages the program and coordinates the appointments of the members of the RIM Committee and provides guidance and direction to regional/local RIM coordinators.

Policy and Procedures		
Procedure No. C04	Section: Corporate	Page 10 of 16
	Records Information Management	
Policy Owner:	Issue/Effective Date:	Replaces previously issued

The RIM Committee shall be responsible for the leadership, planning, overall policy, and general oversight of Records Management. The RIM Committee is made up of representatives from the RIM department, Legal, Finance, Tax, Research and Development, Quality, and others as appropriate. The RIM Committee shall:

1. Incorporate requirements and policies into the Company's overall Information Management Program and planning.

2. Promulgate and communicate policies and guidance that reflect RIM objectives and goals and incorporate statutory and regulatory requirements.

3. Assign overall responsibility for aspects of the centrally provided technology infrastructure, including local area networked applications and databases.

4. Ensure that senior staff are aware of their RIM responsibilities.

5. Conduct periodic reviews and evaluations of RIM policies and programs.

The RIM department shall have formal responsibility for the implementation of the RIM Program, which includes:

1. Leading and managing the program

2. Advising the Chief Information Officer (CIO) and RIM Committee members on the records management issues and developing policies, procedures, guidance, and training as appropriate

3. Coordinating the approval of records retention schedules, records destruction approval process, and records disposition, including destruction

4. Coordinating Records Management issues with other departments such as Legal, Audit, and Tax, including suspension of documents in accordance with the records hold policy and destruction of documents in accordance with the records destruction policy

5. Providing Records Management advice and training to business units and departments establishing and maintaining effective records management programs and procedures

6. Participating in the Company's Emergency Management/Disaster Recovery/Business Continuity Programs.

7. Advising all employees at least annually:

   - Of their responsibility when creating and maintaining records

   - How to identify records and distinguish them from nonrecords

   - Not to remove records from the Company's custody or destroy them

8. Storing archived records received from the business units and departments

9. Maintaining an accurate inventory of the archived records, including their format, location, and status

10. Assisting in the completion and destruction notices with the departmental Record Coordinators

11. Assisting in the disposal of records whose retentions have expired and that have been approved for final disposition

Note: The Corporate RIM manager's role shall be distinguished from that of operational, business unit, or workgroup-level record managers and record-keeping systems administrators, who (in addition to their other duties) shall be assigned identifiable responsibilities for operational records management activities, systems, and services.

Business units and functional departments shall designate a local RIM coordinator to serve as a point of contact for RIM and who shall be responsible for managing and ensuring local implementation of RIM programs and procedures. RIM coordinators' responsibilities include:

- Assisting in the identification of record-keeping requirements for major problematic and administrative record series in all media.

- Evaluating the value of records within their span of responsibility to serve as a basis for assigning records retention and disposition instruction and implementing the most responsive and cost-effective means for managing them.

- Assisting in the development of standardized file plans and indexing approaches where appropriate to simplify the use of, access to, and integration of information within their area.

- Inventorying and scheduling for the disposition of records created and maintained by their area.

- Reporting on a periodic basis to the RIM Committee.

- Ensuring that physical records are properly packaged and labeled for storage, including a description of the contents and date range of the boxes. Ensure that records contained in the same box represent only one fiscal year.

Legal, Audit, and Tax shall assist in the determination of which records are needed to provide adequate and proper documentation of the Company's activities.

The Chief Information Officer (CIO) shall assign responsibility to:

1. Oversee the creation and use of electronic records in keeping with the Company's policies. This includes coordination with the Corporate records manager regarding record-keeping requirements (including retention periods) and the implementation of authorized disposition instructions for technical documentation for networked and other system applications.

<table>
<tr><td colspan="3" align="center">**Policy and Procedures**</td></tr>
</table>

Procedure No. C04	Section: Corporate	Page 12 of 16
	Records Information Management	
Policy Owner:	Issue/Effective Date:	Replaces previously issued

2. Oversee the management of automated data processing resources and notify system mangers and records officers of technology changes that would affect access, retention, or disposition of system records.

3. Incorporate records management requirements into automated information systems development and redesign.

4. Prevent the loss of information in electronic records resulting from the deterioration of the records' medium and software or hardware obsolescence, to the extent possible.

5. Implement systems for backing up electronic records to safeguard against the loss of record information because of equipment malfunctions or human error.

6. Develop and maintain an inventory of electronic record systems specifying the location, manner, and media in which electronic records systems are maintained to meet operational and archival requirements.

7. Develop and maintain adequate and up-to-date technical and informational documentation for data files and databases, which may include:

   - A narrative description of the database or system

   - Database or system's physical characteristics

   - Recording mode for information, including the coding structure (code books)

   - Recording system for information

   - A record layout that describes each field, including its name, size, starting or relative position, and a description of the form of the data (such as alphanumeric, date, or numeric), or a data dictionary or the equivalent information associated with a database management system, including a description of the relations between data elements in relational data fields

The Company's directors, officers, employees, agents, consultants, and independent contractors shall:

- Conduct work in accordance with RIM policies and procedures.

- Create and manage records necessary to their official activities. This includes creating appropriate records, documenting meetings, conversations, electronic mail messages, telephone calls, and other forms of communications that affect the conduct of official Company business.

- Destroy records only in accordance with the approved RIM schedules and in coordination with area records coordinators.

- Ensure that records under their control and eligible for destruction are not affected by a record hold.

- Never remove records from the Company without authorization.

- File personal papers and nonrecord materials separately from official records.

- Coordinate with the area's records coordinators, or the Corporate Records Manager to transfer custody of records when leaving the department or Company.

Procedure

All records, paper and electronic, listed on the retention schedule must be retained, for the specified period of time. Once the specified retention period has elapsed, such record must be discarded, deleted, or destroyed as described within the policy.

- In order to minimize redundancy, one copy of the record or document should be maintained. Local and duplicate records may be maintained and stored within the department as long as they have operational relevancy, and are to be retained in accordance with approved records retention schedules. The department is responsible to ensure the safe storage, secure access and prompt destruction of all records. Unmanaged duplicates or convenience copies are not in compliance with this policy and can cause the Company to incur unnecessary legal and operational expense.

Each functional business area shall have a Records Coordinator, who maintains an inventory list of the records and documents that are within that department's responsibility for safekeeping.

Records required for local or operational use that may not be listed or identified on the retention schedules should be retained as long as they have operational usefulness. If in doubt as to whether the record should be locally or centrally retained contact the RIM department.

Records must be managed throughout their information life cycle.

1. Creation and/or Collection

Records and documents either originate from or are sent to each department. The types of records and documents received or generated should be periodically verified that they are still useful and required for operational purposes. Periodically, an inventory of these records shall be reviewed for continued relevancy. The originating department must be notified to eliminate forwarding records and documents that are no longer required for local operational use.

When records are created, the originator shall consider the appropriate retention medium (e.g., hardcopy, electronic) and duration (usually stated in years). Records should be deleted at the close of the transaction or when the final version of the record is complete, unless it is required to demonstrate a complete audit trail or is subject to a legal hold.

Policy and Procedures		
Procedure No. C04	Section: Corporate	Page 14 of 16
	Records Information Management	
Policy Owner:	Issue/Effective Date:	Replaces previously issued

2. Maintenance and Use

Departments must develop record-keeping requirements for all official records for which they are responsible. Departmental or functional records coordinators shall maintain an inventory control log of records created, collected, and retained within the department and monitor those that are forwarded to central storage.

Local records and duplicate records are maintained and stored within the department as long as they have operational relevancy. Duplicate records **must not** be retained for a period longer than the duration stated on the records retention schedule. The department is responsible to ensure the safe storage, secure access, and, as appropriate, the prompt destruction of the records.

3. Transfers to Central Storage

Inactive records scheduled for off-site storage shall be identified, organized, indexed, and labeled in accordance with records storage procedures. All records prepared and scheduled for storage shall be identified and labeled by record title, as identified in the records retention schedule.

4. Requests for Retrieval from Central Storage

When necessary, departments may request the retrieval of a stored box from central storage.

5. Record Disposition

Records and information must not be destroyed indiscriminately. Records that have met their retention period and are no longer required for operational use and not on "records hold" from Legal, Audit, or Tax are candidates for destruction.

For nonarchived records in nonelectronic and electronic form, the department coordinator should develop local procedures and administer a program to ensure that records are destroyed in a method that ensures that such records and information cannot be recreated, reassembled, or reconstructed. The RIM department provides guidance and support to the department coordinators.

For archived records (in nonelectronic and electronic form), the records manager must receive approval from the department and other authorities e.g., Legal, Tax, and Regulatory to release the records for destruction. An authorized vendor performs destruction and destruction certificates must be obtained and retained.

The Records Information Manager maintains the master listing of retention records eligible for destruction i.e., expired/obsolete records. Prior to releasing the records for destruction, the listing will be distributed to all members of the Records Management Steering Committee for review and approval.

Electronic Documents

Electronic records generated and maintained in company information systems e.g., mainframes, mini- and microcomputing/storage systems must be reviewed at least annually by the applicable information owners and/or custodians to ensure that the RIM handling policies are met.

A technical services administration department is responsible for retaining archived electronic data and records in secured archived electronic storage and for ensuring that electronic systems needed to restore records and information are maintained. Local departments are responsible for identifying data records and documents to be archived electronically.

As referenced in the information technology network security policy, the Company's servers are configured to automatically archive e-mail that has been received and opened more than 185 days prior to such date. Only e-mail messages that comprise a record falling into a category listed on the retention schedule should be retained for a period in excess of the 185 days. Unless otherwise indicated by "legal or records hold," e-mail is destroyed after 365 calendar days.

Personal Computer (PC)-Based Records

PC-based records refer to those documents (e.g., word documents, spreadsheets, presentations) that reside on the local "C" drive or local area networks not linked to the Company's common network.

Original/official records that are also PC-based records are to be considered official records and may not be destroyed except in accordance with the Corporate records retention schedule.

Nonoriginal/official records that are also PC-based duplicate records used for reference purposes or to produce hardcopy documents of company files would not be considered as official records and may be deleted at the discretion of the user. They must be deleted or destroyed **as soon as they are no longer needed, and in no event must they be retained longer than the retention period for the official version of the record.**

Subject to Legal Proceedings

The Company's records, whether in electronic or nonelectronic form, are subject to legal processes, such as discovery or subpoenas. In the event of litigation, Corporate Legal should be notified immediately so that they can notify the appropriate departments if the destruction of certain records must be suspended.

The destruction of records shall be suspended immediately upon notice from senior management and/or the Legal or Audit departments. The request to suspend record destruction should be tailored, to **cover only those documents relevant to the investigation, audit, or litigation,** and upon completion. The department or area that requests the suspension should notify those affected areas on release of the suspension.

	Policy and Procedures	
Procedure No. C04	Section: Corporate	Page 16 of 16
	Records Information Management	
Policy Owner:	Issue/Effective Date:	Replaces previously issued

Notification of the release of the suspension shall be performed in a manner similar to the notification of the suspension.

Penalties for Noncompliance

According to U.S. federal regulations, fines and prison sentences can be imposed on anyone who "knowingly alters, destroys, mutilates, conceals, covers up, falsifies, or makes false entry in any record with the intent to impede, obstruct, or influence the investigation or proper administration of any department or agency of the United States . . ." Employees shall ensure that their retention and destruction activities are conducted in strict compliance with this policy. If employees have any question that documents slated for destruction may be relevant to an anticipated private claim or a federal or state investigation or proceeding, the associate should contact a member of the Corporate Legal department. **When in doubt, contact the RIM Manager and do not destroy.**

Controls/Areas of Responsibility

Employees are to use their discretion or ask for assistance from the RIM department to determine whether a particular record falls within a category of records listed in the retention schedule.

The Records Management Steering Committee, comprised of representatives from the Legal, Audit, Tax, and Records Management and other major business support departments, is responsible for ensuring that the Records Information Management policy is established and implemented throughout all operating business units. The Committee shall review changes proposed or requested to this policy by the records manager and shall be responsible for approving changes to the retention schedule and for the destruction of records.

Division and departmental managers are responsible for the transition of records during departmental or functional changes and associate terminations, and for ensuring the security and integrity of their administrative and operational records at all times.

Records and RIM compliance audits are performed throughout the year. Measures are summarized and reported to executive management for remediation.

Contact

Records Information Management

Index